Comprehensive
Faculty Development

A GUIDE TO
ATTRACT, RETAIN, DEVELOP, REWARD, *and* INSPIRE

ism Publications

"Thinking about hiring in the context of the mission of your school and tied to the entire process of faculty coaching and evaluation is an invaluable perspective. **It's the clarity and articulation of this 'big picture' that makes this book so helpful.** The detailed information on how to design each step of the process makes this an important and accessible guide for any administrator."

Nancy Leaderman, *Upper School Principal*
Golda Och Academy (West Orange, NJ)

The Comprehensive Faculty Development Book

By Michael Brisciana, SPHR

Independent School Management, Inc.
1316 N. Union Street, Wilmington, DE 19806
302-656-4944   *isminc.com*

Disclaimer: Independent School Management, Inc., (ISM) provides management consulting and other services to private-independent schools. ISM is not a law firm. No service or information provided by ISM in any verbal or written form (including this book) should be construed as legal advice. ISM specifically advises schools to consult with legal counsel qualified in their jurisdiction regarding all legal matters (including the hiring, rewarding, and terminating of personnel). All Web links and references in this book are correct as of the publication date, but may have become inactive or otherwise modified since that time.

Printed in the United States of America
ISM Consortium Gold Member: $35   Non-member: $49

ISBN-10: 1-883627-11-7
ISBN-13: 978-1-883627-11-9

Contents

Purpose and Use of This Book

Purpose

ISM developed this guidebook to help private-independent schools attract, retain, develop, reward, and inspire faculty. We believe the best way to achieve these vital goals is to implement, manage, and sustain effective practices for faculty hiring, evaluation, development, compensation, and selective retention. Much of what you are about to read is process-focused. However, in working through each of the processes, it is important not to lose the forest for the trees.

While we strive at all points to support teachers to the fullest, this book is ultimately not about *teachers*—it is really about *students*. We believe, by doing all of the things suggested, the school will *ultimately increase student performance, satisfaction, and enthusiasm*. Thus, it becomes a win-win situation for all involved—by supporting teachers, the school supports students and helps ensure the institution's long-term growth and success.

Balancing Effectiveness and Compliance

In developing these approaches, we have focused on two key criteria, *effectiveness* and *legal compliance.*

With regard to *effectiveness,* it is critical for all employee-related processes to flow from your mission. That is, use these processes to hire and retain qualified, student-centered individuals who are aligned with the school's mission, culture, and values. They should be able to consistently deliver excellence in and out of the classroom. To use these processes effectively, school leaders are encouraged to customize and adapt these generic processes and principles to the specific and unique mission, culture, and values of your school.

With regard to *legal compliance,* school leaders should be aware that educational institutions are bound by nearly all the same laws, statutes, and regulations that govern other private organizations. While it is not necessary for administrators to become legal experts, it is a necessary part of management in the 21st century to be aware of the main parameters within which the school must operate with regard to employment and benefits laws. To this end, we have included a legal overview as part of the book—in addition to inserting compliance-related guidance into all processes and models recommended for your use. Though no process provides 100% protection to any organization, utilizing the methods recommended in this book will help you better protect your school against the risks present when interacting with faculty through the full range of employment activities.

Note: While most of the principles, processes, tools, and techniques outlined in this book apply broadly to the hiring and dismissal of all private school personnel, our focus is on faculty-specific practices. These differ (sometimes slightly and sometimes considerably) from school to school due to the unique culture and role of faculty within private-independent schools.

Connecting Effectiveness and Compliance

In this book, we propose a model (the ISM Comprehensive Faculty Development Model™) that coordinates all teacher-school interactions through an integrated framework. Running through the model is a set of expected behaviors that we define as "Characteristics of Professional Excellence"—performance traits that are used as the basis for hiring, inducting, evaluating, rewarding, developing, and selectively retaining employees.

The characteristics bring the ideas of effectiveness and compliance together. By using the characteristics at each stage of the process, you will base your employment activities on a solid legal footing (ensuring compliance). You will also ensure that your processes are fully aligned with your mission, culture, and values (ensuring effectiveness), for the long-term benefit of the institution and its students.

Using This Book

The discrete sections in this book can stand on their own, but also link to one another. You need not read the book cover to cover like a novel. Get well-acquainted, however, with the introduction and background section (Chapters 1, 2, and 3) that provide important legal information and lay out the general framework (the Comprehensive Faculty Development Model) and the central elements (the Characteristics of Professional Excellence).

After reviewing this information, the reader is well-positioned to focus on the sections of main interest to him/her (e.g., hiring, evaluation, or compensation). Of course, we encourage you to work through the entire text to gain an in-depth sense of how all of the processes fit together. If time is limited, however, focusing only on the section of immediate interest (after absorbing the background information) will still serve your needs well.

Definition: Who is a 'Manager' or 'Administrator'?

Throughout this book, we use various terms to represent private school administrators, including the School Head, Division Director, Manager, Supervisor, and Administrator. As titles and roles vary from school to school, for purposes of discussion in this book, we generally intend these terms to mean:

- *School Head:* The top administrator in your school—the person with responsibility for the entire school operation and who is hired by and reports to the Board of Trustees. Various titles may include Headmaster/mistress, School Head, President, Superintendent, or Principal.
- *Division Director:* Administrators who oversee the operations of a division (e.g., lower school, middle school, upper school). Various titles may include Division Head, Principal, or Director.
- *Manager, Supervisor, or Academic Administrator:* Describes a *function* more so than a level or a *title*. As such, it describes any person responsible for managing faculty members in a school. This may include the School Head, Division Directors, Department Chairs, Grade Coordinators, and Deans of Faculty.

Please note: It is important not to allow title references to distract from the content being presented. That is to say, in virtually all cases, we are using titles for *example* purposes and not for *prescriptive* purposes. We don't intend to (and truly can't) suggest *exactly who* should carry out such-and-such task or hold such-and-such responsibility, other than the general prescription that an administrator with the proper authority, skill, and training should carry out the particular task suggested.

Perspective and Encouragement

We realize that many private school leaders have received outstanding training on *academic* matters, but often less (or no) training on *personnel-related* matters. This often results in administrators who are hesitant to embrace certain of their managerial duties. We hope that reading this handbook will be an empowering experience— because you will have educated yourself about important employee-related principles that are most likely to lead to the greatest success for the students in your school.

Determining exactly what actions are necessary to bring these principles to life in your school may not always come easily (and rarely without deep reflection and assessment). However, by following the processes outlined in this book, you can be confident that you have done your best to ensure that your school's standard of excellence will be achieved this year and sustained into the future—and you will have done so in the most mission-appropriate, legal, and effective manner.

Source Material

This book is written based on ISM's experience since 1975 in guiding private-independent school administrators, as well as from current knowledge of research and best practices in the human resources, performance, evaluation, growth and renewal, management, and leadership fields of study. Key elements are derived from the ISM-led RSM (Research on School Management) and SES (Student Experience Study) research studies, described in the "Characteristics of Professional Excellence" chapter. In addition to introducing never-before-published material, the book draws together content from ISM articles, books, presentations, workshops, webinars, and podcasts published over the years that focus on attracting, retaining, developing, and inspiring faculty. This includes articles and publications such as:

> "Systematically Attracting, Developing, Rewarding, and Retaining Faculty: A Mission-Based Model for 21st Century Schools," *Ideas & Perspectives,* Vol. 37, No. 1

> "A 21st Century Teacher Evaluation Model," *Ideas & Perspectives,* Vol. 37, No. 2

> *The Human Resources Life Cycle: Safe and Effective Faculty Recruitment, Retention, and Dismissal Practices* (Independent School Management, 2008)

> *MFE: Faculty Development and Renewal Reference Book,* fifth edition (Independent School Management, 2008)

> *Xcellence In Executive Leadership: The Teacher's Professional Growth Workbook,* fourth edition (Independent School Management, 2010)

> "ISM's Standards for Professional Growth and Renewal," *Ideas & Perspectives,* Vol. 33, No. 4

"Building Your Faculty's Characteristics of Professional Excellence," *Ideas & Perspectives,* Vol. 32, No. 16

"Purpose and Outcome Statements: Characteristics of Professional Excellence," *Ideas & Perspectives,* Vol. 31, No. 8

"Faculty Evaluation, Student Performance, and School Leadership: An Update," *Ideas & Perspectives,* Vol. 31, No. 13

"The 21st Century School: Faculty," *Ideas & Perspectives,* Vol. 35, No. 11

"Management and Leadership Training for Academic Administrators (Part One)," *Ideas & Perspectives,* Vol. 31, No. 2

"The RSM International Model Schools Project: Final Outcomes," *Ideas & Perspectives,* Vol. 25, No. 9

"A Practical Approach to Broadbanding," *Ideas & Perspectives,* Vol. 30, No. 9

About ISM

Independent School Management (ISM®) is a research entity, publisher, consulting firm, and risk management and insurance services provider—the only comprehensive management support firm for private-independent schools. Founded in 1975 and based in Wilmington, Delaware, our privately held firm has helped guide thousands of schools in North America and throughout the world.

Administrators in private schools of all types and sizes turn to ISM for advice and assistance on an array of management challenges, including student recruitment and retention, fund raising and development, strategic and long range planning, Board/Head relations, scheduling, business operations, leadership training, human resource practices, and risk management. ISM Consultants monitor trends in education, carry out original research, and author the management advisory letter, *Ideas & Perspectives.* In addition to conducting on-campus consultations for more than 100 schools annually, ISM's Consultants lead workshops for school personnel throughout the school year in a variety of settings and at ISM's Summer Institute.

In addition, ISM makes available insurance and benefits programs (such as health benefits; liability insurance; student accident; and other student, employee, and director coverage) that are tailored specifically to the needs of private-independent schools.

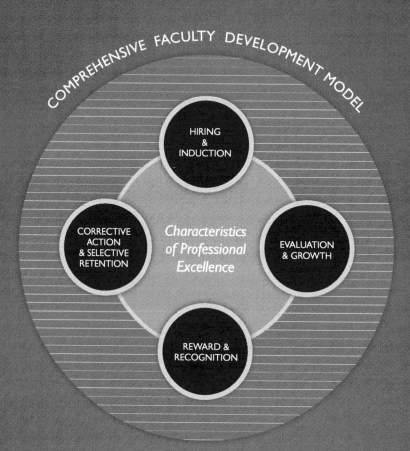

COMPREHENSIVE FACULTY DEVELOPMENT MODEL

HIRING & INDUCTION

CORRECTIVE ACTION & SELECTIVE RETENTION

Characteristics of Professional Excellence

EVALUATION & GROWTH

REWARD & RECOGNITION

"Happiness is the full use of your talents along lines of excellence."

– John F. Kennedy

The Comprehensive Faculty Development Model

The dictionary defines "talent" as "a special ability or aptitude; a capacity for achievement or success;" and, in the collective, as "a group of persons with special ability." Linking this definition with the JFK quote that opens this chapter expresses well the goal of this book. In these pages, we aim to help private-independent schools—through use of tools and frameworks—to engage with teachers in a way that enables them to develop and use their talents along lines of excellence for the benefit of their students, colleagues, the school community at large, and themselves.

To develop these tools and frameworks, ISM engaged in an intensive study of the needs of 21st Century Schools and school leaders, of which this book is one outcome. This examination was comprised of:

- reflecting on changes we have observed while working with hundreds of schools of all sizes, missions, pedagogies, and philosophies during the past decade;

- reviewing the writing and observations of leading educators and management experts; and

- examining societal, generational, technological, and legal changes impacting teachers, students, parents, community members, and schools.

Based on these reflections, we have come to a number of conclusions regarding what is required for schools to thrive in the hyper-competitive 21st century environment. With respect to faculty and administrators, we believe that schools need to:

- view the primary task of academic administrators to be that of increasing the capacity of their teachers (i.e., helping teachers grow);
- measure teacher effectiveness on a regular and ongoing basis;
- establish deeply engaging individual growth and renewal plans that take both a short-term and long-term approach to investing in each teacher's strengths; and
- hold teachers and administrators accountable for their performance.

Holding faculty accountable has three related aspects.

1. Recognizing, supporting, and rewarding mission-appropriate faculty who are working to a standard of excellence;

2. Providing active support for struggling faculty members to reattain and exceed performance standards, such as through coaching and mentoring, and where necessary, formal corrective action; and

3. Identifying and making the hard decisions to terminate the toxic, mediocre, incompetent, and/or mission-inappropriate faculty members (i.e., those who still aren't succeeding even with the school's structured support, either due to skill deficits or misalignment with the school's mission, culture, and values).

We believe that for these aims to be achieved consistently, schools must institute systematic approaches to managing teacher performance, from hiring through retirement. The system we recommend—based on the premise that what is not guided purposefully improves only at random—is the basis for this book.

From the Teacher's Point of View: Experiencing the 'Life Cycle of Events'

Before delving into the details of the systematic approach proposed, first consider the faculty-school relationship from the individual teacher's perspective. Interactions in a teacher's employment experience with the school include responding to a job ad, interviewing, negotiating a salary and benefits package, receiving a performance review, being permitted (or required) to pursue professional development opportunities, and the like. Teachers experience only certain of these activities—such as hiring and termination—once during their tenure with the school, while others—such as performance evaluations and professional development—will likely be experienced on an annual basis.

The following diagram puts these activities into pictorial form, placing the events in roughly sequential order throughout the teacher's career.

Faculty Life Cycle of Events

Mission, Culture, and Values at the Center

You will notice that the words "mission," "culture," and "values" are at the center of the diagram—surrounded by a series of two-way arrows. This is meant to suggest two things.

1. Ideally, candidates and employees sense that mission is the foundation of all interactions with them—i.e., all processes align with and support the school's mission.

2. These interactions both *reflect* and *impact* the school's culture and values—e.g., the hiring of a new teacher reflects the school's values in the selection while also impacting these same values through the new teacher's interactions in the daily life of the school.

Using a Comprehensive Approach to Developing and Sustaining an Exemplary Faculty

When not purposefully designed, the events shown above may feel disparate and disconnected from one another—i.e., things that need to be done for paperwork or compliance purposes, but which don't seemingly connect to or support the school's mission, culture, and values in any way. Such a state of affairs is exactly the opposite of what the school is trying to achieve.

For purposes of effectiveness, the school will want to ensure that all employment-related activities are coming from a common base or starting point (i.e., the school's mission). For efficiency purposes, the school will further wish to design its processes in such a way as to be replicable and repeatable—whether from division to division, or year to year—so that it can ensure that effective practices are being used consistently and continually.

To these ends, ISM's Comprehensive Faculty Development Model is comprised of distinct, as well as overlapping, processes that are connected by a common thread and which individually and collectively aim to support and reflect the school's mission, culture, and values.

- *Hiring and Induction*

  The school begins with a definition of the skills, characteristics, and experience required for the position. With that in place, it can then initiate advertising, interviewing, checking references, and selection. This process extends into effective induction, which actually begins by articulating the school's expectations of faculty during the hiring process. Induction continues post-hire as an 18- to 24-month process of orienting new faculty to the school's mission, culture, and values and supporting them as they acclimate to the responsibilities of faculty at your school.

- *Evaluation and Growth Cycle*

  Starting from describing the school's expectations of faculty during hiring and reiterating them during induction, this process incorporates setting expectations, observing performance, giving feedback, formally evaluating performance, and guiding growth and renewal—all tied together by ongoing coaching and mentoring.

- *Reward and Recognition Process*

  For schools not using merit pay, this process uses evaluation as a way to recognize and appreciate excellence, provide opportunities for leadership within the faculty culture, and enable administrators to publicly and privately acknowledge a job well-done. For schools utilizing merit pay, in addition to the above, this process uses evaluation as a key element in setting individual teacher compensation.

- *Corrective Action and Selective Retention*

  Whereas the school's evaluation and growth cycle helps the school identify highly qualified, mission-appropriate faculty that it seeks to retain, the corrective-action process aims to support struggling faculty in regaining satisfactory performance. "Selective retention" denotes a process to help the school make hard decisions about mission-inappropriate teachers that it must dismiss or whose contracts it will not renew.

From the school's perspective, this systematic approach is represented pictorially by the following diagram.

ISM's Comprehensive Faculty Development Model™

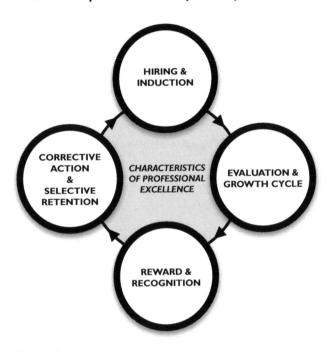

The Common Thread

As we will express in more detail in Chapter 2 and all following chapters, well-defined Characteristics of Professional Excellence (CPEs) serve as the thread tying together each process into an integrated whole. In formal language, we describe these characteristics as "the specific behaviors, values, and attitudes that must be present in strength within your faculty in order for the school's mission to be delivered with excellence to your students." More colloquially, we can describe characteristics as "the how" of faculty life in the school—that is, *how* faculty interact with students, parents, and colleagues to bring your mission to life, and ultimately to fulfillment.

As an example of characteristics serving as a thread, your list of characteristics can form the basis of the school's interview questions and thus help determine which candidates to hire. The same characteristics are reinforced during induction and serve as the basis for the school's evaluation of faculty. Coming full circle, the presence or absence of these characteristics influences merit pay and serves as a key factor in decisions to retain the faculty member, or not.

Implementing This Model

In Chapters 3–8, we walk through each of the elements of the Comprehensive Faculty Development Model in detail for the purpose of helping private school leaders implement this system in their schools in a way that supports, reflects, and sustains the mission, culture, and values of their school. Implementing this model doesn't necessarily require the school to do more than it is doing already—i.e., all schools ordinarily hire faculty, orient them, compensate them, and make decisions as to who will be retained (offered new contracts) each year. What it does require is that the school *think differently,* conceiving of these activities as an interrelated series of events and proactively *managing* these events on that basis. By doing so, the school will be taking significant steps toward ensuring its ability to deliver its mission with excellence to current and future generations of students.

Legal Background and Compliance Issues

It is important for all school administrators to have a basic understanding of the key federal and state statutes that impact hiring, evaluation, pay, and termination practices in schools. They must carry out these processes in a legally compliant as well as effective manner.

Federal, State, and Local Laws Impacting Hiring, Evaluation, Reward, and Termination Practices

NOTE: The scope of this book's legal discussion extends solely to the laws of the United States. Private-independent schools operating in other countries are advised to seek counsel regarding their home country's employment and discrimination laws (which may or may not be similar to or vary from the types of regulations noted here).

In the United States, laws are passed at the federal, state, and local levels. Our discussion in this book primarily concerns *federal* laws that impact employment practices—and, thus, that apply to all 50 states and the District of Columbia. School administrators should be aware, however, that the state in which the school operates may have passed other laws that provide *additional* rights, benefits, and protections to employees—*over and above* those provided by federal law (i.e., state regulations cannot take away rights employees have under federal law but they may extend or expand these rights). The same is true for the localities (e.g., counties, cities, or other local jurisdictions).

For example, the Fair Labor Standards Act (FLSA) provides federal standards regarding minimum wage and overtime pay calculations. Certain states have gone beyond FLSA to set higher minimum wage (e.g., "living wage") and overtime provisions, as have certain cities. Schools are advised to consult with qualified legal counsel (i.e., an employment or labor attorney) with respect to the laws and provisions in their jurisdiction.

NOTE: As indicated on the disclaimer page of this book, ISM is not a law firm and the contributing authors of this book are not attorneys. Accordingly, none of the following may be construed as legal advice. Rather, we are presenting this information as a brief primer on basic employment law. All schools are urged to establish an ongoing relationship with an employment attorney qualified in their state and to seek direct legal advice from this individual (or firm) regarding all employment matters.

Title VII of the Civil Rights Act of 1964

The section of this groundbreaking civil rights era legislation known as "Title VII" refers to provisions of the law pertaining to discrimination in employment. As the foundation for several discrimination laws that were to follow in subsequent years (detailed below), Title VII prohibits discrimination in employment with respect to an individual's

- race,
- color,
- sex,
- religion,
- national origin, or
- genetic information.

These categories are considered to be "protected classes"—so named as they are explicitly protected against discrimination under the law. Title VII is also the statute upon which sexual harassment prohibitions are based. Many states and localities have designed additional protected classes such as medical condition, HIV status, sexual orientation, and gender identity. The number and definition of additional classes protected by law vary considerably from state to state. A table listing current (as of December 2011) state-by-state protected classes is included in the Appendices.

Special Topic: Faith-Based Exemption

Faith-based schools should note that Title VII provides a specific exception with regard to religion for faith-based organizations. If a faith-based school determines that—consistent with its mission—it will use religion as a hiring criterion for some (or all) positions in the schools, it is legally permitted to do so.

TIP: Every school should have an Equal Employment Opportunity (EEO) statement on its employment application, on the job posting page of its Web site, and in its employee handbook that states:

"The school is an equal opportunity employer that makes all decisions regarding employment, compensation, benefits, and all other terms and conditions of employment without regard to a candidate or employee's race, color, religion, sex, national origin, age, disability, veteran status, genetic information, or other characteristic protected by federal, state, or local law."

Schools in states (or localities) that provide additional protected class statuses should include these in their EEO statement.

If a faith-based school uses religion as a hiring criterion, it should eliminate the word "religion" from the above EEO statement and should add the following asterisk:

"As a faith-based institution, the school reserves the right to use religion as a hiring criterion for selected positions, as permitted by law and consistent with the mission of the institution."

The Age Discrimination in Employment Act (ADEA) of 1967

The ADEA prohibits discrimination against employees or candidates aged 40 and older, as well as prohibiting forced (age-based) retirement in most circumstances. While a school may validly specify experience requirements where appropriate to the position (e.g., such as two or four years of experience teaching AP classes for an AP Chemistry position), it should be careful to never set (verbally or in writing) age requirements or to overstate experience requirements that can't be supported.

TIP: The school should make certain that it does not ask for a high school graduation year on its Application for Employment, as this is viewed by courts as a proxy for determining the candidate's age. It should be careful not to use words such as "young," "mature," or similar age-implied phrases in its employment advertisements.

The Equal Pay Act of 1963

Employers are prohibited from discriminating in pay decisions based on gender. One example of a violation of this law would be for a school to provide higher starting salaries to male faculty, due to their perceived status as heads of households, or to pay men more solely on the basis of gender in an attempt to balance gender roles in the faculty.

The Lilly Ledbetter Fair Pay Act of 2009

Acting as a companion of sorts to the Equal Pay Act, The Lilly Ledbetter Fair Pay Act primarily addresses the time periods within which pay discrimination claims must be brought. Under this act, the statute of limitations on initiating a claim is "reset" every time an employee is paid in a way that reflects gender discrimination.

For example: If a school purposely paid a female teacher less than a comparably qualified male teacher when she was hired a number of years ago, the statute of limitations is not based on her first paycheck from years ago. Rather, the statute starts anew every time she receives a new paycheck. Thus, the school can be liable for pay discrimination acts that first occurred in the distant past.

NOTE: Reviewing and addressing past discriminatory pay practices is a complex matter and should be undertaken only under the direct supervision of the school's employment attorney, to ensure the protection of all concerned.

The Americans with Disabilities Act (ADA) of 1990

Different sections of the ADA may apply to a number of different areas of school operations (e.g., regulations regarding physical access to building for the disabled). With regard to employment, the ADA specifically prohibits an employer from discriminating against individuals with disabilities who are "otherwise qualified" for the position. Employers are required to make "reasonable accommodations" to remove barriers to employment (such as making the classroom wheelchair-accessible for a disabled faculty candidate or adjusting work schedules for medical needs).

The "accommodation" requirement is balanced by the provision that accommodations need not be unduly burdensome (financially or operationally) on the school. Defining what is or is not "reasonable" or "an undue burden" is often a difficult matter and should always be reviewed with an employment attorney. Schools should note that courts are becoming increasingly skeptical of "undue financial burden" claims as the sole basis for an employer rejecting an accommodation request by a disabled candidate.

TIP: All applications for employment should include a question that asks, "Are you qualified and able to carry out the duties of this position with or without reasonable accommodations?" (to which the candidate simply answers "yes" or "no"). If the school offers a position to a disabled individual, dialogue should be initiated regarding any necessary accommodations after the job offer has been made. If the employee's recommended solution is not feasible due to cost or operational reasons, then alternative solutions should be sought. Entering into dialogue on accommodations is seen by courts as a matter of good faith, in fulfillment of the intent of the ADA. It may be the case that no mutually reasonable solution is possible—but this conclusion should only be arrived at after full dialogue with the candidate/employee (and your attorney).

Fair Labor Standards Act (FLSA)

Originally passed in 1938 and updated most recently in 2004, the FLSA defines what types of positions qualify for overtime pay. For our purposes in this book, it is most important to note that faculty positions generally meet the "learned professional" exemption criterion under the law and are thus deemed "exempt" positions. This means that faculty positions do not qualify for overtime pay under the law.

In compliance with the "exempt" designation, faculty positions must be paid on a "salaried" (rather than "hourly") basis, and deductions generally cannot be made due to the quality or quantity of work. As a practical matter, this means that faculty members must be paid in full for any days on which they perform work. (Example: If a teacher goes home sick after teaching for three hours and he/she does not have any more accrued sick time available, he/she must be paid for the *full day* of work. If, however, a teacher is absent for a full day, then he/she can be docked for that day—as no work was performed on that day, assuming that no remaining paid time was available.)

Schools should note that some states (California, as one example) have specified additional criteria that teaching positions have to meet to qualify under the exempt status. In addition, schools should be aware that assistant teacher or teacher aide positions do not generally qualify as exempt, and thus must be paid for overtime work.

TIP: Consult with your employment attorney to determine the exempt status of any teacher aide or assistant positions in your school. Misclassification (i.e., not paying overtime when you are required to do so) is a serious matter and can result in fines and penalties of up to $10,000 per incident, as well as overtime pay retroactive up to three years.

Fair Credit Reporting Act (FCRA) of 1970

The FCRA impacts schools with regard to the background screening process. While the statute's name singles out "credit reports," the FCRA also covers many other types of consumer reports, including background screening reports (e.g., criminal, educational, driving records). If the school orders background reports from an outside vendor as part of its screening process, it must observe the guidelines of the FCRA.

The good news is that these guidelines are fairly easily met in most cases. Prior to ordering any background reports, the school must have the candidate complete and sign a Background Screening Consent Form. In most instances, this completes the school's compliance with FCRA. In cases, however, where the school decides against hiring the candidate due (in part or in full) to information contained in the background report (e.g., a past conviction for fraud or harm to children), then it must initiate written notification to the candidate.

Written notification includes sending a certified letter to the candidate, along with a copy of the background report, indicating that the school is considering ending the employment process due to information contained in the candidate's screening report. The candidate has the opportunity to clarify or correct information in the report (usually directly with the report vendor). If correction or clarification does not happen in a reasonable period (usually considered to be five days), then a second letter must be sent, officially informing the candidate that employment consideration is being withdrawn.

> **TIP:** *Review with your background screening vendor the Background Screening Consent Form that the vendor recommends for employers in your state. Certain states also require employers to provide a copy of reports to candidates upon request.*

Immigration Reform and Control Act (IRCA) of 1986

The IRCA resulted in the creation of the well-known I-9 form. This form—which verifies the individual's identity and eligibility to work in the United States—must be completed by all new employees within three days of beginning employment. An employee can meet the law's standards by presenting his/her U.S. passport, driver's license, and Social Security card, or other approved identity and eligibility documents.

The school can be subject to fines up to $10,000 per incident for failure to comply with IRCA regulations. I-9 forms can be printed at the Web site ***www.uscis.gov/files/form/i-9.pdf.***

TIP: Even though new faculty members are typically offered contracts in the spring, the I-9 form should not be given to them for completion until their first day of work (which is usually the preschool Orientation Week in August). This is to avoid any confusion as to what their official hire date is, as well as to avoid inadvertently incurring liability for their employment (such as for Worker's Compensation or insurance purposes) before it actually begins.

Schools may be concerned that they will be left with an empty classroom if they don't find out until right before school starts that an employee cannot work for them because of an I-9 issue (e.g., if a foreign national has not completed the necessary visa paperwork to be eligible to work in the U.S.). For this reason, the Application for Employment (see Appendices for a sample) should include a question pertaining to the candidate's eligibility for employment in the U.S. In addition, the cover letter that accompanies the written contract offer (for those candidates that are hired) should contain a reference to the identity and eligibility verification form (i.e., I-9 form) that they will be required to complete at orientation.

If the employee is not able to provide appropriate proof of identity and eligibility to work in the U.S. within three days of his/her first day of work, he/she is not permitted to work until the matter is resolved.

COBRA Act of 1986

This act, officially known as the Consolidation Omnibus Budget Reconciliation Act (COBRA), pertains to the employee's right to continue his/her employee benefits coverage upon termination of employment or other "qualifying life events" (divorce, dependent reaching maximum age, etc.). COBRA comes into play when a faculty member resigns or is terminated. In addition, there are other nontermination family circumstances that can trigger COBRA (such as decrease in employment from full-time to part-time). Upon termination or ineligibility for benefits coverage, employees must be informed of their COBRA rights (which generally allow them to continue medical/dental coverage at their own expense under the school's policy for up to 18 months).

The School Head should ensure that all COBRA practices are being observed by the Business Office, Human Resources Department, or other staff responsible for employee benefits administration. Due to the complex, evolving nature of COBRA rights, the school may consider outsourcing COBRA compliance to a qualified vendor (such as its payroll or insurance provider or other third-party administrator).

TIP: While a school has the right to decline to offer COBRA coverage to faculty members who are terminated for gross misconduct (fraud, embezzlement, fighting, etc.), we do not recommend that schools invoke this right—as it sets up an often emotionally draining legal battle that detracts from the school's ability to "calm the waters" and attend to the needs of the faculty culture that is disrupted by any termination of this type.

Keeping It Simple: What an Administrator Really Needs To Know About Employment Law

With the exception of the more technically oriented regulations (such as FLSA and COBRA), the majority of the key employment laws described above concern employment discrimination. While there are many nuances to each of these laws, in essence, a school's primary protection against violating discrimination statutes is actually simple. That is, a school needs to take employment actions (hiring, firing, etc.) solely on the basis of job-required skills, experience, and characteristics—and to be able to prove that this is what it has done.

The good news is that this is one of the primary purposes that the Comprehensive Faculty Development Model described in this book serves. By establishing hiring, evaluation, termination, and other faculty-related processes that are based on its operating needs and its mission, culture, and values, the school is doing the best it can to protect itself from lawsuits, claims, and similar penalties and concerns. In the next chapter, we will begin describing exactly how the CFD Model works.

Summary

The school must keep all of the above laws and regulations in mind throughout its hiring process as well every other step in the Comprehensive Faculty Development Model. Practices outlined in the remainder of this book are designed to help the school hire and retain the most qualified, mission-appropriate faculty for the school—and to do so in a legally compliant manner (i.e., in a way that will keep the school from being sued—or if the school is sued, in a way that allows it to prevail in the case).

Characteristics of Professional Excellence

Establishing a mission-appropriate list of Characteristics of Professional Excellence (CPEs) is central to the success of each stage of the Comprehensive Faculty Development Model. It is vital that the school develop a set of characteristics that reflects the best expectations and needs of the school with respect to faculty. These characteristics must be deeply aligned with your unique mission, culture, and values, or they simply will not work effectively for you in this model.

We have two main priorities in this chapter:

1. Share with you ISM's research into characteristics of faculty excellence in private-independent schools; and

2. Guide you toward developing a set of impactful, mission-appropriate characteristics for your school.

ISM's Research-Based List of Characteristics of Professional Excellence for Faculty

ISM has conducted two seminal research projects regarding faculty and student success in the past two decades.

- The RSM (Research for School Management) study, a groundbreaking study of North American private-independent schools in the early 1990s

- The SES (Student Experience Study), a one-year partial replication of the RSM study, conducted in 2010–11

The RSM project ran for six years, from 1989 to 1995, and involved conducting hundreds of interviews annually at each of nine private-independent schools. The project focused upon relevant factors in student performance, satisfaction, and enthusiasm, and, secondarily, on teacher performance, satisfaction, and enthusiasm.

The project's outcomes included ISM's original professional growth and renewal system, known as Meaningful Faculty Evaluation (MFE). RSM also served as the foundation for later ISM studies of School Head leadership and Board President leadership. In addition, the original outcomes and subsequent research projects were layered systematically into the several iterations of the ISM Stability Markers (a framework describing factors critical for school success and sustainability) and, more recently, the 20 ISM Success Predictors for the 21st Century.

In the school year 2010–11, ISM conducted a one-year partial replication of the original project, this time with eight private-independent schools. The mix of schools, as with the original project, included the full range of possible grade configurations, religiously affiliated and secular, single-sex and coed, and boarding and day.

Central Findings—The RSM and SES studies revealed and confirmed the correlations between predictability and supportiveness and student performance, enthusiasm, and satisfaction. In addition, the correlation between a healthy, growth-oriented faculty culture and long-term sustainability of excellence in private-independent schools was brought to light by these studies.

ISM's List—As an outcome of the studies, ISM developed a list of Characteristics of Professional Excellence that we believe to be difference makers for private-independent school teachers. Written from the teacher's perspective, these are:

Classroom-Related Skills

1. *Academic Standards:* I set clearly articulated standards for student academic performance.

2. *Testing:* I create predictable tests (not to be confused either with "simple" tests or with "easy" tests); my students can rely on the test preparation that I offer them.

3. *Grading:* I provide fair, reliable, understandable grade/reward structures for my students; my students are led to understand why they receive the grades they receive—good or bad—and thereby to see how improvement, if they will seek it, might be possible.

4. *Content Knowledge:* I am knowledgeable of cutting-edge content and developmental theory.

5. *Pedagogy:* I have mastered at least one pedagogical approach that is supported by reliable, contemporary research outcomes.

6. *Real-Life Application:* I am practiced in applying any subject matter to real-life conditions beyond the classroom, including applications that may be global or universal in their potential.

Teachers' Attitudes Toward Students and Teaching

1. *Gladness:* I am glad to arrive at school and to see my students each day.

2. *Wishing Success:* I find ways to make it obvious to all students that I wish them success every day, both in school and outside of school.

3. *Encouraging Virtue:* I find ways to make it obvious to all students that I want them to become better, more virtuous people (in ways consistent with our school's stated purposes and projected outcomes for our graduates).

4. *Behavior Standards:* I set reasonable, defensible standards for student behavior.

5. *Bullying Awareness:* I am continually alert to the threat of bullying between and among my students.

6. *Confrontations with Dignity:* In confrontations with students, I conduct myself in ways that leave students' dignity intact regardless of the nature of the issue or infraction.

7. *Enforcing Rules:* I enforce our rules, including the dress code, justly, fairly, consistently.

8. *Predictability and Consistency:* I am able to present myself each day in ways that will be seen by my students as consistent and reliable (i.e., unaffected by outside-of-school problems).

9. *Demonstrated Enthusiasm:* I demonstrate believably high levels of enthusiasm for teaching/learning and for the content of my studies.

10. *Professional Development-Focused:* I pursue career-long professional development as a foremost priority.

11. *Student Engagement:* I am practiced in establishing meaningful emotional/psychological engagement with all my students.

12. *Personal Involvement:* I am practiced in finding creative and appropriate ways to be involved with my students outside the classroom.

13. *Interest in Student Lives:* I am practiced in displaying an overt, conspicuous interest in students' outside-the-class lives—apart from the previous item—without crossing privacy barriers.

14. *Positive Reinforcement:* I am practiced in providing private and public positive reinforcement for individual or group (student) successes.

15. *Parent Communications:* I am practiced in establishing proactive communication with, and service to, each student's parents.

Teachers' Attitudes Toward the School and Colleagues

1. *Commitment to Mission:* I demonstrate through words and actions a genuine, believable commitment to the school, its purposes, its leadership, and my peers.

2. *Colleague Engagement:* I am practiced in giving active support for, and establishing active engagement with, colleagues.

3. *Commitment to Colleagues:* I am practiced in making an overt commitment to the personal and professional well-being of colleagues, administrators, and (other) nonteaching staff.

4. *Commitment to Professional Community:* I am practiced in making positive contributions to a professional, mission-focused sense of community with all constituent groups.

5. *Public Support for School:* I am practiced in giving public support for students, colleagues, and employers (administration and Board).

6. *Socializing Knowledge:* I am practiced in communicating in-class experimentation-and-testing outcomes and findings to colleagues, within and beyond the school.

7. *Professional Academic Community:* I am practiced in routine (yet enthusiastic) participation in outside-the-school academic organizations whose work is supportive of, and pertinent to, my field(s).

Faith-Based Characteristics *(where applicable)*

1. *Commitment to Congregation:* I am practiced in making an overt commitment to the life of my own congregation (church, synagogue, etc.) and its core traditions.

2. *Role Model:* I am practiced in serving as a mature role model for a biblically focused lifestyle.

3. *Personal Faith Commitment:* I am skilled in articulating the personal/ethical implications of a lifelong faith commitment.

4. *Tolerance:* I display appropriate levels of public tolerance of, and respect for, other religious points of view.

5. *Knowledge of Faith:* I am knowledgeable of the developmental history of my school's religious heritage.

6. *Worship Participation:* I actively participate in (and when appropriate, lead) the explicitly religious components of the school's student and community programs.

7. *Personal Religious Growth:* I am committed to growing professionally and personally within the framework of my religious traditions.

Context: It's All About Predictability and Supportiveness

It is important not to lose the forest for the trees when considering ISM's detailed list of characteristics. While our research supports each individual characteristic, the particular characteristics themselves take somewhat of a backseat to the overall finding of the RSM and SES studies—that *predictability and supportiveness correlate with student performance, satisfaction, and enthusiasm.* In a sense, the long list of items simply represents detailed examples of how *predictability and supportiveness* manifest themselves positively in a private school context.

We will explore these ideas further in the "customizing" section below. For now, though, please understand that the primary finding of the study was regarding the importance of predictability and supportiveness—thus, these two behavioral themes should be central to any school-specific list that is developed.

Why Not Use ISM's List?

The question might logically be asked, "If ISM went to the time, trouble, and expense to develop a list of research-based characteristics, why can't we just use this list for our school?" This is a good question, which has a simple answer. Of necessity, ISM developed this research-based list for a generic school (i.e., we weren't thinking of any one school in particular). You don't have a generic school—you have a school with a *unique* mission, culture, and values. Therefore, to work effectively in your school, the set of characteristics that you use must relate specifically to your mission, culture, and values. Thus, you need to develop your own set of characteristics.

Creating a Customized List of Characteristics

When creating your list, we recommend keeping several factors in mind (in addition to the note regarding context, shown above).

- *Size:* When creating the list, *less is definitely more.* Schools should strenuously avoid the temptation to list everything but the proverbial kitchen sink. If the list extends beyond eight to 10 points at most (six is much better), it will take on a length that will weigh it down and risk rendering it inconsequential. For maximum effectiveness, it needs to be a concise, action-packed list that vividly brings the key aspects of great teaching to life. It needs to be of a length that is easily memorized and referenced regularly in the daily operation of the school.

- *Scope:* You will notice that the ISM research-based list includes characteristics that a teacher demonstrates both in and outside the classroom. It is recommended that the school take a similarly broad view of a teacher's responsibilities—identifying the characteristics needed *in and out of the classroom* when developing your own list.

- *Teacher Involvement:* Faculty participation is essential in the creation of the characteristics, since teachers will define the essence of professionalism in your school. Without their significant involvement, the resulting list is likely to feel imposed on the faculty, creating defensiveness and mitigating against teachers embracing the characteristics in a way that gives them meaning in the daily life of the school.

- *Editing ISM's List:* As referenced above, while we believe firmly in the relevance of the ISM list of characteristics for private schools *at large,* we don't believe that our list necessarily lends itself to editing in a way that easily reflects and brings to life the unique characteristics and needs of any one *specific* school. Our experience with schools that attempt to simply edit our list is that they end up with a document that is technically excellent, but which utterly fails to capture the magic of the school and is thus quickly relegated to obscurity, rather than becoming central to the life of the school. Therefore, we strongly recommend that you create your own list from scratch, as described below.

Establishing a Characteristics Design Team

To create a list that resonates most strongly with faculty, we recommend appointing a Characteristics Design Team (or similarly named temporary body). We have found the following approach effective.

1. *Formation:* The Characteristics Design Team should be comprised of three to six teachers (depending on the size of the school and the candidates available), chosen by the School Head. Create a single group—not a group for each academic division—to compile this list, since these characteristics, once formulated, will operationally define what it means to be an exemplary faculty member in your school, across all grades. In a multidivision school, do not allow this definition to be fragmented by division.

2. *Membership:* The design team members are selected because they are bright, energetic, mission-exemplary, respected by their colleagues and their administrators, able to work effectively with adults, and excited about ongoing personal/professional growth. Some may be veterans of many years of distinguished service, while others may be early in their careers. An ideal group will be comprised of members who, when announced, will be greeted by faculty nodding, saying, "Of course, they are *perfect* for this task."

3. *Leadership Involvement:* Usually, the School Head (and possibly Division Directors) meets with the team at least some of the time, particularly in the first session or two during which the group's charge is given, and while the group sorts through and discusses at early stages the implications of the assignment.

   CAUTION: While it is vital that this be primarily a teacher-led project, it is equally vital that the administration not lose touch with the project to the point that it becomes disconnected from the ultimate results and fails to embrace and implement the outcome in meaningful ways. The dynamics of faculty-administration relations will vary by school, of course. Our general recommendation, though, is for the administration to find a nonobtrusive way to stay in close and supportive touch with the project leaders while the team's work is ongoing.

4. *Interaction With Faculty:* As their work proceeds, the design team members will regularly report to—and seek input from—the whole faculty as well as the division that they represent.

The Characteristics Design Team's Work

It is recommended that the School Head designate an informal Chairperson or coordinator to help shepherd the team's work (e.g., scheduling meetings, etc.). Then, the Head meets with the team to initiate the project.

1. *Focus:* Give the design team a written charge, such as: "Develop for our school a list of Characteristics of Professional Excellence that vividly describe teaching excellence at our school." Put more colloquially, the charge might be, "Develop a list that describes what being a great teacher looks like at our school."

   The committee should be aware that the list will be used in several of the school's processes—from hiring to evaluation, to growth and renewal, etc.—but this should only be a background matter for them, not their central concern. Their primary concern is developing a list that fits your school and becomes its living definition of excellence.

   Ensure that the charge includes the idea that this not an exhaustive list, but a succinct (no more than eight to 10 items at most) list that is unique to your school's mission, culture, values.

2. *Perspective:* Noted management author Stephen Covey (*The Seven Habits of Highly Effective People*) recommends to "begin with the end in mind." ISM suggests that all schools establish what we call "The Portrait of a Graduate"—three to five points that describe what a student looks like (in terms of personal attributes and behaviors) by the time he/she graduates from your school. As such, the portrait is the "end" that you have in mind.

   The Committee may wish to work backwards from the end—to consider what behaviors (i.e., characteristics) are required on the part of faculty to bring the portrait to fulfillment in your graduates. In this way, they can consider the characteristics to be the actions (or the "how") that the school (faculty) takes to deliver your mission with excellence to the students, a mission that reaches its ultimate end in your graduates.

   See the "Portrait of the Graduate" article in the Appendices for further details regarding how to develop this document.

3. *ISM's List as a Point of Reference:* You may find it helpful to share with each committee member a copy of ISM's list of characteristics (above). Explain, however, that this is offered solely as a point of reference and no attempt should be made to merely edit the list (as explained above). Rather, they may draw general inspiration from the list, keeping in mind the central finding of ISM's research that characteristics and behaviors that denote predictability and supportiveness correlate strongly with student performance, satisfaction, and enthusiasm. The final version of your school's list should speak to predictable and supportive behaviors in some measure, to ensure

the maximum impact of the characteristics on student performance, satisfaction, and enthusiasm (the ultimate goal of the Comprehensive Faculty Development Model as a whole).

4. *Time Limits:* Discuss time constraints, if any. While many schools find that six to eight weeks is sufficient to bring the project to a successful conclusion, it may take some committees longer. The quality of the team's product is paramount. It should not become a race to the finish because they have run out of time. At the same time, a drawn-out process has its own downside, as this may inadvertently drain the passion and enthusiasm of team members. Whether and how to prompt a committee that is moving too slowly (or to slow down a committee that may be moving too urgently) is a matter of judgment on the part of the School Head.

5. *Review and Feedback:* When a completed draft has been delivered by the committee, jointly review the list with your academic leadership team (e.g., Division Directors, etc.) and the design team to ensure that the characteristics (a) are complementary with the school's mission, culture, and values; (b) reflect teaching excellence in your school; (c) are appropriately informed by and infused with predictability and supportiveness; and (d) will be useful as guideposts throughout the Comprehensive Faculty Development Model (e.g., useful in hiring, evaluating, growing, rewarding faculty).

   If the document presented doesn't meet your expectations, *tread lightly here.* Redirection calls for a well-crafted, thoughtful, and tactful response that guides the team carefully on this, lest they lose heart or feel that their efforts have been unappreciated.

6. *Publication:* When the final document is ready for public unveiling, schedule a whole-faculty meeting and ask the design team to present its work. Provide a brief introduction yourself, and then sit down while the members do the actual presentation. It is their time to shine—help them do so by accepting the finished product with appropriate expressions of private and public gratitude.

7. *Moving Forward:* Now the hard (and exciting) part begins. With the list of characteristics set, it is time to start using them in the daily life of the school. See all of the following chapters—starting with the hiring and induction process—for details.

Additional Observations

Based on our experience helping schools create their own list of characteristics, we would like to offer a few additional reflections for your consideration.

- *Skepticism:* In schools where a culture of trust between administration and faculty doesn't currently exist, faculty may be skeptical about the project's purpose or utility—especially if their prior experience has been serving on committees whose work was put on a shelf and not implemented or accepted. If such a culture exists in your school, the Head may wish to acknowledge the earned skepticism at the public kickoff of the project and use effective collaboration with the design team and support of their work as one means of demonstrating a changing culture on an ongoing basis.

- *Jump-Starting the Process:* If the team is stumped as to how they can start getting the right characteristics on paper, they might consider thinking of the most exemplary faculty members at your school. By identifying the characteristics displayed by these outstanding teachers, they may find that they have put the heart of their list on paper quickly.

- *An Administrator-Created List:* Not all administrators choose to appoint committees to develop the school's list of characteristics. Some hold the view that their faculties are so overloaded with essential instructional responsibilities, or with some inescapable set of additional responsibilities (e.g., such as preparing for an accreditation review), that this assignment would be a crushing burden for them. In these instances, the Management Team will develop the initial Characteristics of Professional Excellence themselves, presenting a draft to the faculty prior to finalizing their work.

  While this approach is highly *efficient,* its *effectiveness* is questionable. Faculty may easily perceive the resulting document as something that will be used to control (or, in extreme cases, even penalize) them, rather than something that will be used to support and uplift them—spurring resentment and defensiveness rather than inspiration, growth and renewal. Most Heads, realizing the implications, will choose effectiveness over efficiency and find a way for the faculty to vigorously participate in developing the characteristics.

- *Making the Characteristics List New Again:* The Characteristics of Professional Excellence list should not be regarded as set in stone for the remainder of the school's history. It should be examined regularly—perhaps every fourth year or so—with an eye toward updating and further refinement. A renewed design team is the logical entity to spearhead that ongoing refinement.

- *Further Work for the Design Team:* Once the team's work is completed and the school has adopted a set of Characteristics of Professional Excellence, the committee may be disbanded. The characteristics that are developed may be used immediately in the school's next hiring cycle, which is described in detail in Chapters 4 and 5. Additional uses of the school's list of characteristics occur in the three remaining stages of the Comprehensive Faculty Development framework—the evaluation and growth cycle, the reward and recognition process, and corrective action and selective retention process.

In both the Evaluation and Growth Cycle and Rewards and Recognition Process, additional work needs to be done to form the school's evaluation, growth and renewal, and merit-pay criteria. Accordingly, the Head may choose to appoint a new design team when each of these remaining projects is initiated—or, she may choose to reappoint some or all of the original design team members for these tasks, depending on the needs of the school and the talents and temperaments of those involved—as well as the timing involved. We will discuss these further adaptations later in this book.

CODA: Characteristics of Professional Excellence for Aegis Academy

For purposes of illustration, we have written an eight-item list of Characteristics of Professional Excellence for Aegis Academy—a fictional K–12 private-independent coed day school. This sample set of characteristics will be used as the backdrop to an example we will carry through the next five chapters—the hiring and induction, evaluation and growth, reward and recognition, and corrective action of an upper school history teacher at Aegis Academy.

Characteristics of Professional Excellence

*The faculty of Aegis Academy commit to these characteristics as the foundation
of our efforts to serve the needs of our students, colleagues, and school.*

- **Professional Growth:** I dedicate myself to daily and lifelong professional development, continually seeking opportunities to improve my teaching in service to my students and colleagues.

- **Setting and Maintaining Standards:** I set and support clear and appropriately challenging standards for both student academic performance and student behavior. My students know what they're accountable for and are confident that they will be held to these standards.

- **Real-Life Applications:** I strive to relate all of my lessons to real-life conditions and events to help students make the connection between the subjects we are studying and the world they observe and experience outside the classroom.

- **Enthusiasm:** I bring my "A" game every day, passionately and energetically demonstrating my enthusiasm for teaching and learning, and striving to engender similar enthusiasm in all my students, so that they may become lifelong learners, seekers, doers, and innovators.

- **Commitment to Mission:** I strive to live the mission in word and deed, working every day to help make our mission come to fruition in the lives of our students, families, and graduates.

- **On Their Side:** In all of our interactions inside and outside the classroom, I find ways to make it obvious to all students that I am eager to teach them, I believe in their abilities, and I work for their success every day.

- **Engaging and Supporting the Whole Person:** I strive to have meaningful and healthy emotional engagement with my students and colleagues regarding their out-of-school lives, without crossing privacy barriers—so that we can support each other in the most vibrant, professionally appropriate ways possible.

- **Healthy Learning Community:** I work hard every day to contribute to a healthy learning, growing, and mutually supportive environment for and with my colleagues—sharing knowledge, resources, insight, and aid freely, openly, and energetically.

▲▲

Special Note:

In Chapters 4 to 8, we examine a distinct process within the Comprehensive Faculty Development (CFD) Model, in the order in which the steps would ordinarily occur with respect to a new employee.

- Chapter 4: *Mission-Based Hiring Process*

- Chapter 5: *Induction Process*

- Chapter 6: *Evaluation and Growth Cycle*

- Chapter 7: *Reward and Recognition*

- Chapter 8: *Corrective Action and Selective Retention*

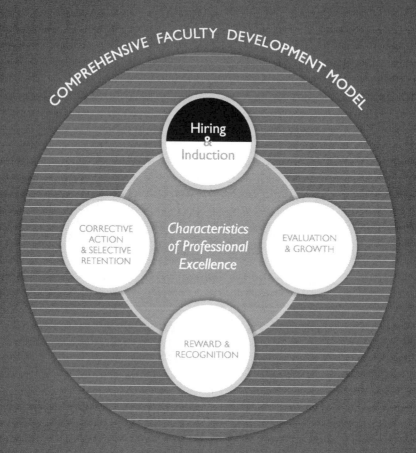

COMPREHENSIVE FACULTY DEVELOPMENT MODEL

Hiring & Induction

CORRECTIVE ACTION & SELECTIVE RETENTION

Characteristics of Professional Excellence

EVALUATION & GROWTH

REWARD & RECOGNITION

Begin with the end in mind.

- Stephen Covey, The Seven Habits of Effective Leaders

A Mission-Based Hiring Process

The goal (or "end") of the hiring and induction process is to identify and select the right person for the right job in an effective and legal manner—and then to retain, engage, and inspire him/her throughout the course of his/her career at the school. Breaking down the first part of this goal, we observe the following.

- *The right person* is a candidate whose skills, characteristics, experience, and credentials are a strong fit with the needs of the position and with the school's mission, culture, values, and definition of professional excellence.

- *The right job* is a position in which responsibilities and required skills, experience, and characteristics are well-defined (for all involved on both sides of the hiring process) and well-designed to carry out the mission of the school.

- *An **effective manner*** is a process that:

  - respects the time commitments of the candidates and the school;

  - maintains communication and good will with the candidates throughout the process;

  - honors the dignity of all candidates, whether selected or not; and

  - reaches a selection decision with proper care and deliberation.

- *A **legal manner*** is a process that:

  - is in compliance with both the letter and the spirit of federal, state, and local regulations regarding antidiscrimination; and

  - minimizes the likelihood of the school experiencing (or losing) employment-related claims or litigation

Addressing the second part of the goal—retaining, engaging, and inspiring faculty throughout the course of their career at the school—is where induction comes into the picture. This will start to be examined in detail in Chapter 5. We believe that only with all parts of the model working together in a planned, integrated way will a school be ensured of achieving its goal of attraction and retention of energized, mission-appropriate faculty on a regular basis.

A Mission-Based Hiring Process

As with any organization, the hiring process in a private-independent school should take on a logical sequence of events, such as:

- identifying an opening,

- defining the requirements of the job,

- advertising the opening,

- receiving résumés,

- selecting candidates to be interviewed who have the required qualifications and experience,

- interviewing candidates about their qualifications and experiences,

- screening the backgrounds of the finalist candidates, and

- selecting the candidate who most clearly meets the job requirements in all respects.

This general flow of events is described in the following diagram.

Mission-Based Hiring Process

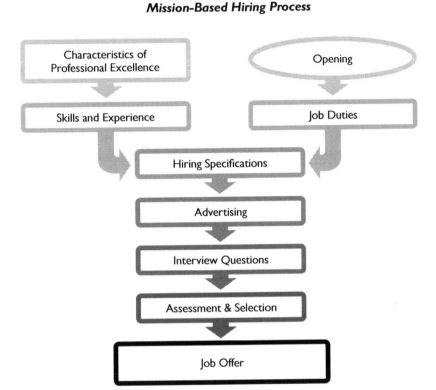

Developing a List of Characteristics: A Practical Matter

As noted in Chapter 3, ISM recommends a process in which the Head appoints
a faculty committee (i.e., the Characteristics Design Team) and charges it with
developing a list of characteristics of excellence, to be used in all areas of school life
involving teachers. Ideally, development of this list would take place well before
beginning the hiring process. This is so that the list is not influenced by the pressure
of "coming up with something" in the heat of the moment—i.e., when the need
to hire is imminent and urgent.

As a practical matter, we understand that schools don't often have the benefit of
operating under ideal conditions. Therefore, if the School Head finds that the hiring
season will soon be upon them and time does not permit the recommended faculty
committee-oriented process, the following is recommended as a short-term alternative
(after which a full-fledged, faculty-involved process can be embarked upon during
the following term).

- **Initial Meeting:** Prior to the beginning of the hiring season, the School Head should meet with his/her academic administrators to discuss and reflect on the school's mission, culture, and values as they pertain to hiring faculty.

- **Focus of Discussion:** The discussion—which may take up part or all of several meetings—should conclude only when each member of the Management Team has a firm and consistent view of what the school's mission, culture, and values look like in action and understands how these elements relate to hiring new faculty (i.e., the group shares a common vision of "what we are looking for" and why).

- **End Result:** For practical purposes, these Management Team discussions need to result in a list of well-defined characteristics pertinent to faculty excellence in the school.

- **Communication and Use:** These characteristics must be communicated to—and absorbed by—all individuals participating in the hiring process (i.e., including the person responsible for drafting the job posting, all those involved in interviewing, all those involved in planning for guest teaching demonstrations, etc.).

The most important element in the process is ensuring that all individuals involved have a common picture of what faculty characteristics are most important for success at the school. (See Chapter 3 for further details.) Once these characteristics are defined, then the hiring process can begin in earnest.

Hiring Process Overview

The following list represents the key steps in a mission-based hiring process. We will lay these out in short form here to help give you a sense of the flow of the process without interruption. Then, we will review each step in detail.

1. Determine the Head's role in the hiring process.

2. Determine members of the recruiting team (aka "hiring committee").

3. Define the job requirements and performance characteristics.

4. Develop your recruitment marketing strategy for the open position.

5. Write and place recruitment advertising in appropriate venues.

6. Receive and acknowledge candidate résumés.

7. Screen résumés against the established job requirements.

8. Select candidates for initial telephone screening interviews (optional).

9. Conduct telephone (or video/Skype) screening (optional).

10. Select candidates for on-campus interviews.

11. Prepare for the interviews (write questions in advance).

12. Conduct on-campus interviews.

13. Assess results of interviews against the established specifications (i.e., job requirements and performance characteristics).

14. Invite final candidate(s) for guest teaching demonstration.

15. Check professional references and conduct background verification on finalist candidate(s).

16. Select the final candidate.

17. Determine the job offer.

18. Make verbal job offer to the finalist.

19. Upon acceptance of offer, issue the contract and notify nonselected candidates.

20. Receive signed contract; set up personnel file and close recruiting file.

21. Launch the orientation/induction process.

Hiring Process: Step-by-Step Details

The following provides detailed recommendations and guidance regarding each of the 21 steps noted above.

Step 1: Determine the Head's Role in the Hiring Process.

The Head will want to clarify his/her expectations as to his/her own role in the process—e.g., will he/she participate as an active and equal team member in all hires; serve as ultimate arbiter, deciding among the small group of finalists; meet with only the final candidate (selected by the committee) for formal approval purposes; or, have some other role in the process.

Step 2: Determine Members of the Recruiting Team.

Depending on the Head's role and other related factors—such as the size and composition of the school's Management Team and the number of openings to be filled—the Head may designate a team to handle all faculty hiring for that season, or may designate a team for each opening. It is critical to ensure that all persons involved in the process have received appropriate training as to pertinent laws. (See Chapter 2 regarding federal and state employment laws.) All team members should have clear understanding of their roles and responsibilities in the school's hiring process.

Step 3: Define the Job Requirements and Performance Characteristics.

This is the most critical part of the entire employment process. The hiring team must ensure that the essential skills, responsibilities, qualifications, and characteristics for the position are well defined, as these elements will be central to each remaining step of the process.

Tools

ISM recommends two tools to aid schools in defining job requirements:

- the Faculty Job Description Template, and

- the Faculty Hiring Specifications Form.

The use and purpose of each form is described below.

Faculty Job Description Template

The job description template is intended to help the school capture the primary responsibilities of the particular teaching position, including any physical, educational, or certification requirements. Avoid the temptation to include a detailed laundry list of all possible tasks associated with the job and focus on the three to five primary duties of the position.

NOTE: The following Faculty Job Description is completed based on an opening for a history teacher for grades 11 and 12. This example will be carried through the rest of this book.

Aegis Academy

Faculty Job Description

TITLE AND REPORTING RELATIONSHIP	
Job Title	History teacher, grades 11 and 12
FLSA Status	☐ **Nonexempt** *(eligible for overtime pay)* ☑ **Exempt** *(not eligible for overtime pay)*
Department	History
Reports To	Department Chair, History

SUMMARY *(1–2 sentences describing the main purpose of the job)*
Teaches a full load of grade 11 and 12 history courses. Serves as coach or assistant coach of athletic teams. Serves as a moderator of club(s). Advises students as part of the school's advisory program.

ESSENTIAL FUNCTIONS *(List 3–5 key duties/responsibilities and the time spent on each)*	
Function 1	Full-time teaching load: grade 11 and 12 history courses, including American History; AP American History; Special Topics: 20th Century America; Special Topics: Capitalism and Democracy
Function 2	Serves as head coach for a sport one semester and assistant coach for another sport the following semester (or vice versa).
Function 3	Advises students with regard to academic and personal matters as prescribed in the Aegis Faculty Advisers Handbook. (Typically 6-8 students per year).
Function 4	Serves as the moderator/sponsor of one student club, to be determined based on faculty member's interest and school's need.
Function 5	Participates fully in the life of the school in terms of academics (i.e., providing high-quality instruction to upper class students); professionalism (i.e., constant focus on professional development); mission (i.e., serving as an appropriate role model for lifelong leading and global citizenship); and culture (i.e., mentoring junior colleagues; engaging in collaborative work projects; supporting all members of school community).

•••▶

OTHER FUNCTIONS
(Briefly describe)

Serves on at least one faculty committee during the academic year, as selected by the Division Head.

MINIMUM REQUIREMENTS

Education	Bachelor's Degree (required); Master's Degree (preferred)
Years Experience	6 years of teaching history (required); at least two years of private-independent school teaching experience (preferred).
Specific Skills *(technical or interpersonal)*	☐ Fulfills "Basic Teacher Expectations" (see below) ☐ Academically current in discipline (history) ☐ Special expertise in at least one or more topic (e.g., American History) ☐ Strong coaching skills in competitive athletic environment
Licenses or Certifications	First Aid certification required within 3 months of hire
	State-sponsored coaching certification preferred

BASIC TEACHER EXPECTATIONS

These requirements apply to all faculty members at Aegis Academy.
* Demonstrate alignment with school's mission in all interactions with students, parents, colleagues, and other community members
* Carries out thoughtful planning and preparation for all classes taught
* Evaluates students' progress predictably, fairly, and consistently
* Demonstrates professional presentation, communication, and instructional skills
* Maintains professional credentials and academic currency in subject area

PHYSICAL CONDITIONS

Work Environment	Classroom; indoor and outdoor athletic facilities (daily); field trips (occasional)
Physical Requirements	Lifting (10 lbs) of athletic equipment; walking (coaching); occasional exposure to heat and cold (coaching)

▲▲

Faculty Hiring Specifications Form

The Faculty Hiring Specifications Form is intended to capture all data that is necessary to carry out an effective recruiting process, but which is not otherwise captured in the job description.

NOTE: Readers will notice considerable overlap between the content of the job description and that of the Faculty Hiring Specifications Form. While a job description has other uses beyond that of the hiring process (i.e., as a centerpiece of conversations with new employees regarding job duties at time of hire and during performance evaluation discussions), as a practical matter, we would suggest that—when time is of the essence in the hiring process and if job descriptions have not previously been developed in the school—the school may choose to use *only* the Faculty Hiring Specifications Form, confident that this captures the key data points necessary for carrying out a successful hiring process.

Hiring committees are encouraged to select four to six Characteristics of Professional Excellence that will have the most impact for the position at hand. These characteristics are most critical in helping the hiring team separate those candidates who are qualified for the position (based on education or experience) *but* who are not a fit or match with your culture from those who are qualified *and* who match with your culture.

NOTE: Readers may wonder why—if the school went to so much time and effort to develop a full list of up to 10 characteristics—we don't recommend using the full list in the hiring process. This is simply due to time and focus—i.e., the need to use every available minute of interviews to the best possible purpose. If the school has a 10-item list of characteristics, for example, 10 is ordinarily too many characteristics to discuss in one interview. Rather, by focusing the interview on the four to six characteristics most important to the particular job under discussion, the school can keep the interview to a reasonable time period while losing little by not touching on the "left out" characteristics.

Faculty Hiring Specifications Form

POSITION TITLE	TODAY'S DATE
History Teacher	Jan. 24, 20XX

DIVISION/DEPARTMENT/GRADE LEVEL	STARTING DATE
Upper School/History/Grades 11 and 12	Fall, 20XX

REPORTS TO NAME/TITLE
Kristen Grainger/History Chair

POSITION FACTS

Reason for Opening	❏ New Position		☑ Replacement
Designation	☑ Faculty	❏ Staff	❏ Administrator
Employment Status	☑ Full-time	❏ Part-time	❏ Temporary
Overtime Status	☑ Exempt	❏ Nonexempt (overtime eligible)	
Supervisory Duties	☑ No	❏ Yes	___ Direct reports

POSITION DESCRIPTION (LIST MAIN DUTIES OR ATTACH JOB DESCRIPTION)

Teaches full load of grade 11 and 12 history courses. Coaches athletic teams (as head coach/assistant coach). Advises students. Participates in life of school.

EDUCATION/CERTIFICATION REQUIREMENTS

Education	❏ H.S./GED	❏ Associate's	☑ Bachelor's	☑ Master's (Preferred)	❏ Doctoral
Certifications	First aid (within 3 months of hire); state coaching cert. (preferred)				
Experience	Teaching upper school history (6 years) is required. Teaching in private-independent school (2 years) is preferred				

•••▶

CHARACTERISTICS OF PROFESSIONAL EXCELLENCE (SELECT 4–6 FROM REVERSE SIDE)
Professional Growth
On Their Side
Setting and Maintaining Standards
Real-life Applications
Enthusiasm
Healthy Learning Community

SOFTWARE/HARDWARE	SKILL LEVEL/YEARS OF EXPERIENCE
Smartboards	Intermediate–2 years experience preferred
Tablet computers	Intermediate–2 years experience preferred
Power Point	Expert
MS Office or Mac Keynote	Intermediate–2 years experience preferred
General	Comfortable in an interactive technology environment

APPROVAL	NAME	SIGNATURE	DATE
Division Head	Robert Jones	*Robert Jones*	1-28-20xx
School Head	Eleanor Smith	*Eleanor Smith*	1-29-20xx

•••▶

Characteristics of Professional Excellence

Select four to six characteristics to be the focus on the interview process.

❏ *Professional Growth:* I dedicate myself to daily and lifelong professional development, continually seeking opportunities to improve my teaching in service to my students and colleagues.

❏ *Setting and Maintaining Standards:* I set and support clear and appropriately challenging standards for both student academic performance and student behavior. My students know what they're accountable for and are confident that they will be held to these standards.

❏ *Real-Life Applications:* I strive to relate all of my lessons to real-life conditions and events to help students make the connection between the subjects we are studying and the world they observe and experience outside the classroom.

❏ *Enthusiasm:* I bring my "A" game every day, passionately and energetically demonstrating my enthusiasm for teaching and learning and striving to engender similar enthusiasm in all my students, so that they may become lifelong learners, seekers, doers, and innovators.

❏ *Commitment to Mission:* I strive to live the mission in word and deed, working every day to help make our mission come to fruition in the lives of our students, families, and graduates.

❏ *On Their Side:* In all of our interactions inside and outside the classroom, I find ways to make it obvious to all students that I am eager to teach them, I believe in their abilities, and I work for their success every day.

❏ *Engaging and Supporting the Whole Person:* I strive to have meaningful and healthy emotional engagement with my students and colleagues regarding their out-of-school lives, without crossing privacy barriers—so that we can support each other in the most vibrant, professionally appropriate ways possible.

❏ *Healthy Learning Community:* I work hard every day to contribute to a healthy learning, growing, and mutually supportive environment for and with my colleagues—sharing knowledge, resources, insight, and aid freely, openly, and energetically.

▲▲

Step 4: Develop Your Marketing Strategy for the Open Position.

Target your advertising based on the position being marketed. Determine first whether you will be posting the opening internally for consideration by current employees. Also, consider whether your search is local, regional, or national. Identify the best vehicles (or combination of vehicles) for that search—from the school's own Web site, to national employment Web sites (e.g., CareerBuilder.com), to the local newspapers, to industry-wide forums (e.g., national publications such as ISM's Career Corner, search firms, or other industry publications), to more contemporary options such as Facebook, Twitter, LinkedIn, or whatever the latest popular social media sites are that accept employment advertising.

Factors such as scarcity (demand and supply of candidates) and budget restraints will play a considerable role here. For example, for the majority of faculty positions in your school, you may already have the benefit of a strong pool of local applicants eager to see which positions your school posts each hiring season. In this case, a posting on your Web site may more than suffice in generating a qualified, enthusiastic hiring pool. For harder-to-fill positions with particularly exacting requirements (for example, an AP Physics teacher with 10 years of experience), the school may need to consider a broader regional or national search—which warrants advertising in national or industry publications, educational Web sites, and job boards, etc.

Step 5: Write and Place Recruitment Advertising in Appropriate Venues.

Employment ads should be consistent—in look, style, and tone—with the brand image that the school promotes in all of its external student/parent marketing and communication materials. This serves several purposes—giving prospective candidates a much clearer sense of who you are as a school (and why they would want to work there), as well as furthering your school's image and message in the community at large. Irrespective of the medium, branding should be central to your considerations at this point in the process.

Upper School History Teacher

Aegis Academy, a coeducational college preparatory school, seeks an experienced and dynamic educator to join its faculty as history teacher, coach, and adviser in our upper school. We enroll 400 students in three divisions (K–5, 6–8, and 9–12) and commonly place a large portion of our graduates in Ivy League or other elite colleges and universities nationally. Our campus is located in the Anytown suburbs and consists of 40 acres of well-maintained buildings, athletic facilities, and a nature preserve. Our school motto, "Integrity, Service, Scholarship," sums up our deep passion for preparing our students for future leadership roles in society.

In three or four sentences, "tell the story" of your school: key factors, overview of your mission, and why it is special to work here.

Duties and Responsibilities

This position involves teaching a full load of grade 11 and 12 history courses, in addition to serving as head or assistant coach for two sports, sponsor of one club or extracurricular program, and adviser to six to eight upper division students. We expect all faculty members to be fully engaged in the life and mission of the school, in and out of the classroom.

Briefly describe the job duties.

Education and Experience

Educational requirements include a bachelor's degree, with a master's preferred. Due to the rigors of our academic program, we require faculty who have made a deep, career-long commitment to teaching. In particular, this role requires a minimum of six years of teaching experience, with at least two years of experience teaching in the upper division of a private-independent school.

State the educational and experience requirements or preferences.

Skills and Characteristics

Teaching, advising, and personal skills and traits required for success in this position at our school include:

– cutting-edge knowledge of latest approaches for bringing history to life in the upper school classroom;

•••▶

– ability to engage students creatively in and outside the classroom, helping all students achieve their fullest academic and leadership potential;

– enthusiasm and dedication to contributing to our healthy learning community, energetically supporting colleagues, sharing ideas and resources, and being there for others

Identify the Characteristics of Professional Excellence (adapted from the Faculty Hiring Specifications Form).

Summing it up, we're looking for a "natural" teacher who loves teaching history to upper division students with a deep-seated, can't-be-contained enthusiasm, who will be energized by our collegial, collaborative, technologically advanced environment.

We encourage schools to include a summary statement that engages the reader and makes your school (and this position) stand out from other, more generic ads the candidate is reading. Here's where you can unleash your creativity!

We offer a competitive salary and top-flight benefits program, in addition to full relocation expenses.

Highlight key features of the compensation and benefits package.

Interested candidates should forward a cover letter and résumé by e-mail to:

Eleanor Smith
Head, Aegis Academy
esmith@aegisacademy.org

Clearly state the application procedures. If written references are required at this point in the school's application process, it should be stated here.

Application deadline is: March 1, 20__

Clearly state the application deadline (if applicable).

Aegis Academy is an Equal Opportunity Employer

If the school is actively seeking diversity candidates, it may elect to add, "We encourage applications from all qualified candidates, including those from diverse backgrounds." Schools should be careful not to use the phrase "Affirmative Action Employer" unless they have established a formal affirmative action program (which is highly unlikely at most schools).

▲▲

This model represents a fully developed advertisement. It may not be feasible for a school to place such an ad for all positions due to the expense of print ads (as well as some online ads). In cases where a more limited ad is necessary, the school may choose to:

– limit the ad to the school name, mission, and position title—and direct the candidates to the school's Web site (where the full position details can be posted); or, similarly,

– if you have several positions open, simply list them and, again, direct candidates to the school's Web site for further details.

The key issue is to make the full details of the opening (i.e., duties, skills, experience, mission, etc.) available to the candidate in some venue. This prompts qualified candidates to apply because they have a good sense of what the school is looking for (both in terms of credentials and mission-related characteristics).

Step 6: Receive and Acknowledge Candidate Résumés.

Before résumés begin flowing in, work with your IT person to have an "automated reply" set up. That way, when candidates submit their résumés to your e-mail address, such as jobs@yourschool.org, they will receive an automatic reply acknowledging receipt of the résumé and notifying them of how they will be informed of the next steps in the hiring process. For example:

Thank you for your interest in our school. We have received your submission and will be reviewing your background against our needs for this position. We will be in contact shortly should we decide to invite you to campus for an interview or if further information is required. We wish you the best in all your endeavors.

Step 7: Screen Résumés Against the Established Job Requirements.

The hiring team then begins reviewing all résumés received against the skills, experience, and characteristics requirements that you established in Step 3, above. The team may use any number of approaches to narrow the field of applicants. One common approach to conduct the initial screening is to separate résumés into "A," "B," and "C" piles.

- *A:* Candidates that you definitely want to speak with, as their backgrounds appear to be a close fit with the requirements of the position.

- *B:* Candidates who may be a fit, but whose credentials aren't as strong as the "A" candidates.

- *C:* Candidates who do not meet the requirements.

Depending on the strength of the applicant pool—i.e., how many "A" and "B" candidates you have for the position—you may decide to extend the application period and/or place additional advertising in an effort to strengthen the potential candidate list before beginning the interview process.

Step 8: Select Candidates for Initial Telephone Screening Interviews (Optional).

Depending on the nature of the position and the number of viable candidates, you may find it helpful to conduct an initial screening by telephone. For example, if your initial screening resulted in eight or 10 "A" list candidates, you may wish to use telephone interviews to whittle this group down to a more manageable pool of four or six semifinalists. If, however, the size of the candidate pool is such that the hiring team can arrive at a workable group of candidates (e.g., four to six) directly from the résumé screening process, then the telephone screening step can be skipped. In this case, proceed directly to Step 10.

Step 9: Conduct Telephone (or Video/Skype) Screening (Optional).

The telephone screening interview is a 20-minute conversation designed to:

– tell the candidates a little more about the position;
– gauge their interest level, salary requirements, and other expectations; and
– ask them two or three questions about their background/skills to confirm that they meet the general requirements for the position.

The telephone interview process will ordinarily help the hiring team focus its efforts on the candidates whose skills, interests, and expectations best fit with the school's needs. For example, some candidates may decide to self-select out of the process after hearing more about the school's requirements or because their salary expectations vary significantly from the range the school is considering.

Step 10: Select Candidates for On-Campus Interviews.

Candidates whose interests and requirements seem a match after the telephone interview (or résumé screening) stage would then be invited for an on-campus interview. Conversely, candidates who received a telephone screening interview but who will not be invited for an on-campus interview must be notified that they are no longer under consideration. Depending on the culture of the school and the "touch factor" it wants to employ, this contact can be made by e-mail, letter, or telephone. The most important thing, regardless of the medium used, is that the "loop is closed" with the candidates—in fairness to them and so that the school maintains good will with all candidates as a reflection of its professional, caring culture.

Step 11: Prepare for the Interview—Write Questions in Advance.

For the legal protection of the school, interview questions must be strictly job-related—i.e., based on the required skills, experience, and characteristics identified for the position. As a reminder, interviewers must avoid illegal questions pertaining to race, sex, national origin, and other nonjob-related factors (see "Legal and Illegal Interview Questions" in the Appendices).

The following represent some brief tips on developing and asking interview questions. Many books have been written on the subject of interviewing; we strongly encourage hiring committee members and all others involved in interviewing to seek out additional written and live training resources to further develop their interviewing skills and knowledge.

Interview Question Sources

The hiring team should develop interview questions stemming from these key sources:
- the candidate's résumé and employment application, and
- the Faculty Hiring Specifications Form.

The résumé and application provide information about the candidate's job history, skills, and experience, which should be reviewed during a structured interview (see details below). The Faculty Hiring Specifications Form provides information regarding the school's required skills, experience, and characteristics for the position.

Behavioral Interviewing

Behavior-based interviewing operates from the premise that past performance/behavior is the best predictor of future performance/behavior. That is, how someone has acted in past situations is the best (but not the only) indication of how he/she will act in future, similar situations. For this reason, behavior-based interviewing emphasizes having candidates describe, in as much concrete detail as possible, the actions they took in specific situations similar to those they will encounter in your school and in your classrooms.

For example, a typical behavior-based question in a faculty interview would be, "Tell me about a time when a parent reacted defensively in a conference with you about his/her child. How did you handle the situation, and what were the results?" Questions that begin with "Tell me about a time when …" will most often represent appropriate behavior-based questions.

Additional Interviewing Techniques

In concert with behavior-based techniques, we recommend that interviewers:

  - strive to ask open-ended rather than yes-no questions;

  - take notes during the interview to recall specific examples that the candidate described;

  - prompt the candidate for additional details with follow-up questions where appropriate (to give the interviewer a full picture of the situation or outcome being described);

  - exercise discipline when asking questions, allowing silent time for the candidate to reflect on his/her answer before speaking (as opposed to the interviewer jumping into brief, awkward pauses and asking the next question prematurely, which often doesn't allow the candidate the opportunity to provide a thoughtful answer); and

  - actively probe for contrary evidence—that is, if a candidate displays a strong tendency in one direction, probe if he/she also has tendencies in the opposite direction, which provides the interviewer with a more well-rounded view of the candidate. For example, if a candidate's answers demonstrate a repeated tendency to violate school rules, instead of asking a follow-up question regarding any additional times the candidate has violated school rules, the interviewer should ask a contrary question such as, "Tell me about a time when you followed school rules, even if you didn't agree with them."

Conducting a Structured Interview

For purposes of effectiveness and compliance, we recommend that the administrator conduct the interview in a methodical, planned manner. Working in a structured sequence of questions, the interviewer methodically covers all the bases, from confirming the candidate's experience, to gaining a deeper understanding of his/her skills, to assessing how well the candidate seems to fit with the school's mission, culture, and values.

As indicated on the following Interview Planning and Evaluation Form, the interview should follow a logical sequence, covering:

1. *Welcome and rapport-building*
   Exchanging pleasantries; taking care of candidate's comfort (coffee, water, restroom break, etc.).

2. *School's expectations for this position*
   Summarize the school's needs and expectations for this position, and for faculty members in general. (Note: Be careful to talk for less than 20% of the interview; the candidate should speak for at least 80% of your time together.)

3. *School's mission, culture, and values*
   Probe the candidate's understanding of—and alignment with—the school's mission.

4. *Candidate's work history (résumé-based questions)*
   Have the candidate briefly walk you through his/her résumé. Ask one or two clarifying questions (e.g., for items on the résumé that weren't clear or which are particularly relevant to the school's needs in this position).

5. *Required performance characteristics*
   The hiring team should develop one or two questions for each of the Characteristics of Professional Excellence that were identified on the Faculty Hiring Specifications Form.

6. *Candidate questions, status, and next steps*
   For purposes of good will and clarity, it is important to confirm where you are in the process and when you plan to notify the candidate of next steps.

All told, a thorough interview generally lasts from 45 to 60 minutes.

By approaching the interview process in this structured fashion, the hiring team:
   - protects the school by engaging in a consistent, job-related, nondiscriminatory interview process for all candidates;
   - ensures that the most important skills, experience, and characteristics relevant to the job are being covered in the interviewing process; and
   - provides the team with the ability to make apples-to-apples comparisons of all candidates to help it arrive at an appropriate hiring decision regarding the candidate who most closely meets its requirements.

Tools

Interview questions should be recorded on a form such as the Interview Planning and Evaluation Form (shown on the next page). This form serves several purposes, including:
   - helping the hiring team plan for the interview process in an organized fashion;
   - recording a consistent set of questions to be asked of each candidate (for legal documentation purposes);
   - helping search committee members know "who is going to ask what" of each candidate;
   - providing a place for each interviewer to take notes on the candidate's responses; and
   - summarizing each interviewer's feedback for review by the School Head or decision-maker.

Aegis Academy

Interview Planning and Evaluation Form

Candidate's name:	*Annette Richardson*
Date:	*February 15, 20xx*
Position to be filled:	*Upper School History Teacher*
Interviewer's name and title:	*Kristen Grainger/History Chair*

> *Note: One person from the hiring team can use this form to record the questions that the team agrees will be asked of all candidates for the position. When completed, it can be copied or e-mailed to all hiring team members, so that all members are operating from the same source when conducting interviews.*

1. Introduction

- Welcome; beverages; restrooms, etc.—making the candidate feel comfortable
- Explain that the interviewer will take notes during the discussion and that the candidate will be asked to provide *specific details* regarding past work performance.

2. Brief Description of the School and Position

- School's mission; key facts and brief history
- Overview of main duties/expectations (e.g., teach five classes, coach two sports, etc.)

3. Mission-Related Questions

Questions designed to assess how closely aligned candidate is with the mission

Q1 *Aegis' motto is "Integrity, Service, Scholarship." Can you tell me a little about why you would want to teach in a school with this mission and how it resonates with your own goals and interests?*

Q2 *We strive to educate students to be "global citizens." What does this mean to you?*

Candidate Responses:

R1:

R2:

Aegis
Academy

4. Résumé-Based Questions
Questions designed to confirm the candidate's job history, as indicated on his/her résumé

Q1: I see from your résumé that your first teaching position was at XYZ School. Can you tell me about one or two of the most important things that you learned about teaching at XYZ that prepared for your next role with the Prep?

Q2: Your résumé says that you "created and implemented a History Careers Speakers Series" while you were at the Prep. Can you tell me about your role in organizing the series and what the impact was on students?

Candidate Responses:

R1:

R2:

5. Questions About Skills And Characteristics Of Excellence
Behavioral questions developed from the skills and characteristics of excellence selected as being the most important elements for success in this role at this school

Q1: Professional growth is an important priority here. Can you tell me about the most important professional growth experience you've had thus far in your career? What brought it about? And, what impact did it have on you in the classroom?

Q2: It's a fact of life in teaching that some students are easier to engage with than others. Can you tell me about a student who challenged your patience on a regular basis? How did you ensure that you supported his/her needs just as energetically as the needs of other students?

Q3: Can you tell me about a time that you struggled with applying the school's rules consistently? What was the point of concern and how did the situation turn out?

Q4: Tell me about the most exciting lesson you've given or project you've led that applied "real life" experiences to the topic you were discussing in the classroom.

Q5: Can you tell me about the times you felt you were bringing the most and the least enthusiasm to the classroom? What affected your enthusiasm level? And how did this impact the student learning experience?

Q6: Do you find yourself seeking out colleagues for joint projects or do you prefer to go-it-alone most times? Can you tell me about the joint project or collaboration that you're most proud of?

Candidate Responses:

R1:

R2:

R3:

R4:

R5:

R6:

6. Candidate Questions and Next Steps

- Ask the candidate what questions he/she has about the position and the school.

- Inform the candidate about what he/she can expect from this point forward—i.e., if another round of interviews is planned; when/how they will be informed about his/her status; etc.

Interview Planning and Evaluation Form: Page 3 of 4 ••• ▶

NOTE: The final page of this form, where the interviewer evaluates the candidate, is shown later in this chapter (after Step 13).

Step 12: Conduct On-Campus Interviews.

When candidates visit campus, they should complete two forms prior to interviewing:

- – Application for Employment, and
- – Background Screening Consent Form.

Application for Employment

Schools sometimes shy away from using employment applications in their faculty hiring process, feeling (or fearing) that prospective faculty members see it as unnecessarily "bureaucratic" and beneath their dignity as professionals. They believe—incorrectly—that it is "just the same as a résumé." However, applications provide protections for the school that résumés do not, making them an important part of a safe and effective hiring process. The application form offers numerous benefits.

- ■ *Provides consistency:* One of the most serious legal risks for schools is an employment process that varies from applicant to applicant. By requiring all candidates to complete an application, the school is ensuring that it is collecting consistent data—allowing it to compare applications on a fair and equal basis and avoiding inadvertent discrimination due to different treatment.

- ■ *Communicates EEO commitment:* By including the school's Equal Employment Opportunity (EEO) statement (noted previously) on the application, the school is prominently communicating its commitment to EEO principles in the hiring process.

- ■ *Identifies work eligibility:* Applications should ask the question "Can you, after employment, submit verification of your legal right to work in the United States (yes/no)?"—which forewarns the candidate that he/she will need to comply with the I-9 requirements (noted previously) if hired.

- ■ *Identifies criminal history:* While virtually no candidate will indicate his/her criminal history on a résumé, the application requires disclosure of felony and misdemeanor convictions—providing information that may be relevant for screening purposes and may disqualify him/her from further consideration, even before a background check is run. For example, if a candidate indicates a recent felony conviction for a violent crime or a crime against children, it is unlikely that you will wish to proceed further in the interview process. (See the following "Background Screening" section for further details and guidance.)

- ■ *Provides past salary information:* This is a quick indication to the school as to whether the candidate's past salary is in line with (or significantly above or below) the potential salary being offered, helping provide an initial gauge as to how likely it is that the school's offer might be accepted by the candidate.

- *Identifies reasons for leaving past jobs:* Few candidates indicate reasons for leaving past positions on their résumé. By requiring this on the application, the school can better understand the circumstances surrounding the candidate's career moves (e.g., whether he/she resigned to pursue greater responsibilities in a new school or was terminated or dismissed from a school).

- *Signing to verify accuracy:* All applications should include a statement in which the candidate vouches for the accuracy and completeness of all information contained on the application. By way of this statement, the school notifies the candidate that misrepresentations will be grounds for the rejection of his/her application (or termination, if discovered after the person is hired).

None of the protections noted are gained by the school if candidates are allowed to submit résumés without completing applications. Therefore, as both a matter of legal protection (to avoid discrimination or wrongful hiring claims) and good practice (being able to compare candidates on the basis of the same data points), requiring candidates to complete employment applications is essential.

Background Screening Consent Form

As noted previously, the school must comply with the Fair Credit Reporting Act (FCRA) regulations if it plans to order background screening reports (such as criminal history reports) from a vendor. To do so, it must have the candidate's written consent *before* it conducts any reference checks (including calling any professional references) or orders any background reports. To comply with FCRA, the school should have all candidates who are brought to campus for an interview complete the one-page Background Screening Consent Form at the time of the interview.

NOTE: The Background Screening Consent Form requests the candidate's birth date (commonly required by screening vendors to verify background information) and thus indicates the candidate's age. Therefore, this form must not be shared with anyone involved in the hiring decision to avoid age discrimination concerns under the Age Discrimination in Employment Act (ADEA). Accordingly, after completion, this form should be handled only by the person or office (usually the Business Office) responsible for ordering background reports on finalist candidates. It should be maintained in the recruiting file and should not be transferred to the candidate's personnel file when the person is hired.

TIP: States may have background screening notification provisions that exceed federal law. Check with your school's background screening vendor to ensure that the consent form your school is using complies with your state's requirements.

The Interview Setting

The school will want to ensure that interviews are conducted in a quiet, private setting that is not likely to be subject to interruptions, excessive noise, clutter, etc., none of which is conducive to putting the candidate at ease and conducting an effective interview. The interview should proceed according to the general outline indicated on the Interview Planning and Evaluation Form.

Closing the Interview

In bringing the interview to a conclusion, the interviewer should:

– thank the candidate for his/her time;

– explain the next steps in the process as well as the anticipated time frames (i.e., whether the candidate will be interviewed by others that day and the names and positions of those whom he/she will be meeting; at the conclusion of the day, the approximate date when the candidate can expect to hear from the school); and

– personally guide the candidate to the next interview or see him/her to the door (if it is the candidate's final interview of the day).

VIGNETTE: Conducting An Interview

To wrap up our discussion of interviewing methods, we wanted to offer a vignette to bring several of the key points to life in a vibrant way. Imagine, if you will, the following scene:

SET-UP: Stephanie is an applicant for the position of English Teacher in Aegis Academy's middle school. On paper, Stephanie is the leading candidate, as her education, skills, and experience appear to closely match the school's established requirements. Consider the interview that Robert, the School Head, conducts as part of the school's hiring process. What does he do right? What does he do wrong? Are any parts potentially illegal or discriminatory, or just ineffective?

NOTE: We provide comments, observations, and recommendations regarding Robert's interview questions and techniques in the "commentary" column. You may wish to read the "dialogue" column in full, then loop back to the "commentary" column for notes and perspectives on the dialogue.

Dialogue

Robert (Interviewer): Good morning, Stephanie. Thanks for coming in today.

Stephanie (Candidate): My pleasure. It's great to be here.

Robert: Please have a seat. Is there anything I can get you—coffee, juice, water?

Stephanie: Water would be great. Thank you.

Robert: Did you have any problem with traffic this morning?

Stephanie: No. I'm a morning person. Ever since I finished rehab, I've disciplined myself to run at least two miles four times a week. So, I was up and out early—just as the sun came up.

Robert: That's great. What was the rehab for—knee surgery? ACL?

Stephanie: Oh, no—the other kind of rehab. I've had a few struggles with some issues in my life. I don't mind talking about it, if you'd like—it's part of the recovery process.

Robert: [to himself] Oh, my. I didn't see that one coming. I probably don't want to go down that path. How can I get us back on track?

Robert: [out loud] I appreciate your candor, but that won't be necessary. (Pause). I see that you went to UM as an undergrad. Great school. I started work on my doctorate there. Beautiful campus.

Robert: [to himself] There—that wasn't too bad. This seems a lot safer ground.

Stephanie: It sure is a great school—what I remember of it, that is. You know—always a party going on somewhere. I could tell you some stories, believe me! But that was a long time ago in a different life, it seems. Anyway, it's funny how life goes—my oldest is considering colleges now and she's interested in their Junior Year Abroad program. She wants to study our family heritage firsthand.

> *Sometimes, even the most innocent question brings potentially controversial and discriminatory information in reply. Interviewers should be ready for this and prepared to gracefully deflect the question. In this case, a simple question about the morning traffic leads to a disclosure of a past disability. As is the case here, the key issue is not following up with a question that is likely to prompt disclosure of potentially discriminatory information (regarding medical condition).*

> *This is an example of gracefully redirecting the interview back to its core purpose without offending the candidate who has offered too much personal information.*

> *Sometimes candidates just want to talk and tell you everything about their lives, even if you haven't asked. In this case, the school needs to decide if Stephanie's candor and openness is a quality that aligns well with the school's mission, culture, and values—or if it is an example of poor judgment that may not reflect well on her ability to maintain appropriate boundaries.*

Robert again prompts a dangerous line of questioning regarding national origin, which is a "protected class" under Title VII of the Civil Rights Act of 1964. While it is somewhat safer if the candidate brings up discriminatory information than if the school actively seeks it out, the fact that it comes up at all puts the school at risk. This heightens the need to have a structured interviewing process based on the requirements of the job—so that a potential defense if a lawsuit is brought is the fact that all candidates were asked the same questions during the interview process.

Again, it is reasonable for Robert to wonder if Stephanie's candor is appropriate for the job she would be hired for. If discretion is an important requirement for the job, though, it probably should be asked about directly—as in a behavioral question specifically addressing the candidate's skill in keeping private information private and confidential.

It is appropriate for Robert to share with Stephanie the general interview approach that he will be using. This is helpful in "training" Stephanie on the fact that Robert will be seeking specific answers about Stephanie's past experiences that are relevant to the job. This helps emphasize to her that she can "shine" best in the interview by relating specific, substantive details about how she demonstrated a particular skill or philosophy in the past.

Robert: What heritage is that?

Robert: [to himself] Ooops! Should I have asked that? I'm just trying to make small talk. How bad could it be?

Stephanie: My father is from Eastern Europe and my mother is from Argentina. They met while studying in Mexico City during graduate school.

Robert: I see from your résumé that you're fluent in Spanish. Were you born in Mexico?

Stephanie: Actually, I was born in Costa Rica, where my parents were living at the time—we emigrated here when I was a year old. I hold dual citizenship.

Robert: Very interesting. That's terrific. Well, we've got a lot of ground to cover today, so what do you say we dive right in.

Stephanie: Sure thing. I'm an open book.

Robert: [to himself] She sure is an open book. I wonder if our parents would be happy with someone who is so "open" about her life. Hmmmmm. Anyway, we've made it this far—I guess I should just keep asking the questions and we'll see where we end up. I'm glad I wrote out the questions in advance or who knows what we might end up discussing.

Robert: [out loud] Before we begin, Stephanie, I just wanted to share with you a little about our approach to interviewing. I'll be taking notes as we talk. It helps me recall our conversation in more detail later on.

Stephanie: No problem at all.

Robert: Great. The other thing that I want to explain is that we use what we call a "behavioral" interview style here. I'll be asking you for examples of your experience in several key areas. You can help me by giving specific examples. Do you have any questions before we begin?

Stephanie: No. Sounds good. Fire away.

Robert: Wonderful. OK, then. As you know, grammar and sentence structure are strongly emphasized in the 9th and 10th grade here. We realize that studying grammar is often a dry lesson. Can you tell me about any creative approaches in this area that you've taken in the past? What has worked? What didn't work? And what did you learn from it? And what would you suggest if a new colleague asked you for advice on this?

Stephanie: Great questions. OK, I'll take them one at a time. To start with, I do agree. Grammar is often very dry.

Robert: [to himself] That was a great question. I remember when I was starting out and struggled teaching grammar. I'll be interested to hear what she has to say. Oh—I think she started talking. I better pay attention to her answer.

Stephanie: Earlier in my career, after struggling through what even I thought were dull lessons with the 9th graders I was teaching at the time, I had an idea for a "quiz show" to help the students with . . .

After the interview proceeded for another 30 minutes or so, Robert was ready to wrap things up.

Robert: Stephanie, we've covered a lot of ground today, and I appreciate your candid answers. I don't mind telling you that I've been very impressed. We'll finish our last interviews on Friday. We want to get our staffing plan in place for next year as quickly as possible—so we'll be in touch with you the middle of next week with our decision.

Robert: [to himself] Well, I'm glad I didn't get scared off by the way she opened the interview. Stephanie really impressed me with the depth of her experience and her self-awareness. She might be exactly what we're looking for.

Stephanie: So, how did I do?

Interviewers should ask only one question at a time. In this case, Robert somewhat breathlessly runs four or five questions together into one, making it difficult for the candidate to remember and respond to each question appropriately.

The interviewer must use active listening skills during the interview.

Stephanie does a good job of starting to give a substantive answer, telling a story about a specific, relevant experience she has had in the past.

> *While rapport-building and maintaining good will are two critical elements of a successful hiring process, at the same time, it is important not to mislead or overstate the candidate's chances to be hired. In this case, Robert has gone too far. While he is trying to be appropriately upbeat and complimentary, his comment about "if the others' impressions are as favorable as my own …" he has created the impression that the job is virtually a lock to be offered to Stephanie. If this is still an open question behind closed doors at the school, it is best to say less rather than more. Otherwise, the candidate will feel misled or "used" if he/she doesn't ultimately receive a job offer.*

Robert: I want to consult with the others you spoke with—as well as the School Head, of course. However, if their impressions are anything like my own—well, it all looks very favorable.

Robert: [to himself] Always leave them on a high note, they say. Right? I've got to say, I think I did a good job with this one.

Stephanie: Thanks. I'm really excited about the opportunity. I hope to hear from you soon.

Step 13: Assess Results of Interviews.

Each interviewer should complete a written assessment of the interview as soon as possible after it is complete, while the facts are still fresh. A tool that can help interviewers record their assessment in a consistent fashion—see the final page of the Interview Planning and Evaluation Form on the next page.

Note that, while the interviewers are asked for substantive *feedback* on the candidate, the form does not ask them to *vote* on whether the candidate should be hired or not. The exact use of this feedback will vary by school. Depending on its culture, some schools may in fact grant each member of the hiring team a vote, with the candidate with the most votes being offered the positions. However, in many schools, the School Head serves as the ultimate arbiter—gathering the feedback and insights of the hiring team, but making the final decision as to which candidate will be hired.

Interview Planning and Evaluation Form (cont'd)

CANDIDATE	INTERVIEWER
Annette Richardson	Kristen Grainger

A. Does the candidate appear to be a good fit with the mission, culture, and values of our school? Why/why not?		
☑ Yes	❑ No	❑ Undetermined

COMMENTS

Annette spoke passionately about her commitment to developing "global citizens" in a way that aligns closely with our mission. She presented herself in a professional but friendly and engaging manner that is very consistent with our culture.

B. Does the candidate appear to possess the skills and Characteristics of Professional Excellence required by the position? Why/why not?			
Skill/Characteristic	Demonstrated		
1. Professional Growth	☑ Yes	❑ No	❑ Undetermined
2. On Their Side	☑ Yes	❑ No	❑ Undetermined
3. Consistency and Reliability	☑ Yes	❑ No	❑ Undetermined
4. Real Life Applications	☑ Yes	❑ No	❑ Undetermined
5. Enthusiasm	☑ Yes	❑ No	❑ Undetermined
6. Healthy Learning Community	☑ Yes	❑ No	❑ Undetermined

COMMENTS

The quality that stood out the most during the interview was Annette's passion for bringing "real-life examples" to the classroom. One example was her bringing a recently retired politician into class to discuss the legislative process.

Interview Planning and Evaluation Form: Page 4 of 4

Step 14: Invite Final Candidate(s) for Guest Teaching Demonstration.

Asking candidates to demonstrate their teaching practice in your school's setting is a traditional aspect of faculty hiring processes in many schools. We recommend this as an excellent way of viewing the candidate's skills—particularly his/her interaction with students—on a firsthand basis. While the demonstration lesson is admittedly an artificial situation even under the best circumstances, it still provides the best opportunity for gaining a "live" look at the candidate's interactions and classroom presence.

NOTE: Some schools choose to conduct guest teaching sessions as part of the initial on-campus interview rather than at the finalist stage. While this may create scheduling challenges (due to the larger number of candidates in the initial stage of the process), this is perfectly appropriate—and may serve as an early double check mechanism to screen for candidates who interview well but teach poorly, or vice versa.

To position the teaching demonstration for the greatest possible success, the hiring team should take these two steps.

- Provide the candidates with clear expectations well in advance of the demonstration lesson to allow adequate time for preparation. Specifically, describe what you are looking for (e.g., lecturing ability, engagement with students, leading class discussions) so that they can plan their lessons accordingly.

- Play to each candidate's strengths (i.e., ask him/her to demonstrate a class in his/her specialty area) insofar as this is possible within the context of the overall curriculum of the class to be visited. Keep in mind the need to:
  - have the various candidates teach equivalent classes (e.g., all honors sections in a high school, or the same subject in an elementary homeroom setting);
  - prepare the students appropriately by being transparent about the purposes of the class. As much as possible, have the guest's topic relate to the students' curriculum to ensure that the students will be as focused and engaged as possible;
  - prepare the candidate properly, in terms of providing perspective on how the lesson fits into the class's regular curriculum, what they've worked on in the few days leading up to the lesson, etc.; and
  - allow time on-site for the candidate to prepare him/herself prior to giving the class (at least an hour).

Step 15: Check Professional References and Conduct Background Verification on Finalist Candidate(s).

Depending on how closely the finalist candidates are rated after the guest teaching demonstration, the school may decide to check references and conduct background screening on multiple candidates (if two or more candidates are closely rated), or only on the finalist candidate (if one is clearly above the others). In all cases, though, it is imperative that both professional references (for qualitative, mission-appropriateness reasons) and background verifications (for legal, safety reasons) are checked scrupulously before offering or confirming a position for a candidate.

There are important distinctions between "professional reference checks" and "background screening"—terms that are often (mis)used interchangeably, but which actually represent two distinct processes.

Professional Reference Checks

We recommend that the candidate's professional references be personally checked by the hiring manager (i.e., the person to whom the candidate will report). The purpose of checking references is to gain qualitative information about the candidate from supervisors and colleagues—i.e., those in the best position to assess the candidate's on-the-job skills and behaviors. Candidates are ordinarily asked to provide the names and contact information for three professional references who will be able to discuss the candidate's performance (which may be supplemented by written reference letters, if available).

Tools

The following Reference Check Script is provided as a guide to the reference check conversation. It focuses on the same Characteristics of Professional Excellence that were identified in Step 3 and which have been guiding the hiring process throughout.

Telephone Reference Check Script

Candidate	Annette Richardson
Opening	Upper School History Teacher
Reference	Samuel Andrews
School/Organization	Central Prep
Title	Chair, History Department
Telephone	811.555.1212

1. In what capacity have you known this candidate?
Professional. For 4 years

2. Briefly describe the position the candidate is applying for.
Question: "How do you feel the candidate would work in this type of role and environment, and why?"
Very well. Annette is highly committed to educating children on their role as global ambassadors. I believe that she will excel in your culture.

3. What would you list as the candidate's top three or four characteristics on the job?
Dependability; energy; perseverance; commitment.

4. Can you tell me something about the candidate's on-the-job behavior and performance regarding:
Healthy Learning Community: Reported that Annette is considered to be one of the most supportive and engaged colleagues on the entire faculty, constantly being sought out for quiet, confidential guidance by peers.

Consistency and reliability: Early in her career, Annette was prone to giving too many "special exceptions" to students that inadvertently lowered standards. She has focused on becoming much more consistent in enforcing standards in recent years, an effort that has had very positive results.

••••▶

5. *If you had to suggest one area, skill, or characteristic for the candidate to work on or enhance in the future, what would it be and why?*

Sometimes her passion can lead Annette to raise her voice with colleagues, which is interpreted as conflict or confrontation. Being mindful of this will help her be a better colleague.

6. *Is there anything we haven't talked about that you feel would be pertinent if the candidate became an employee of our school?*

Her extensive volunteer work with a global charity aligns very closely with the school's mission.

NOTE: *If the reference is a current or former supervisor (e.g., the teacher's current or past School Head), a closing question might be,* **"If you had the opportunity to rehire this individual, would you?"** *This would not be relevant or appropriate, of course, if the reference is a current or former peer.*

Closing Statement: *"Thank you for your time and consideration. Reference checking is an important part of our hiring process, and we appreciate your assistance a great deal."*

▲▲

Background Verification

Background verification involves confirming the information the candidate has provided regarding prior employment, education, criminal record, and driving record. Due to the requirements of the Fair Credit Reporting Act (FCRA) regarding use of information contained in background reports (see Chapter 2 for further details), ISM recommends that schools contract with outside vendors for this service.

We also strongly recommend that background results should be tightly controlled for the school's legal protection. For example, the School Head or Division Head may be responsible for notifying the Business Manager that a background check should be ordered on a finalist candidate. The Business Manager would then ensure that the appropriate report is ordered, and the results—when received—are transmitted directly to the individual at the school who is responsible for assessing whether or not the candidate's background meets the school's standards. We ordinarily recommend that this be the school's Business Manager, as this position is outside the faculty hiring chain of command and is least susceptible to claims of using the background information for discriminatory purposes in the future, if the candidate is hired.

The hiring manager is informed solely of the candidate's "pass/fail" status. He/she is not informed of the reasons for the determination, for his/her own protection, as well as that of the candidate and the school.

Verification Reports to Be Ordered

The school must determine the extent to which it will check the candidate's background. For example, if the candidate has lived in three states in the past seven years, will the school request that the vendor check the criminal records in all three states—or just the last state of residence? The same questions exists for motor vehicle records (assuming that the faculty position requires driving—such as to/from field trips, athletic contests, and the like).

Ultimately, this becomes a risk management question for the school—determining the relative cost-benefit relationship between the safety of greater knowledge versus the time/expense of securing additional reports. Accordingly, we recommend that schools develop a standard protocol, a sample of which is shown below. Review and modify these parameters based on the school's needs and interests.

Sample Background Screening Plan

SCREENING REPORT	WHEN ORDERED	PARAMETERS
Criminal	For all openings	Order a national search plus sex offender registry check
Employment	For all openings	Check the last three employers (up to 10 years)
Education	For all openings	Verify the highest degree
Motor Vehicle	For all openings in which driving on school business is a reasonable expectation	Check DMV records in state of current residence plus any states lived in over past three years

Background Screening Criteria

Similarly, schools should establish criteria by which the screening report reviewer (e.g., the Business Manager or HR professional) can determine whether or not the candidate meets the school's standards with regard to criminal history and other background report elements. The exact criteria used will depend in large measure on the school's culture and values—i.e., its views on youthful transgressions and the question of forgiveness versus the value of protecting its students, employees, and community members. A sample criteria chart is shown below.

REPORT	CRITERIA
	Absent significant mitigating circumstances, the following criteria will ordinarily disqualify a candidate for employment consideration.
Criminal	• *Any convictions for violent acts* • *Any convictions involving fraud or embezzlement* • *Any convictions requiring registration as a sex offender* • *Any convictions for acts involving minors* • *Any felony convictions within the past seven years*
Employment	*Any material misrepresentation regarding dates of employment, position title, or duties*
Education	*Any material misrepresentation regarding completion of degree or type/level of degree*
Motor Vehicle	• *Three or more moving violations within the past 36 months (including speeding, driving without a license/insurance, etc.)* • *Any convictions for DWI, DUI, or similar impairment within the past three years*

REMINDER: No references should be contacted nor any background reports ordered prior to the candidate signing a Background Screening Consent Form.

If a candidate passes the background screening, the hiring manager should be advised immediately. If the candidate fails the screening, the hiring manager should be so advised and the FCRA notification process (see Chapter 2 for details) should be triggered immediately.

NOTE: Federal and state agencies and laws are increasingly limiting the type and extent of background information that may be used in the hiring process (e.g., the use of credit checks and even criminal background checks is increasingly coming under scrutiny). Please consult with your employment attorney concerning the state of the law on this point in your jurisdiction.

A Caution Regarding 'Googling' a Candidate or Checking His/Her Facebook Page

As social media continues to evolve, more and more employers are "Googling" candidates, checking their Facebook public pages, etc., prior to inviting them for interviews. As this practice becomes more widespread, we are beginning to see court decisions regarding the legalities of using social media information in the hiring process. As we go to press, the matter is far from settled legally.

We caution all schools to consider the risks involved in obtaining potentially discriminatory information regarding a candidate (i.e., pertaining to protected characteristics such as race, ethnicity, sexual orientation, etc., described in Chapter 2). Possessing such information may place the school at risk of a discrimination lawsuit should the candidate not receive an offer of employment. Schools are advised to consult with their employment attorney before engaging in social media checks of this type.

Step 16: Select the Final Candidate.

After all the interviewing, data-gathering (e.g., guest teaching), and reference-checking and background verification processes have concluded, the hiring team reconvenes to select the final candidate. As noted above, this process will vary based on the School Head's desired approach. The Head may choose to have the hiring team:

- recommend a candidate for his/her approval;
- offer a small slate of candidates for him/her to select from; or
- select a candidate to be hired by "vote" or consensus.

No matter which process is used to arrive at a final decision, all decision-makers (and all of those with input) consider all final candidates in terms of how they compare against the school's desired skills, experience, and characteristics of excellence. While no hiring process is 100% foolproof, we strongly believe that continual references to mission/culture/values when making hiring decisions is the best and most effective course for schools to take—and will ultimately lead them, when consistently applied, to the faculty that they desire.

Step 17: Determine the Job Offer.

Upon selection of the final candidate, the school is in a position to determine the terms of the job offer. It is most important that the offer is consistent with your school's policies, salary structure, culture, and expectations. (See Chapter 7, Reward and Recognition Process, for a detailed discussion of compensation structures within private-independent schools.)

Step 18: Make a Verbal Job Offer to the Finalist.

Once the salary offer is determined, the appointed administrator (usually the Division Head or School Head) will call the candidate with the offer. The person making the verbal job offer should be trained to avoid inadvertently making *promises* that can later be construed as *verbal contracts*—e.g., *"I'm sure* we can revisit your salary needs after six months"—unless the promise is going to be included as a term of employment in the offer letter or contract. By sticking to the terms approved by the Head, the school will protect itself against making unintended contractual promises.

Candidates may accept "on the spot," or they may ask for a few days to consider the offer. The school should be clear with the candidate as to what it considers an acceptable time frame for response.

Step 19: Upon Acceptance of an Offer, Issue the Contract and Notify Nonselected Candidates.

When the candidate has verbally accepted the job offer, a written contract can then be prepared. At that time, all remaining candidates should be notified that they have not been selected, to bring closure to the process and maintain good will. Remember, the candidate who finished "second" may be your top candidate for another opening next year.

Tools

ISM has developed the following Sample Faculty Contract.

NOTE: Sample contract language is shown in black. Commentary and "tips" are shown in the gray boxes within the contract.

Sample Faculty Contract

THIS AGREEMENT is made and entered into by and between the School Head, as the duly authorized agent of Aegis Academy, Inc., a nonprofit corporation of the State of ___ (hereinafter called the "School") and NAME _____(hereafter called the "Educator"). The parties agree as follows.

1. Term of Contract:

The School will employ the Educator for the 20___–20___ School Year, commencing August 15, 20___ and ending August 14, 20___. Both parties agree that neither the Educator nor the School owes any subsequent contractual obligation or services to the other after the ending date of this contract. There are no restrictions whatsoever on either party's right to choose to seek or refuse to seek another contract with the other party after the expiration of this agreement, and both parties are free to negotiate future employment on an equal basis.

> *Whether the school elects to use a 10- or 12-month contract (as referenced here), in all cases the starting and ending dates should be selected to include all dates on which the teacher's services are needed (i.e., the contract should start on or before the preschool orientation week and should end on or after the end-of-school meetings).*

2. Void Contract:

In the event that any existing employment contract between the parties is terminated prior to expiration, the contract set forth herein shall be null and void and neither party shall owe any compensation or services to the other.

> *If the School has signed this contract for the next school year (i.e., starting in September) but after signing determines that the teacher must be let go in the current year (e.g., March, April, May, or June), this clause ensures that the new contract is automatically voided before it goes into effect (thus avoiding the messy situation where you terminate someone but he/she still has a valid contract for next year and you need to buy him/her out of a full year's salary).*

●●●▶

3. Position and Duties:

The Educator is appointed to the position of _____ in the _____ division of the School. The Educator shall perform all reasonable duties as assigned by the School Head or his/her designee appropriate to the Educator's skills and position and as needed to fulfill the School's plans, programs, and standards. The Educator understands and agrees that he/she may be regularly called on to perform duties—including but not limited to cocurricular duties—that may often take place outside of what is generally considered to be the standard school day. The Educator agrees to attend all required meetings, keep all records, and prepare and file all reports customary for his/her position and as required and directed by the School.

> *The School may wish to specify particular classroom, coaching, and cocurricular duties within this section—or include an "addendum" (referenced and incorporated as part of the contract) that spells out duties and requirements in detail. However, schools should act with caution when spelling out duties too exactly. Few schools can predict the shifting operational needs that develop during the spring and summer after a contract has been signed. Thus, the School should avoid language that unnecessarily restricts it from changing the teacher's duties within reason if the needs of the School change.*

4. Duty of Compliance:

The Educator agrees to perform these duties to the best of his/her abilities to the School's satisfaction, in accord with the laws of the State of _____, and in compliance with the policies and procedures of the School (as spelled out in the School's employee handbook and other relevant documents). In addition, the Educator agrees to abide by the rules, regulations, and requirements established by the Board of Trustees of the School. In any instance where the School's policies and procedures are deemed to be in conflict with the terms and conditions of this contract, the contract's terms and conditions shall take precedence.

> *The School should explicitly reference the employee handbook policies and procedures, incorporating those policies and procedures as terms and conditions of the contract. In doing so, however, the School should review the employee handbook carefully to ensure that its policies are not in conflict with the provisions of this contract.*

••••▶

5. Compensation:

In consideration of the Educator's services (as set forth in this contract), the School agrees to pay the Educator the sum of $_____ during the term of this contract.

Compensation shall be subject to all deductions and tax withholdings required by applicable federal, state, and local law.

Paid Time-Off: The Educator will be eligible for ____ sick days and ____ personal days during the term of this contract. Use of sick and personal time will be governed by provisions stated in the employee handbook.

> *The School may choose to specify here whether unused sick/personal days can be carried over to potential future contracts, or if unused sick/personal time is paid out at the conclusion of the contract. Alternatively, the School may choose to leave these details for the employee handbook.*

Overtime Status: The Educator's position has been determined to be exempt from federal and state overtime regulations and thus he/she is not eligible to earn or be paid additional compensation (commonly referred to as "overtime") for additional hours worked.

The Educator's compensation may be reduced by periods of unpaid leave or for other legally permissible reasons set forth by the School Head.

> *It is vital to clarify the exempt/nonexempt status of the teacher's position, so that there is no confusion or dispute regarding eligibility for overtime pay. (As an exempt employee, please note that a teacher's salary may only be reduced or stopped for reasons permissible under FLSA.)*

School Breaks: The Educator will be paid his/her full salary during regularly scheduled school breaks (such as Winter or Spring Break) when classes are not in session.

The School shall pay the Educator over 10 months or 12 months at the Educator's election, in accord with the School's ordinary payroll practices. To comply with Section 409a of the IRS tax code, the Educator will be required to complete a written election of his/her selection.

> *If the School permits the faculty member to choose to be paid over 12 months instead of 10, a written "election" is required to comply with Section 409a of the tax code (or else the school and the employee will risk penalties on deferred compensation). A 12-month contract avoids this issue.*

●●●▶

6. Benefits:

The Educator shall be permitted to participate in all employee benefits programs available to faculty for which he/she otherwise qualifies, as per the guidelines of the plans that comprise the School's benefits offerings. The cost, if any, of participating in the employee benefits which the Educator elects will be deducted from the Educator's pay with his/her authorization, according to the established procedures of the School.

Some schools may choose to recite all of the faculty member's benefits options in this section— or as an addendum to this contract. Where benefits plans are recited in detail, the school should be careful to add a clause to the contract indicating that:

"While brief descriptions of the plans are provided here for summary purposes, the provisions of the official plan documents govern the administration and eligibility criteria of the plans. Where there is any discrepancy between these brief descriptions and the official plan documents, the terms of the official plan documents will prevail."

The Educator understands that benefits plans may be created, modified, or eliminated from time to time, as permitted by law and the agreements between the school and its benefits providers—and that such changes may occur during the term of this contract. The Educator will be eligible to participate in the benefits plans as per the then-current terms of the individual plans.

7. Confidentiality:

The Educator acknowledges that during the course of employment, he/she may obtain or have access to confidential information that is important to the School's business. This includes but is not limited to matters related to students, parents, employees, donors, and volunteers and may include student, parent, employee, volunteer, and donor names, academic records, addresses, financial information, and other personal information. The Educator may also become aware of marketing and academic plans and other information proprietary to the School. This is all herein referred to collectively as "Confidential Information."

The Educator acknowledges that such Confidential Information is the property of the School. The Educator agrees that during the term of this Agreement and thereafter, for so long as the pertinent information remains confidential, the Educator shall not divulge or otherwise make use of any Confidential Information, directly or indirectly, personally, on behalf of any other person, business, organization, or entity, without the prior written consent of the School.

A similar confidentiality statement should be included in the School's employee handbook.

8. New Employees:

If the Educator has not previously been employed by the School, this contract is contingent upon the following:

The Educator must complete a full application for employment. The Educator represents and warrants that all of the statements and facts set forth on the application are true and correct and that there has been no omission of material facts therein. Any false or misleading statement(s) of material fact(s) in the application or omission of material fact(s) shall be grounds for termination of employment and concurrent voiding and termination of this contract.

By the time a contract is offered to a new employee, the School should have already ensured that an Application for Employment was completed and signed by the candidate—ordinarily at the time he/she was first interviewed on campus. Accepting a résumé only without a signed application provides insufficient protection for the School, as the candidate's résumé is not signed by the candidate and thus he/she is not certifying the accuracy of its contents.

The Educator must also successfully complete all requirements of the School's pre-employment screening process, including but not limited to: criminal background and/or fingerprint checks, reference checks, and pre-employment drug testing. The Educator understands and agrees that the school may obtain consumer credit reports (commonly known as "background screening reports") for legally permissible screening purposes.

In compliance with the Fair Credit Reporting Act (FCRA), the School should also ensure that a Background Screening Authorization Form is completed by every candidate who is interviewed by the School.

9. Termination Provisions:

With the best interest of the School's students in mind, both parties intend for all aspects of the Educator's duties to be carried out for the full term of this contract. However, if grave circumstances or events compel one or both parties to seek to terminate this contract prior to its ending date, the following provisions will apply:

It is vital that the contract provide explicit termination provisions. If it does not, it may easily be construed that the School must pay the teacher for the full term of the contract (even if it validly terminated the employee midyear for performance or behavior issues).

●●●▶

Educator Resignation: If the Educator desires to resign his/her position, the Educator must give thirty (30) days written notice to the School Head. If the Educator successfully carries out his/her duties during the notice period, he/she will be compensated through the end of the notice period.

If the Educator does not provide thirty (30) days notice, compensation will terminate as of the Educator's last day worked.

> *The 30-day provision is recommended to avoid sudden, unexpected resignations, which may significantly disrupt the classroom and continuity of student education. As an incentive to faculty members to avoid sudden resignations, schools may wish to state that references will be withheld if proper notice is not provided by the faculty member.*

The parties agree that the School, at its sole discretion, may elect to pay the employee for the thirty (30) day notice period in lieu of the Educator working through the notice period.

> *Conversely, based on its culture and values, the School may determine that it will pay out the contract in full regardless of whether or not the termination is for cause. In such a case, by leaving this provision in the contract, the School is placing itself in a position to validly execute a "Separation Agreement and General Release" when terminating the employee. The release— which provides protection against future discrimination or wrongful termination claims by the employee—is validly offered because it provides valuable "additional consideration" (in the form of pay for the remainder of the term) that is not otherwise required.*

Educator Termination for Cause: If the School, at its sole discretion, determines that it will terminate the Educator's employment for cause (defined for purposes of this contract as behavior which brings disrepute on the School; insubordination; or actions which place the School's students, employees, parents, volunteers, or visitors in physical, emotional, or other danger), the School will provide written notice to the Educator of such termination. In this event, this contract and all compensation due to the Educator will terminate as of the last day worked.

> *The School may wish to list several more examples of for cause reasons for termination. This clause is intended to protect the School from having to pay out the remainder of the contract by distinguishing for-cause terminations from dismissals (described further below).*

Temporary or Permanent Discontinuance of Operations: If the School determines the need to cease operations temporarily or permanently for financial, operational, or safety reasons (such as due to enrollment decline, legal action, or unsafe conditions

●●●▶

due to flood or earthquake), the School will notify the Educator in writing and shall continue the Educator's compensation for thirty (30) days beyond the last day worked or thirty (30) days beyond the date of written notice, whichever is later.

Educator Dismissal: If the School, at its sole discretion, determines the need to terminate the Educator's employment for reasons other than those outlined above, the school will provide written notice to the Educator and shall continue the Educator's compensation through the end of the term of this contract.

> *As noted above, the School may determine it is most consistent with its culture and values to pay a terminated employee in full when dismissing a faculty member midyear.*
>
> *As the School doesn't want to inadvertently create (or deny) benefits termination or continuation rights that are different from existing practices and federal and state COBRA laws, it should review all benefits provisions in the contract carefully.*

Termination of Employee Benefits: In all cases in which this contract is terminated prior to the end of its term, the Educator's ability for employee benefits provided by the School shall terminate according to the regular provisions of the School's employee benefits programs.

10. Ability to Enter into Contract:

The Educator hereby affirms that he/she is not under contract with any other school covering a part or all of the same period as contemplated by this contract, nor is he/she bound by any other restriction preventing him/her from legally entering into this binding contract.

> *This affirmation is intended to prevent the teacher from entering into contracts in violation of existing contractual terms (e.g., signing a contract with your School in March after having signed a contract with another school in February for the coming school year).*

11. Entire Agreement, Modifications, and Severability:

Both parties expressly acknowledge that this contract expresses the only agreement between the parties hereto, unmodified and unaffected by any other understanding whatsoever. Any other perceived representation by the Educator or the School (including its agents or employees)—except for written documents explicitly incorporated by reference into this contract, such as the School's employee handbook—are not part of this contract or contractual representations.

This contract may only be modified in writing, signed by both the Educator and the School Head (or his/her designee), and entitled, "Modification of Contract."

••••▶

Should any provision of this contract be invalidated by a court of law with proper jurisdiction, the remaining provisions shall remain in full force and effect.

These are standard legal provisions in most contracts.

12. Jurisdiction:

The parties agree that this contract shall be interpreted in accordance with the laws of the State of _____, and that the venue for any action concerning this contract shall be the state or federal court having jurisdiction over these matters in the County of _____.

Similarly, this is a standard legal provision.

In consultation with its legal counsel—and depending upon its philosophy—the School may elect to specify that contract claims will be mediated by an arbitrator (rather than through a court proceeding). Please consult with legal counsel to determine if a mandatory arbitration clause is permissible or advisable under your state's laws.

13. Modification and Expiration of Contract Offer:

The School reserves the right to modify or rescind the above offer of employment prior to acceptance by the Educator.

This contract offer shall be null and void unless the Educator returns an executed copy of this contract to the School by _____ (date), unless this deadline is extended in writing by the School Head or his/her designee.

For practical purposes, most schools need to have contracts signed (or declined) by specific deadlines so that hiring vacancies can be accomplished in a timely manner.

Signatures and Dates

_____

NAME   DATE

NOTE: *ISM's Sample Faculty Contract (above) should never be used as is.* This sample is provided for discussion purposes only. All contracts and other legal documents should be drafted and reviewed by an employment attorney qualified in your state or jurisdiction.

Step 20: Receive Signed Contract—Set Up Personnel File (and Close Recruiting File).

Upon receipt of the signed contract, the school will need to:

- close out the recruiting file, and
- create an individual personnel file for the employee.

Recruiting File

The school should maintain a recruiting file that contains a complete record of the recruiting process for the position, including:

- job description and/or Faculty Hiring Specifications Form,
- the recruitment advertising and job posting,
- all résumés received,
- all Applications for Employment (copies) and Background Screening Consent Forms (copies) received from candidates who interviewed for the position, and
- interview notes and comments—in the form of completed Interview Planning and Evaluation Forms—from all members involved in the interviewing process.

This file should be maintained for two years after the *completion* of the hiring process (i.e., two years after the position is filled or a decision not to fill is made).

Personnel File

The school should establish individual personnel files for all new employees containing:

- Application for Employment (original),
- Background Screening Consent Form (original),
- résumé, and
- employment contract.

All other recruiting-related forms related to the *position* and not the *employee* (such as the Faculty Hiring Specifications Form) should remain in the recruiting file for the position.

Once the employee is hired and begins working, numerous additional documents will be entered into the individual's personnel file, including:

- I-9 form,
- W-4 (payroll/taxation) form,
- performance evaluations, and
- employment contracts for subsequent years.

TIP: To comply with myriad regulations pertaining to different aspects of personnel records (such as maintaining performance evaluations until discrimination claim statutes of limitations expire), schools should maintain personnel files for seven years after the employee terminates employment with the school.

Step 21: Conduct Orientation/Induction Process.

We know that almost 50% of teachers new to the profession leave within the first five years, and that the average annual turnover rate for teachers in private-independent schools is around 20%. The two major reasons for teacher turnover are:

- compensations issues, and
- lack of administrative support.

An effective orientation to the school's policies, processes, culture, mission, etc., is important for ensuring that all employees get off to a good start with the school. A comprehensive and sustained induction process helps a new faculty member acclimate to—and utilize his/her full skills within—the school's mission, culture, and values much more quickly and effectively than would otherwise be the case. This is the topic of the following chapter.

Summary

A mission-based hiring process is admittedly an intensive one—requiring substantial commitments of time, energy, and reflection on the part of the School Head and his/her Management Team. Yet, given the central role that faculty play in the long-term viability of the school and the successful delivery of mission to students, it is vital that all concerned approach the process with the greatest vigor and dedication possible.

While no process for hiring will be successful 100% of the time, the mission-based hiring process is designed to give schools the greatest likelihood of hiring mission-appropriate faculty in every possible case.

COMPREHENSIVE FACULTY DEVELOPMENT MODEL

Hiring
&
Induction

CORRECTIVE
ACTION
& SELECTIVE
RETENTION

Characteristics
of Professional
Excellence

EVALUATION
& GROWTH

REWARD &
RECOGNITION

The Induction Process

The process of introducing a new teacher to the school and its norms and expectations goes by different names in different schools, including "orientation" (most common) and "induction" (less common, but gaining in usage). Consulting **dictionary.com**, we find the following:

- *orientation (noun):* an introduction, to guide one in adjusting to new surroundings, employment, activity, or the like: *"New employees receive two days of orientation."*

- *induction (noun):*
  Origin: late 14th century, from *inductionem* (Latin), noun of action from *inducere* (to lead).

The definitions above give us insight into the important differences between orientation and induction processes. As a practical matter, we see this distinction clearly when comparing traditional New Teacher Orientation meetings (one-time, 3-day event at the beginning of each school year), and New Teacher Induction (a systematic growth and support plan that runs over the course of two years and incorporates a variety of processes and events designed to help the teacher grow).

While the terms are often used as synonyms, we view orientation as a *part* of induction, but not the whole thing. The New Teacher Orientation Meeting is an important kickoff of the induction process, but in essence it is exactly what the name implies: a *one-time* orientation event. If this event represents the sum total of the school's induction efforts, it falls far short of its potential impact on the life of the new teacher and the life of the school.

Rather, orientation should only be the *beginning* of what is ideally an 18- to 24-month sequence of events designed to effectively inculcate the new teacher into the culture and norms of the school (as articulated in large measure by the Mission Statement, Characteristics of Professional Excellence, and Portrait of the Graduate documents referenced earlier—see Chapter 3 for details). In essence, a true induction program draws its purpose from the origin of the word "induction" shown above—that is, *to lead the new teacher into the life of his/her chosen vocation/profession, and into the life of the school.*

When carried out planfully and systematically, an effective induction program maximizes and accelerates a new faculty member's chances of long-term success within the school. It is the observation of induction experts that schools with effective induction programs produce teachers who feel (and are) well supported; have a clear view of the values, norms, and processes of the school; are more likely to establish ongoing peer networks; and are much more likely to be enthusiastic (bonded) to the school in meaningful ways for extended periods of time (even lifelong). We fully concur.

SPECIAL ACKNOWLEDGMENT: We tip our cap to induction experts Harry Wong and Annette Breaux, authors of ***New Teacher Induction: How to Train, Support, and Retain New Teachers*** (Harry K. Wong Publications, 2003) and primary influencers of our thinking on induction.

Inducting New Teachers

Your New Teacher Induction program has two primary audiences:

- – teachers who are new to the profession of teaching; and
- – teachers who are new to your school, but are not new to the profession of teaching.

The main differences between these two groups as it relates to New Teacher Induction are time and emphasis.

New teachers (i.e., those who are coming to your school directly from undergraduate or graduate programs or who are making career changes into the teaching profession) should have a systematic induction program that lasts two years—some effective programs last three! These programs should encompass guidance on all aspects of teaching both in and out of the classroom (e.g., advisory, club work, coaching, parent relations and internal marketing, time and stress management, and service learning). In terms of core skills, special emphasis ordinarily should be placed on classroom management and parent relations skills (two nonnegotiable skills for private-independent school teachers).

Depending on available resources, these programs may include:
- model classrooms,
- heavy peer observation,
- group interaction and reflection
- significant readings and discussions of those readings, and
- both general and skill-specific mentoring relationships.

Administrators should increase the frequency of both formal and informal observations as part of an effective induction program for these fledgling professionals—providing extra amounts of coaching, mentoring, support, and encouragement on an ongoing basis. In our experience, providing support to new teachers on a random, intermittent, and infrequent basis is highly ineffective. New teachers need *sustained support* for at least the first two years. This support must come from both school leaders and peers.

As a practical matter, administrators must recognize that there is a tension that exists for academic leaders related to a teacher's first two years. On one hand, new teachers need heavy doses of encouragement, skill building, and guidance to learn and negotiate the private-school culture—i.e., support. On the other hand, effective administrators realize that they must also use the first two years to determine if the new teacher is in fact a good fit with both school and profession—i.e., evaluation.

This tension between the need to provide high support and careful evaluation and assessment is particularly acute during the first two years. There is no way to resolve this tension—both parts are necessary. It simply needs to be acknowledged by the administrator, and shouldn't cause him/her to hold back from either duty (i.e., to support and to evaluate).

Inducting Experienced Teachers Who Are New to Your School

While the *orientation* of experienced teachers is the same as those new to the field (i.e., participating in beginning-of-year meetings), **induction** for these teachers is significantly different from those new to the field. The primary difference is a much more accelerated move toward an individualized growth plan in the first year. Whereas with teachers new to the field it is safe to assume the need to cover all the classroom basics in detail, with experienced teachers that are new to your school the emphasis is:

– on determining if there are any deficiencies and remediating those as soon as possible; and
– inculcating them as an individual into the school's mission, culture, values, and norms.

Thus, experienced teachers have a far more individualized program, which is worked out between the teacher and the administrator within the first month of school and adjusted as needed as the teacher acclimates to your culture throughout the year.

Experienced teachers ordinarily should take no more than a single year to effectively acclimate. The emphasis here is ensuring that they make the transition from the missions, values, and norms of their prior school(s) to those of your school. This means that much of your work with these teachers may include "un-teaching" approaches and behaviors that were acceptable (or even encouraged or required) at their prior school but which are misaligned with the needs and expectations of your school.

Returning to the theme of predictability and supportiveness, we see that what this looks like is determined by your unique mission, culture, and values. In one school, teachers may be expected to ensure that all the students come to class in uniform, stand up when an adult comes in the room, and address all adults as "Mr. or Mrs." In another school, there may be a relaxed dress code and a much more casual approach to student/teacher relationships (with students even referring to teachers by their first name).

As it is possible for a teacher to excel in one context/culture and fail in another, it is vital that your induction program help experienced teachers make the transition from their former context to the culture of your school. In this sense, experience can be a great advantage, but it is of little good if that experience cannot be translated into the existing context and mission. Academic leaders will need to help experienced teachers translate their experience into your culture in ways that mesh well with your norms and needs, by being clear about what is or is not expected (and enforced) at the school.

A Sample Two-Year Induction Calendar

In planning your **New Teacher Induction Program**, you might use the following as a guide.

Year One

- *August:* Welcome back meetings for all faculty, New Teacher Orientation, assignment of mentor, model classroom exercises

- *September:* New teacher workshop (effective classroom management), peer observation

- *October:* New teacher reading and reflection group (e.g., reading on parent relations), peer observation

- *November:* Formal observation by academic administrator, post-meeting discussion, focused mentoring relationships established, new teacher reading and reflection group

- *January:* New teacher workshop (e.g., developing your Parent Retention and Education Plan)

- *February:* New teacher reading and reflection group (e.g., effective assessment), peer observation

- *March:* Formal observation; peer observation, new teacher reading and reflection group (e.g., 21st Century Schools)

- *April:* New teacher reading and reflection group (e.g., effective assessment)

- *May:* Annual evaluation meet, Professional Growth and Renewal Plan for next year developed (see Chapter 6 for details), multiple end-of-year celebratory events with accolades for new faculty

NOTE: ISM recommends that, due to the overwhelming nature of being new to the teaching profession and/or being new to the school, the induction program should take the place of a formal growth and renewal program for the teacher's first two years with the school.

Year Two

- *August:* New Year, New Teacher Meeting (focus on classroom management and parent relations/communications from last year)

- *September:* New Teacher Workshop (e.g., effective student-led teacher/parent meetings), peer observation

- *October:* New teacher reading and reflection group (e.g., homework that really works), peer observation

- *November:* Formal observation, peer observation

- *January:* New teacher workshop (e.g., 21st Century Schools)

- *February:* New teacher reading and reflection group (e.g., differentiated instruction), peer observation

- *March:* Formal observation, peer observation, new teacher reading and reflection group

- *April:* New teacher reading and reflection group, peer observation

- *May:* Annual evaluation meeting, Professional Growth and Renewal Plan for next year developed, multiple end-of-year celebratory events with accolades for new faculty

Summary

Thoughtfully segueing from the hiring process into a well-planned, 18- to 24-month induction program will give your school the best opportunity possible for keeping your energetic new hires engaged, aligned, and passionate about delivering your mission every day.

Notes:

COMPREHENSIVE FACULTY DEVELOPMENT MODEL

HIRING
&
INDUCTION

CORRECTIVE
ACTION
& SELECTIVE
RETENTION

Characteristics
of Professional
Excellence

Evaluation
&
Growth

REWARD &
RECOGNITION

Evaluation and Growth Cycle

Once new faculty members have been interviewed, hired, and inducted, it is time to set them loose to do the job for which you've hired them—i.e., delivering your mission to students. When we say "setting them loose," though, we need to note that this is both the correct and incorrect image:

- **It is correct,** insofar as teachers are highly autonomous. Once they close the classroom door (actually or metaphorically, given the rise of virtual environments), they are the only adult in the room, and they are in charge. In addition, teachers are increasingly being empowered to drive their own curriculum, collaborate with colleagues, etc., according to their own discretion.

- **It is incorrect in this sense:** At no time should being set loose feel like being neglected or unsupported by their administration or fellow teachers (which would be the opposite of the predictability and supportiveness principles emphasized earlier).

This is where the evaluation and growth cycle comes in—providing teachers with predictability and support from administrators, while retaining appropriate autonomy. As we will see, this cycle also provides a framework of accountability—ensuring that both the teacher and the administrator are constantly striving to expand the teacher's ability to deliver the mission with excellence.

Purpose and Goals of the Evaluation and Growth Cycle

Most 21st century competitive pressures require faculty and administrators to be laser-focused on enhancing student performance, satisfaction, and enthusiasm— a situation which requires schools to think differently about managing teacher performance. Returning to our assertion that processes need to be planned and guided to bring about consistently excellent results, we believe that it is critical that a school establish a systematic approach to enhancing the capacity of each teacher. If not, faculty growth that does occur will only meet the needs of the school and its students at random.

This belief is the foundation of ISM's Evaluation and Growth Cycle, which is designed to systematically help:

- weaker but qualified teachers improve and succeed;

- average teachers progress toward excellence;

- outstanding teachers to continue to grow, develop, and remain energized and engaged;

- identify (and ultimately remove) toxic, incompetent, or mission-inappropriate teachers; and

- provide legal protection when corrective action or nonrenewal needs to occur.

The primary purpose of the cycle, then, is performance improvement in the broadest sense—the enhanced performance of the individual teacher, the faculty as a whole, and ultimately, the students.

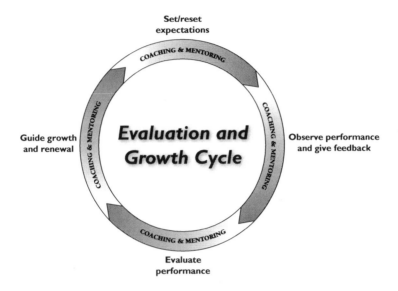

This cycle is segmented into four distinct but interrelated steps.

- *Step 1: Setting Expectations*

  The school's defined Characteristics of Professional Excellence (see Chapter 3 for details) and its day-to-day operating needs (termed "Basic Teacher Expectations," as explained below) inform the expectations that are articulated to faculty.

- *Step 2: Observing Performance and Giving Feedback*

  Administrators observe faculty performance in a variety of settings. These formal and informal observations provide the content for frequent coaching conversations (feedback) between the administrator and teacher.

- *Step 3: Evaluating Performance*

  Administrators write and discuss a formal performance evaluation with each faculty member on an annual basis. The written evaluation may indicate required or suggested skill enhancements that—along with the teacher's own reflections— serve to launch the teacher's growth and renewal plan.

- *Step 4: Guiding Growth and Renewal*

  The administrator and faculty member collaborate on a robust growth and renewal plan, which the teacher is responsible for carrying out and the administrator is responsible for supporting with time and attention, encouragement, and resources.

Point of Reference: Traditional Teacher Evaluation

The Evaluation and Growth Cycle we are proposing in this book differs considerably from traditional teacher evaluation methods, which ordinarily take the following form.

1. The evaluator (such as a Division Head or Department Chair) informs a faculty member that he/she will be evaluating the teacher's class at a particular date and time (e.g., during second period on Tuesday).

2. The teacher prepares a lesson intended to impress the evaluator and asks students to be "on their best behavior" during that class.

3. The evaluator may hold a preconference meeting with the teacher to go over the checklist to be used in evaluating his/her class.

4. The evaluator observes the scheduled class, makes notes, and schedules a follow-up conversation with the teacher.

5. The evaluator and teacher meet to discuss the review.

6. The review is filed and commonly isn't referenced again (or, at least, not until next year's performance review).

This stands in sharp contrast with the Evaluation and Growth Cycle, as shown below.

ASPECT	TRADITIONAL TEACHER EVALUATION	ISM'S EVALUATION AND GROWTH CYCLE
Time period covered	*Evaluation is based on teacher performance during one class period*	*Evaluation is based on an entire year's performance*
Aspects of performance that are evaluated	*Evaluation is based solely on classroom observation*	*Evaluation is based on observation of the teacher's interaction with students, parents, colleagues, and administrators both inside and outside of the classroom*
Nature of observation	*Teacher and students are conscious of being observed*	*Teacher and students become accustomed to observers in their classroom and tend to act more naturally during the administrator's frequent, informal visits*
Teaching to the evaluation	*Teacher is aware of the date/time of the observation and can prepare a lesson and teach in a style geared specifically to gaining rating "points"— whether or not this is the type of lesson or style of teaching that he/she ordinarily engages in*	*Due to the administrator's frequent, unannounced visits, the teacher's actual performance is more accurately gauged (i.e., one cannot "put on an act" on a continual basis)*

Process vs. event	*The evaluation is a single event*	*The evaluation is one aspect of an integrated cycle of events that includes expectation-setting, observation, frequent feedback, written evaluation, developing and carrying out a professional growth plan, and ongoing coaching and mentoring*
Follow-up mechanisms	*Beyond a post-evaluation conference with the evaluator, there is no follow-up mechanism in place to ensure that recommendations are put into effect or that any needed support actually occurs*	*The evaluation is only one part of the administrator and teacher's ongoing conversation. The administrator is responsible for coaching and mentoring (supporting) the teacher throughout the year, as well as for holding the teacher accountable for implementing any required changes/behaviors*
Consequences of a positive evaluation	*Teacher is glad to "get it over and done with"*	*Ideally, the teacher's spirit is buoyed by the genuine, demonstrated support from the administrator*
Consequences of a poor evaluation	*None—unless the situation deteriorates to the point that a decision is made not to offer the teacher a contract for the following year*	*A poor review (or even an overall satisfactory review with unsatisfactory elements) will ordinarily trigger corrective action and/or a required goal in the teacher's growth plan—potentially leading to nonrenewal of contract in the future if performance issues remain unresolved*

Managers' Core Role: Enhancing the Capacity of Faculty

The Evaluation and Growth Cycle described here is not something new, but is rather a process that occurs between employees and managers in high-performing schools and other organizations every day. However, the notion that academic administrators need to actively manage this process may be a new perspective for some schools. The maxim that "managers must manage" is, in fact, the primary assumption underlying this process—and the central point on which it will succeed or fail. This requires, then, an examination of the manager's role in a private-independent school.

It is unfortunately true in some schools that hard-working academic administrators are consumed with managing urgent but not necessarily difference-making tasks—i.e., becoming entwined in virtually all conceivable administrative matters other than guiding the performance and growth of their faculty. ISM believes, however, that the core responsibility of school administrators is to enhance the skill and capacity of the faculty on behalf of their students, which results in the increased performance, satisfaction, and enthusiasm of students (and thus the long-term success and viability of their school).

As such, enhancing faculty capacity is "the thing itself." Without this focus on the part of academic administrators, a school runs the risk of placing the administrator in a position where his/her efforts—though vigorous and well-intentioned—have little or no long-term impact on the life of the school.

Predictability and Supportiveness Within the Evaluation and Growth Cycle

ISM has long written on the critical role that predictability and supportiveness play in student and faculty performance (see Chapter 2). To excel, faculty (just like students) require an environment in which they can reasonably anticipate what is likely to occur in various circumstances (predictability) and in which the administration actively demonstrates care for their needs (support).

Specific to the Evaluation and Growth Cycle:

- Predictability means that faculty members are aware of the school's expectations of them, know the basis on which they will be evaluated, and understand the consequences of succeeding or failing to maintain the school's standards.

- Supportiveness means that teachers are given the resources, encouragement, and guidance necessary to develop their skills for the benefit of their students and in support of colleagues.

Coaching and Mentoring

In the Evaluation and Growth Cycle diagram shown previously, you will notice the words "coaching and mentoring" repeated throughout the inner circle of the cycle. This is meant to depict the integral role that coaching and mentoring plays in uniting all steps in the performance process. Coaching and mentoring is not a *step* in the process, but rather something that occurs regularly throughout all steps in the cycle. In private-independent schools, predictable and supportive administrators manage through coaching and mentoring. This approach is explored in more detail in a separate section at the end of this chapter.

Counterpoint: Managing Doesn't Mean Micromanaging

A concern might be raised as to whether managing faculty performance is consistent with private-independent school culture and the reality of faculty working as autonomous professionals (i.e., the only adults in the classrooms, increasingly empowered to drive their own curriculum). To this, we note that managing is not meant to imply micro-managing or other nonproductive, control-oriented behavior.

Rather, it implies leadership and inspiration of faculty—i.e., guidance rather than control, and encouragement rather than limitation. Thus, an administrator's view of his/her role should be one of helping faculty continually raise their performance to the next level of excellence, rather than feeling that he/she needs to constantly be on guard to "catch" faculty doing things wrong.

In a school context, managing means that the administrator is engaged in collaborating with, coaching, and mentoring the faculty member to enhance his/her skills and abilities to increase his/her impact on students. In a nutshell, this is managing through coaching and mentoring. This involves articulating and reinforcing the school's mission, culture, values, goals, and expectations in a way that inspires and supports faculty, individually and collectively.

At the same time, there is, of course, the hard edge of holding faculty accountable for performing to the level expected by the school, which is a necessary aspect of management. Control measures are necessary from time to time, as they are in managing any enterprise. Poor performance will demand that the supervisor hold the teacher accountable through a corrective-action process, potentially extending up to and including termination of employment where warranted (see Chapter 8 for details).

The good news is this, though: The vast majority of the administrator's time and effort will be expended coaching and inspiring—not penalizing—faculty.

For Long-Time ISM Readers: A Word About MFE

Long-time readers of ISM publications may wonder how introducing the Evaluation and Growth Cycle—and more broadly, the Comprehensive Faculty Development Model itself—impacts ISM's well-known MFE program (formally known as "MFE: Professional Growth and Renewal"). Readers should have no worries that we have, in any way, backed away from the core tenets of MFE regarding the central role of professional growth and renewal in the health of a faculty culture and the long-term sustenance of the school.

In essence, we are simply clarifying MFE's role as an exemplary growth and renewal program and placing it within the context of a more comprehensive, integrated cycle of events (of which formal evaluation is a now established as a distinct but connected element). As such, we now recommend teacher evaluation in the form described in Step 3, below, and growth and renewal (i.e, MFE) as described in Step 4.

Main Elements of the Evaluation and Growth Cycle

We have divided the remainder of this chapter into five sections, reflecting the main elements of the Evaluation and Growth Cycle:

- *Step 1: Setting Expectations*

- *Step 2: Observing Performance and Giving Feedback*

- *Step 3: Evaluating Performance*

- *Step 4: Guiding Growth and Renewal*

- *Common Element: Coaching and Mentoring*

Step 1: Setting Expectations

For purposes of predictability, effectiveness, and fairness, it is important that expectations are communicated consistently. We recommend defining two types of expectations:

    – Basic Teacher Expectations, and

    – Characteristics of Professional Excellence.

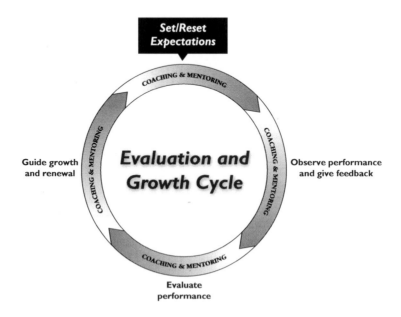

Basic Teacher Expectations

These are nonnegotiable tasks required of teachers for the school and classroom to operate effectively—such as maintaining a professional appearance; submitting grades in a timely manner; showing up to school on time every day; and the like. A sample list of Basic Teacher Expectations (BTEs) for Aegis Academy, the fictional school we are using for example purposes throughout this book, includes the following.

Expectations of Teachers

All teachers at Aegis Academy are expected to:
- act in accordance with the school's mission and values;
- plan and prepare properly for instruction (including submitting lesson plans for review, as required);
- maintain a classroom atmosphere that inspires learning;
- uphold professional standards of appearance, punctuality, courtesy, and discretion;
- carry out all cocurricular responsibilities, including: leading advisory programs, assigned supervision duties (lunchroom, playground, etc.); and
- maintain professional credentials and/or certification.

Developing Your Basic Teacher Expectations

Whereas we suggest a committee be appointed to draft the school's list of Characteristics of Professional Excellence (see Chapter 3), Basic Teacher Expectations (BTEs) are more limited in nature and can ordinarily be developed in one meeting by the school's academic leadership team. The team may review the school's faculty handbook, typical annual memos to teachers, and other similar documents as source material to spur its development of the school's BTE list.

Characteristics of Professional Excellence

As a reminder, this set of characteristics defines the higher-order behaviors or actions that bring your mission to fulfillment in the lives of your graduates—i.e., describing "how" your mission is delivered to students. (See Chapter 3 for further details.)

As a reminder, we are using the sample list below for purposes of example throughout this book.

Characteristics of Professional Excellence

The faculty of Aegis Academy commit to these characteristics as the foundation of our efforts to serve the needs of our students, colleagues, and school.

- **Professional Growth:** I dedicate myself to daily and lifelong professional development, continually seeking opportunities to improve my teaching in service to my students and colleagues.

- **Setting and Maintaining Standards:** I set and support clear and appropriately challenging standards for both student academic performance and student behavior. My students know what they're accountable for and are confident that they will be held to these standards.

- **Real-Life Applications:** I strive to relate all of my lessons to real-life conditions and events, to help students make the connection between the subjects we are studying and the world they observe and experience outside the classroom.

- **Enthusiasm:** I bring my "A" game every day, passionately and energetically demonstrating my enthusiasm for teaching and learning, and striving to engender similar enthusiasm in all my students, so that they may become lifelong learners, seekers, doers, and innovators.

- **Commitment to Mission:** I strive to live the mission in word and deed, working every day to help make our mission come to fruition in the lives of our students, families, and graduates.

- **On Their Side:** In all of our interactions inside and outside the classroom, I find ways to make it obvious to all students that I am eager to teach them, I believe in their abilities, and I work for their success every day.

- **Engaging and Supporting the Whole Person:** I strive to have meaningful and healthy emotional engagement with my students and colleagues regarding their out-of-school lives, without crossing privacy barriers—so that we can support each other in the most vibrant, professionally appropriate ways possible.

- **Healthy Learning Community:** I work hard every day to contribute to a healthy learning, growing, and mutually supportive environment for and with my colleagues— sharing knowledge, resources, insight, and aid freely, openly, and energetically.

▲▲

Communicating Expectations

The school will ideally communicate its expectations to faculty early and often throughout the academic year and throughout their careers at the school. In practical terms, we would suggest that this occur in several ways, including:

- providing the list of basic expectations and characteristics as an addendum to the teacher's contract offer or renewal letter;
- reviewing expectations as part of the annual back-to-school orientation sessions;
- discussing expectations in direct, individual conversations between the teacher and supervisor throughout the school year;
- in writing in the faculty handbook; and
- discussing a different expectation during each faculty meeting throughout the year. Example: A vibrant discussion of "What do we really mean by 'healthy emotional engagement'?" would be a growth-oriented feature of a faculty meeting.

By communicating expectations on a regular basis, the school:

- helps the expectations become embedded in the school's culture and standard way of operating;
- helps the teacher inculcate these expectations in his/her own mind and practice;
- helps the faculty move toward a common understanding of what the expectations look like within the school's culture; and
- solidifies its legal credibility when holding underperforming teachers accountable for these standards should a lawsuit or other claim ever arise.

Step 2: Observing Performance and Giving Feedback

Once expectations are established and communicated, the teachers go forth and teach, and the supervisors go into observer, coach, and mentor mode—providing regular feedback and guidance to their teachers. The "observing" part of this can occur in a variety of ways, including:

- frequent, unannounced, brief visits to classrooms; and
- observing interactions between teachers and students, teachers and colleagues, and teachers and parents in the hallways, on the ball fields, in the carpool lane, etc.

Insights, patterns, trends, and ideas gleaned from these observations provide the content for coaching conversations between the administrator and teacher.

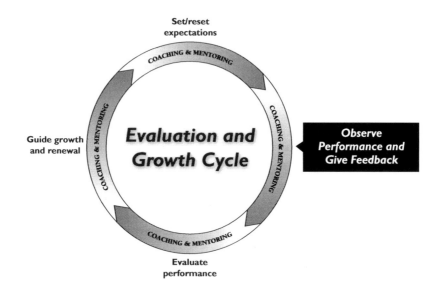

The Purpose of Observation

While we don't believe that observation of one class period has any validity when used as the sole basis of evaluation (such as under the traditional evaluation method), we are not suggesting that classroom observation should never occur. To the contrary, we believe that visiting classrooms (as well as ball fields, carpool lines, cafeterias, etc.) should be a regular part of the administrator's day. By doing so, administrators can gain firsthand knowledge of life in each teacher's professional world, for coaching and mentoring purposes—positioning their observation time as an opportunity for supporting rather than evaluating the teacher, per se. While the accumulation of observational anecdotes will provide important fodder for the formal evaluation, the primary purpose is still coaching-focused.

If the school agrees that expanding the capacity of faculty is the primary role of the academic administrator, these visits should then represent a significant portion of the administrator's daily routine—consuming upwards of 25%–50% of the administrator's time. One way of putting this approach into practical effect is managing by walking around, as described below.

The Benefits of 'Managing By Walking Around'

Supervisors may observe actively by using the technique of Management By Walking Around (MBWA). Made famous by authors Peters and Waterman in their work, *In Search of Excellence* (HarperBusiness, 1984), MBWA involves being out of your office and involved in the daily life of the school. Using this approach, administrators make it a point to be on the grounds, in the hallways, and in the classrooms of the school on a regular (daily) basis. This accomplishes several goals, including:

- creating a culture of observation in which faculty and students are used to seeing and interacting with administrators as part of the daily course of events and are thus less conscious of being observed;
- establishing an environment in which feedback becomes embedded as a regular, positive, and sought-after experience (in its most ideal form, teachers—excited by the genuine support they're receiving—will invite the administrator into their classroom regularly to share in and comment on innovative new techniques they're trying out); and
- providing the administrator with a wide range of views into the faculty member's performance both inside and outside the classroom, which they use in their ongoing coaching of the teacher (eventually serving as source material for the teacher's annual evaluation).

When observing faculty in this manner, we suggest that administrators keep in mind the Basic Teacher Expectations and Characteristics of Professional Excellence described previously, as these items provide the frame of reference against which observed behavior should be compared.

NOTE: Administrators may wish to focus their attention on observing students during their observations of teachers. That is to say, for administrators to pay careful attention to how students are reacting to the teacher inside and outside the classroom. This may provide excellent fodder for coaching discussions with the teacher, helping him/her gain a broader perspective on the impact of his/her actions as judged through the verbal and nonverbal reactions of the students.

Keeping Notes

Except for the few among us with photographic memories, it is virtually impossible for most administrators to recall with ease all of the significant interactions they have had with an individual faculty member during the course of the year—a difficulty that is multiplied by the number of direct reports that they may have. For this reason, we recommend that each administrator keep a file of their coaching notes on each of their direct reports. The content of the notes can range from a few words on a sticky note to detailed log observations maintained in an application on a Smartphone. The format of the notes doesn't matter at all; the fact that notes are kept matters greatly.

Supervisor Files vs. Official Personnel Files

For purposes of organization and confidentiality, notes should be maintained in a file. Depending on the administrator's comfort with technology, this file may be either hardcopy or electronic. Whatever the medium, the supervisor's file must not be confused in any way with the official personnel file maintained by the school's Business Manager or Human Resources Manager. The supervisor's file is used solely for the administrator's purposes—containing only notes, comments, and the like that the administrator has jotted down or compiled throughout the year.

The supervisor's file should not be considered an official school document and thus should not be readily subject to subpoena. Of course, however, care should always be taken to avoid recording notes that focus on nonjob-related or discriminatory factors. (See Chapter 2 for further details on discrimination laws.) Please consult with your school's Business Manager or Human Resources Manager to ensure that the manner in which you are keeping notes appropriately protects the school's interests.

Moving From Observing to Giving Feedback

As we have been describing, observing teacher performance isn't an end in itself; rather, it is intended as the source and impetus of the supervisor's coaching of the faculty member. We will discuss the ins and outs of coaching and mentoring in greater detail at the end of this chapter. For now, we would just like to note the goals of feedback, including:

- – reaffirming the school's standards and expectations (predictability);
- – furthering the supervisor's coaching relationship with the teacher (supportiveness);
- – giving the administrator regular opportunities to collaborate with the teacher in enhancing his/her skills, capabilities, and techniques (growth);
- – expanding the capacity of the teacher (as an individual) and faculty (as a whole) to deliver the school's mission with excellence (growth); and
- – engaging with teachers in a way that inspires them to higher levels of professional skill and expertise (renewal).

Feedback Example: '10-24s'

We would like to share this example of an exemplary use of feedback that was related to us by a school leader with whom we've worked closely.

- This academic administrator plans to visit the classroom of each teacher in her group at least once every two weeks.

- She commonly slips into the back of the room unannounced and observes whatever is going on for 10 minutes or so.

- Teachers and students know this is her modus operandi and are quite used to—and have come to welcome—her visits.

- The leader's commitment to the faculty member is that she will return within 24 hours to have a private (10-minute) discussion with the teacher, where she shares her thoughts and invites the teacher's reflections and comments in dialogue.

- The administrator finds that teachers usually are engaged in these discussions and are eager to share their thoughts, reflections, fears and questions regarding best practices, new techniques, etc.—to the point that the leader has remarked, "I learn something important from the conversation almost every time."

This is "observing performance and giving feedback" (Step 2) in its most ideal form.

Step 3: Evaluating Performance

To recap our progress through the four-step Evaluation and Growth Cycle thus far, we have:

- set and communicated expectations regarding teacher performance (i.e., including the Basic Teacher Expectations and Characteristics of Professional Excellence);
- observed teacher performance in a variety of settings throughout the academic year; and
- regularly given feedback and guidance to each teacher, based on our observations.

Having done so, we are now ready to develop and discuss with the teacher a formal, written evaluation of his/her performance over the course of the full school year.

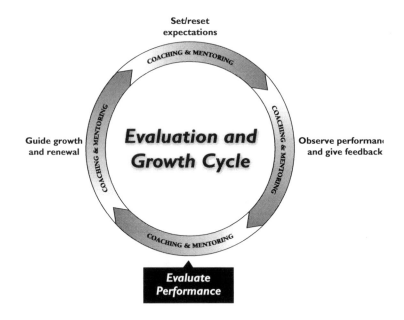

The Legal Protection Provided by Annual Written Evaluations

To address a sensitive issue right up front, while school administrators should be aware that performance improvement is the primary driver of the Evaluation and Growth Cycle, it is necessary to acknowledge the impact that legal matters also have on this process. In an age of litigation and increasing federal and state regulation of employment matters (see Chapter 2), for its protection, the school must have a substantive, written evaluation of each faculty member's performance on an annual basis.

As a point of fact, there are no federal or state regulations that *require* employers to conduct annual evaluations. However, without these, the school has very little with which to protect itself if a discrimination or wrongful termination claim is brought. An evaluation that addresses the critical elements of the job and fairly assesses the employee's performance goes a long way in helping a school *prove* that its employment decisions are based solely on job-related, rather than discriminatory, considerations—thereby potentially saving the school untold legal expenses and financial judgments, to say nothing of preventing the damage to community reputation that public lawsuits engender.

What Is Evaluated

As the private school teacher's role extends well beyond the classroom, schools should view and evaluate a teacher's performance comprehensively, considering the full range of a teacher's interactions with students, parents, colleagues, and administrators, both inside and outside the classroom. From a practical perspective, in keeping with our prior recommendations for expectations to be consistently communicated and applied, we recommend the following as appropriate standards on which to base faculty evaluation:

- *Basic Teacher Expectations (BTEs)*:
  These are nonnegotiable tasks required for the school and classroom to operate effectively. Examples include professional appearance, timely submission of grades, excellent attendance record, and the like.

- *Characteristics of Professional Excellence (CPEs)*:
  These are the higher-order behaviors, values, and attitudes demonstrated by your faculty—the actions they take are "how" your mission is delivered to students with excellence. Examples include creating a predictable and supportive environment for students, collaborating with colleagues, and constantly focusing on professional growth and development.

As you will note, the "Basic Teacher Expectations" and "Characteristics of Professional Excellence" used to evaluate teachers are exactly the expectations that we recommended communicating in Step 1 of the Evaluation and Growth Cycle at the beginning of this chapter. These are the same lenses through which we suggested observing performance and giving feedback in Step 2.

Why Use These Criteria for Evaluation?

There are many possible things that can be evaluated, of course. Why have we selected the items noted above? Our reasoning is simple: By comparing a teacher's actions against the school's expectations regarding "what's most important here," you can best evaluate whether a faculty member's efforts are meeting the school's needs, and by extension, the needs of your students. And by using these criteria consistently, you are creating an environment of predictability (i.e., faculty know what your expectations are and see them being consistently reinforced), one of the hallmarks of a healthy faculty culture.

We don't believe that student test scores or other similar measures appropriately reflect a teacher's performance; we do believe that observing their actions and comparing them against well-communicated expectations is a fair, defensible, and effective way to judge teacher performance.

Teacher Evaluation Template

It is important for a school to implement this new evaluation model in a consistent and practical manner for all faculty members. To that end, the evaluation template shown below is designed to assess the primary elements of teacher performance in a way that is clear, consistent, and user-friendly for both teachers and administrators.

To illustrate what a well-formed written evaluation might look like, we continue our example of an upper school history teacher at Aegis Academy, our fictional K–12 private-independent school.

Aegis Academy

Faculty Evaluation

Name	Annette Richardson	School Year	20XX - 20XX
Position	Faculty, Upper School	Division/Dept.	History
Supervisor	Kristen Grainger	Supvr. Title	Dept Chair

Section 1: Basic Teacher Expectations

All faculty members at Aegis Academy are expected and required to:
  – overtly support and act in accordance with the school's mission and values;
  – demonstrate appropriate planning and preparation for instruction;
  – develop and maintain a classroom atmosphere that inspires learning;
  – uphold professional standards of personal presentation, punctuality, professional courtesy, and discretion;
  – appropriately carry out specific assignments, including but not limited to service learning, advisory programs, assigned supervision, and other areas as determined by the Head; and
  – maintain professional credentials and/or certification.

Rating:

☑ Meets expectations ☐ Doesn't Meet Expectations

Comments

Annette has quickly become a role model of professionalism for her colleagues, attending to the "nuts and bolts" of daily responsibilities in a timely, accurate, and thoughtful manner at all times. As an example, she consistently submits well-developed lesson plans and accurate grade reports on or before deadlines, while also taking time to mentor junior colleagues needing assistance and guidance in these areas. She more than fulfilled all of her assigned duties—teaching five sections, advising 12 students, moderating the Government club, and serving as Assistant Field Hockey Coach in the fall and Coach of the junior varsity Softball Team in the spring.

••••▶

Section 2: Characteristics of Professional Excellence

The faculty of Aegis Academy commit to these characteristics as the foundation of our efforts to serve the needs of our students, colleagues, and school.

- *Professional Growth:* I dedicate myself to daily and lifelong professional development, continually seeking opportunities to improve my teaching in service to my students and colleagues.

- *Setting and Maintaining Standards:* I set and support clear and appropriately challenging standards for both student academic performance and student behavior. My students know what they're accountable for and are confident that they will be held to these standards.

- *Real-Life Applications:* I strive to relate all of my lessons to real-life conditions and events to help students make the connection between the subjects we are studying and the world they observe and experience outside the classroom.

- *Enthusiasm:* I bring my "A" game every day, passionately and energetically demonstrating my enthusiasm for teaching and learning, and striving to engender similar enthusiasm in all my students, so that they may become lifelong learners, seekers, doers, and innovators.

- *Commitment to Mission:* I strive to live the mission in word and deed, working every day to help make our mission come to fruition in the lives of our students, families, and graduates.

- *On Their Side:* In all of our interactions inside and outside the classroom, I find ways to make it obvious to all students that I am eager to teach them, I believe in their abilities, and I work for their success every day.

- *Engaging and Supporting the Whole Person:* I strive to have meaningful and healthy emotional engagement with my students and colleagues regarding their out-of-school lives, without crossing privacy barriers—so that we can support each other in the most vibrant, professionally appropriate ways possible.

- *Healthy Learning Community:* I work hard every day to contribute to a healthy learning, growing, and mutually supportive environment for and with my colleagues—sharing knowledge, resources, insight, and aid freely, openly, and energetically.

••••▶

COMMENTS:

Enthusiasm and Engagement: Annette has demonstrated her skill in engaging indifferent or borderline students, in part by sharing her passion for history and in part by finding an aspect of the topic that each student can respond to. As an example, she consistently worked with one student in her American History course this fall during study periods, after-school extra-help sessions, and the like. The student, who had C-minus grades in History courses in prior years, earned steadily increasing marks in her course, ultimately deciding to enroll in AP American History next semester.

Real-Life Applications: Annette is very skilled in bringing the past to life in her classes. One example occurred in her Government course this fall, where she had the students perform snippets of speeches from famous politicians from the past. She collaborated with the Media teacher to turn the videotaped performances into political "commercials," which the students then distributed via YouTube and Twitter.

Professional Growth: In February, Annette participated in a national conference of History teachers. She came back with many new approaches to teaching World War I history (her area of special interest), which she shared with her departmental colleagues in an engaging presentation at our Spring In-Service.

Teacher Signature/Date	Annette Richardson/5-1-20XX
Supervisor Signature/Date	Kristen Grainger/5-1-20XX

NOTE: If the faculty member disagrees with elements of this evaluation, he/she has the opportunity to provide a written statement of disagreement. This statement will be attached to the evaluation and will be considered an official part of the employee's evaluation and record.

 Download an unfilled Faculty Evaluation Template: www.isminc.com/cfd-evaluation

NOTE: Over the next few pages, we will analyze several of the key elements (ratings, comments, etc.) that we have included in the sample teacher evaluation above. We will then proceed to offer some suggestions regarding customizing these elements to the school's mission, culture, and values.

The Use of Ratings

With one exception (noted below), we do not recommend incorporating ratings into your teacher evaluation process. This is primarily intended to emphasize the *content* of the evaluation rather than reducing the evaluation to a simple rating or label that can significantly distract the teacher from the true purpose and value of the evaluation as a learning tool. In our experience, it is much more useful for a teacher to know that his/her Division Director valued *specific actions and results* he/she produced during the year (as seen through the comments), rather than to simply know that he/she gained a "meets expectations" rating with no guidance as to what was done well or poorly.

The Basic Teacher Expectations are an exception. By their nature, they are cut-and-dried items that a teacher is either complying with or not complying with—and thus lend themselves to simple pass-fail or meets-doesn't meet designations. By contrast, the Characteristics of Professional Excellence take on higher-order behavioral aspects and thus have room for more nuanced and subtle distinctions. Accordingly, they do not readily lend themselves to fixed labels or simple ratings. For the characteristics, developing well-written, well-chosen examples is the key to effectively communicating your assessment of the teacher's performance.

The Use of Comments

As contrasted with simple ratings, substantive comments are far more meaningful and effective communication and learning tools. Well-formed comments provide specific examples of how the teacher is or is not bringing the characteristic to life in his/her daily work—and thus can be learned from and replicated by the teacher in the future, which is the primary purpose of the evaluation, and more broadly, of the Evaluation and Growth Cycle as a whole.

Well-written comments should include examples of behavior or accomplishments during the year that indicate either the presence or absence of the characteristic. For example, in addressing a characteristic such as "Emotional Engagement," the administrator would draw on his/her observations of the faculty member (both inside and outside the classroom) over the course of the year and remark on a specific instance or activity (or two) that accurately illustrates how the faculty member regularly interacts with students—i.e., commenting on instances that illustrate either desirable or inappropriate ways that the teacher has engaged with students during the year.

It is appropriate for a comment to *start* with a generality (e.g., "Annette is very skilled in bringing the past to life in her classes")—but an effective comment can't *end* there. It must go on to provide an example (or several) to illustrate how the teacher demonstrated this skill or characteristic. Thus, the words "For example," followed by a short story describing the teacher's efforts on this point, are critical to making the evaluation a teaching tool. Well-written examples will make it clear to the teacher why what he/she did was (or was not) consistent with the school's expectations—thus, giving the teacher the information he/she needs to replicate that action again in the future (or not).

The Number of Comments Needed

Administrators will need to use their judgment as to how many comments are enough to form a well-developed evaluation. It is not necessary to include long "laundry lists" of the teacher's activities—rather, a small number of examples should be chosen that appropriately represent the whole. Ordinarily, to be appropriately comprehensive and substantive, an administrator should provide a total of at least three to four examples related to the CPEs to effectively tell the story of the teacher's performance during that year.

It is not necessary to comment on every individual characteristic (especially if the school has adopted a long list of characteristics), lest the review become overwhelming both for the administrator to write and for the faculty member to receive. Rather, a small handful of meaningful examples that are well-chosen to aptly and fairly illustrate the teacher's performance can be used to strong effect.

Preparing to Write the Evaluation

In preparation for writing formal teacher evaluations, administrators will want to:
  - reflect on their numerous formal and informal coaching conversations with the teacher throughout the year;
  - review the notes that they have maintained describing these conversations;
  - identify appropriate examples of the teacher's performance that will serve as appropriate, substantive anecdotes for comment purposes; and
  - consider whether any patterns, themes, or trends (positive or negative) are apparent in the teacher's performance over the year.

Upon reflection, they will formulate these notes, observations, and reflections into a summary document using the evaluation template shown previously.

Where to Draw Examples: Supervisor's Desk File

Staring at a blank evaluation template is a cause of great angst for many new (and even experienced) administrators, not being sure exactly where to start. This can be remedied to large degree by drawing on the notes contained in the supervisor's file described in the "Observing Performance" section (Step 2, above). As a reminder, these are informal notes kept by the supervisor in his/her "desk file" for each employee who reports to him/her. This file may contain "sticky notes," copies of e-mails, comments recorded on a Smartphone, etc.—in whatever form the administrator is comfortable keeping notes. The notes may contain:

- the administrator's observations regarding the employee's performance (such as from "management by walking around" and other views of the individual;
- observations made by others that the administrator deems credible and that serve to provide a well-rounded view of the teacher's performance;
- commendations (or complaints) shared with the administrator regarding the teacher; and
- reports, summaries, or other descriptions of projects or initiatives that the teacher has undertaken or completed during the year—including clippings from school newsletters or publications, stories in the school's publications featuring the teacher's work, and the like.

A word of caution is in order regarding the selection and use of examples, particularly those describing actions and events that the administrator has not personally observed. Quite simply, judgment must be used. Not everything that was reported to the administrator is accurate—and, even if it is accurate, it is not necessarily reflective of the teacher's overall work or accomplishments during the year. As a practical matter, some of the administrator's compiled notes will be used in the evaluation, and some will not. The review should cite examples that are most illustrative of the teacher's performance during the year. Fairness, credibility, and balance should guide the administrator in selecting the specific examples to be used.

Goal: No Surprises

Conforming to the principle of predictability, ideally there won't be any surprises for the teacher contained in the written evaluation. That is because the evaluation contents should represent a *summary* of the year's coaching conversations between the teacher and the administrator—i.e., they should have already discussed all of the points in the review. As long as the teacher and administrator have been engaging in regular informal and formal coaching sessions during the year, they will likely have discussed each of the situations used as examples in the review. In this way, the examples serve as reaffirmation of prior positive comments, as well as reminders regarding areas for performance improvement that have been previously discussed.

Discerning Trends and Patterns

The only exception to the "no surprises" principle noted above has to do with discerning trends and patterns. In many cases, it is difficult to identify trends or patterns in the moment; often, it is only by standing back and reflecting on a series of events that we are able to identify themes and patterns of behavior. This is one of the benefits of writing an evaluation—it gives the administrator a chance to step back and assess whether he/she sees a pattern of improvement, decline, or other variation in the teacher's performance over the course of time.

Ideally, these patterns would be discussed in coaching sessions once they are identified. It is sometimes the case, though, that patterns are not identified until the administrator sits down to write the review. In these cases, it is perfectly appropriate to include a discussion of trends or patterns in the written review—citing previously discussed situations as examples. It is important to discuss the meaning and direction of these trends during the evaluation meeting (discussed below) and in subsequent coaching conversations, so that the insights gained during the review can be utilized going forward.

Negative Examples

In the sample evaluation shown above, the reader may notice that all of the examples cited described positive performance. However, one shouldn't infer from this that only positive performance should be noted in the review. Rather, performance should be described as accurately as possible, whether it was positive or negative. Administrators should not hold back from commenting on areas of performance that require improvement, for fear that they may offend or alienate the teacher.

"Accurate assessment compassionately delivered"—a core principle of ISM's coaching philosophy for many years—is the best tack that an administrator can take in coaching and evaluating teachers. Administrators should consider that only in providing genuine feedback to teachers can they help teachers grow and improve. Sugar-coating performance deficiencies is not helpful or desirable from any perspective.

Examples of negative assessments delivered compassionately include:

- *Enthusiasm: Annette carries out her duties with great self-discipline, attention to detail, and professionalism. On a technical basis, Annette's teaching this year was excellent, as always. However, for the majority of this year, Annette struggled with demonstrating enthusiasm for teaching and for her students.*

  Example: Stopping in her classroom after school on several occasions, I observed Annette tutoring students. Whereas in the past, students would be hanging on her every word, enthralled with the new worlds they were discovering, this year the atmosphere was much more strained, as Annette patiently reviewed the material but spoke not a word more, missing significant opportunities to engage the students' interests and imaginations.

  We discussed my concerns several times during the year, and Annette indicated that certain personal matters may be impacting this situation. The school wants to do everything it can do to appropriately support Annette. At the same time, she is aware that "joyful teaching" is an important value at Aegis. We will continue our conversations during the fall and look forward to helping Annette regain the joy in her teaching.

- *Setting Standards: Annette struggled with communicating the scope of particular tests and preparing students adequately at different points this year. On a handful of occasions, students complained of being tested on material that was never taught. At those times, Annette and I discussed the matter and she agreed that she decided to skip certain material but did not revise the test accordingly. She understands that clearly communicating testing scope is an important element of teaching at Aegis and she has assured me that this will no longer be an issue in her classroom.*

Just as with positive comments, it is appropriate to start with a somewhat general statement, and then use an example to make your point concretely. As in the sample comments above, it is vital that critical comments be delivered accurately, but in a tone that clearly conveys "I'm on your side" and "I want to help you succeed." In this way, even negative assessments are likely to be taken seriously and acted up on in a positive manner.

Customizing a Teacher Evaluation Process for Your School

This template shown above is a sample. How, then, should the school go about creating an evaluation form of its own? We recommend the following approach:

1. **Form an Evaluation Design Team.** This may be comprised of the same individuals who previously created the school's Characteristics of Professional Excellence (see Chapter 3). Or, the Head may choose to appoint a completely new committee for this purpose—or appoint some mix of former Characteristics Design Team members and new members.

   NOTE: Due to the nature of the team's task—i.e., designing/customizing an *evaluation* system—the Evaluation Design Team differs from other similar teams suggested in this book. That is, we recommend that this team include all of the school's Division Heads (or similarly positioned administrators) and that the *administrators* drive the team's work. The Head is still encouraged to include faculty members on the team, so that faculty have a direct voice in the process. However, it is often most appropriate for administrators to take the lead in guiding this effort.

2. **Charge the Team with Developing an Evaluation Format and Process.** Using the following template as a guide, the team is asked to make any and all modifications necessary for ISM's generic template to become the school's own. This would include wrestling with topics such as ratings (or not); comments (how many and what type); when would be the most practical time of the year to conduct evaluations; and how the evaluation links to self-reflection and professional growth and renewal efforts (discussed in the next section of this chapter).

3. ***Review and Approve the Template and Process.*** When the team's work is complete, the Head thanks them for their service and disbands the team. He/she then reviews the proposed template with the Academic Administrative Team and, when there is concurrence that the modified template meets the school's needs, approves the template for use.

4. ***Train the Academic Administrative Team on the Template's Use.*** As the final step before implementation, all administrators who have faculty reporting to them need to be fully trained on use of the template. Training may be provided by the school's Business Manager, Human Resources Manager, Head, or an outside consultant, as appropriate.

5. ***Implement the Format and Process.*** Once the template and process are finalized, it can be communicated to all faculty (such as in a faculty meeting). Ideally, this would occur in the fall, so that teachers would have many months to get used to the idea that this is how they are being evaluated from now on. Most important, this allows the coaching and mentoring conversations to begin as soon as the system is ready for use.

These conversations—which are the bedrock of this approach to evaluation and growth—not only provide the content for the evaluation's examples, they also provide credibility for the evaluation process as a whole. That is to say, if a teacher meets regularly with his/her administrator and they are engaging in productive coaching conversations, the teacher is much more likely to take the evaluation seriously and be receptive to the guidance provided by someone whom she views as engaged, caring, and credible.

The Evaluation Meeting

Once written, the evaluation should be discussed with the faculty member in a formal meeting. This meeting can serve as the launch for creating the succeeding year's growth and renewal plan. For example:

– if the evaluation noted particular themes or interests of the teacher, then the teacher can be invited to suggest potential growth opportunities he/she would like to pursue in those areas of interest; or

– if the evaluation identified an aspect of the teacher's performance that is lacking, the teacher and administrator could determine that this is a goal the teacher must include in the upcoming year's professional growth plan.

NOTE: Significant deficiencies identified in the evaluation may trigger a performance warning within a corrective-action process, depending on the severity and urgency of the issue. (See further details in the following section, "Step 4: Guiding Growth and Renewal," as well as in Chapter 8.)

VIGNETTE: Conducting the Evaluation Meeting

When implementing this evaluation model for the first time, you may experience resistance and skepticism from faculty members who aren't yet convinced of the benefits of this approach—as well as from those who are suspicious of school leadership's motives. In essence, the model's credibility can only truly be established by effective use of the system over the course of years. By clearly, consistently, and confidently articulating the model's best purposes, you can help faculty acclimate to—and ultimately embrace—this form of evaluation, leading to growth and renewal.

Set-Up:

Joan is in her 10th year teaching the 4th grade at Aegis Academy. She is meeting with Elaine, the Lower School Principal who is in her second year at the school and her 12th year in administration after a long teaching career. They are meeting to discuss Elaine's evaluation of Joan's performance during the current school year.

NOTE: You may wish to read the "dialogue" column in full, then loop back to the "commentary" column for notes and perspective.

Dialogue

It is always recommended for the evaluation meeting to be scheduled in advance, and for it to be held in a quiet, private location (such as the Division Head's office) where the discussion won't be interrupted.

Joan (teacher): Hi, Elaine. Is this still a good time?

Elaine (Principal): It sure is. Thanks for coming, Joan. Have a seat, please.

Joan: Thanks.

Elaine: How are things going today?

Joan: Fine, thanks. A little exhausted, actually. I have a really good group this year … but they were definitely a little rambunctious today. The long weekend will be good for everyone.

Elaine: Very true. Well, let's dive right in, shall we? As you know, we instituted a new performance evaluation system this year, and I wanted to share the results of your evaluation with you.

Joan: [skeptically] Hmmmm …

It is important for the administrator to use active listening to stay alert to verbal and nonverbal clues that indicate the employee's state of mind, demeanor, etc., so that she may engage the teacher fully.

Elaine: Is something the matter, Joan? You seem a little concerned.

Joan: Well … I don't know. (pause) It's really not my place to say.

Elaine: Sure it is. It's *your* evaluation. We can talk about anything that concerns you. What's on your mind?

Joan: It's just, well … a few of the teachers were talking, and, well … we're just not sure what this is all about.

Elaine: "All about"?

Joan: I mean, what are you really trying to get at with the evaluation? It just seems like, well, things have been running very well for years now—and then all of a sudden there are these forms and requirements. Are you trying to force someone out?

Elaine: "Force someone out?" No. Nothing like that. We're just trying to build up the skills of the faculty in general, and …

Joan: [interrupting] You think we're *unskilled?*

Elaine: No. I didn't say that at all. What I mean is, if we evaluate performance effectively, it will help us coach faculty members to grow and develop. We talked about this before we rolled out the program last fall, didn't we?

Joan: I guess so. I just didn't think you'd actually go through with it. I mean, every year, someone says something about evaluation—but nothing ever happens.

Elaine: I understand your skepticism. That's fair. But I can tell you that it's something that the current leadership team really believes in. Barbara, Julia, and I spent all summer working on the system before we rolled it out to everyone during the orientation meetings last August.

Joan: Hmmmm.

Elaine: Ok, then. Why don't we take a look at what we have here?

Elaine hands a copy of the review to Joan and they begin looking at the written evaluation document.

> *It is important not to take negativity toward the evaluation process personally. As a matter of human nature, people are ordinarily fearful or suspicious of change (i.e., the new evaluation model) and it is not uncommon for it to require persistence to get everyone on board with the change.*

This remark may indicate that the concept of "Basic Expectations" wasn't clearly explained when first introduced. With any new concept—particularly one related to evaluation, which a faculty member will take personally—consistent and repeated communication is needed before full acceptance will occur.

Ratings are a particularly sensitive topic in most evaluations. We recommend using ratings only in the "Basic Teacher Expectations" section, so that most of the discussion can be focused on the characteristics that are difference-makers in the lives of students. Elaine does a good job of turning the conversation toward her substantive comments.

Progress in building credibility for implementing a new evaluation process is often slow. Resilience and a willingness to tell the same story multiple times from multiple angles are often necessary.

Elaine: As you see, the review is divided into a few sections. First, there's "Basic Expectations." Then …

Joan: Don't you think that's a little offensive? I mean, this is my 10th year of teaching. I think I'm a little beyond "basic expectations" at this point—and I have been for many, many years.

Elaine: Yes, that's true. Of course. It's just that we need to communicate across-the-board expectations for everyone— "rookies," experienced teachers, and everyone in between.

As Joan looks over the evaluation, she points to a section and remarks:

Joan: That's pretty sad.

Elaine: What's that?

Joan: I see my first rating. Ten years' experience and all I get is a "meets expectations" on basic requirements. Really?

Elaine: That's true, Joan. But there are only two rating levels: "Meets Expectations" and "Doesn't Meet Expectations." The value in the evaluation isn't in the ratings. They are really just labels. Where we focus most of our attention is on the comments. As you can see, I specifically made note in the comments of how you're very timely with submitting report card grades. In fact, you're usually the first teacher in the lower school whose grades I receive. That helps me a lot in doing what I do and I appreciate it.

We fast-forward a few minutes to when Joan and Elaine begin discussing another section of the evaluation.

Joan: OK, I have another issue.

Elaine: What's that?

Joan: Well, this next heading says, "Engagement With Students." How can you judge my excellence in engaging students? I mean, 99% of the time I'm alone with the children. You only come by once a week, popping your head in for five minutes. How can you possibly know whether I'm engaging the children effectively or not?

Elaine: Fair question, of course. You're right in saying that I wasn't usually in your classroom for all that long at any one time. But every time I was in the classroom, I made note of something you were doing that day with the children. As you'll recall, most weeks I dropped by to chat with you after school. Those visits were to discuss things—in most cases, terrific things—that I had noticed you doing in the classroom. I kept notes on those visits, and they add up over the course of a year. That's where I drew my examples from.

Joan: So, you were spying on me and making notes, is that it? That's pretty sneaky, don't you think?

Elaine: No, Joan—you're taking this all wrong. Yes, I did make notes … but no, I wasn't spying on you. Rather, I was gathering firsthand information for our coaching sessions.

Joan: If you say so.

Elaine: [undeterred] In fact, the first comment here is a good example. One of our characteristics is "Cutting Edge Knowledge." The example I used is how you are constantly talking about research studies or education-related books that you're reading, which is a great picture of how you keep up-to-date. That's an important value here.

Also, I was happy to tell the story of how you went to the "Social Media in Education" conference at your own initiative—because it's an area you think is important. That says a lot about your dedication to staying up to date with the latest and greatest in your field, so I wanted to make note of it.

Joan: [quietly] Thank you.

Elaine: My pleasure. Now, the next comment has to do with …

Elaine and Joan continue talking through the next sections of the review. As they're finishing up, we return to the conversation.

Elaine: As it says in the comments, I really appreciated how you went "above and beyond" in not only helping James R. get diagnosed with hearing issues, you were a great source

> *The hoped-for outcome is for both the teacher and the administrator to feel that they had a discussion that paves the way for further performance growth and enhancement.*

of comfort to his parents as they went through the surgery and recovery process with him.

Joan: Thanks for mentioning it. They're nice folks. They deserved the support.

Elaine: That wraps up the review for the most part, Joan. There is one more thing I want to discuss with you. But before I do, do you have any questions or comments about the review?

Joan: Well, I have to admit to being a bit skeptical about the process when we started out with this discussion. I've never really been evaluated this way before—it takes some getting used to. There is one thing I've been thinking about, though.

Elaine: What's that?

Joan: Well, I've been wanting to learn more about using certain types of technology in the classroom. Do you think I might get some support on that?

Elaine: Funny that you ask. Your growth plan was actually the last thing I had on my agenda to talk with you about today. Absolutely. Technology is not one of our school-wide goals right now—but I think it likely will be in the coming year. In the meantime, why don't we plug that in as one of your two goals for the year in the growth and renewal plan?

Joan: That would be terrific. I would look forward to that.

> Another hoped-for outcome is for the teacher and administrator to be on the same page regarding the teacher's growth needs and interests. Often, the written performance evaluation can serve as the springboard that propels the teacher and administrator to creating a truly vibrant growth and renewal program for the following year.

More details about recommended growth and renewal practices are provided in the following section.

Having completed the "evaluation" step of the Evaluation and Growth Cycle, we now proceed to Step 4, Guiding Growth and Renewal.

Step 4: Guiding Growth and Renewal

Step 4 is, in a real sense, the culmination and fulfillment of the prior three steps of the cycle. By reflecting on the school's expectations, the administrator's evaluation, and the coaching and mentoring conversations that they have engaged in during the year, the teacher and administrator will be well-positioned to identify the teacher's interests, needs, and opportunities for growth, and to set his/her course of renewal for the year. Once the plan is formed, the teacher is responsible for enthusiastically carrying it out, and the administrator is responsible for vigorously supporting his/her efforts with time, attention, encouragement, and resources, as appropriate.

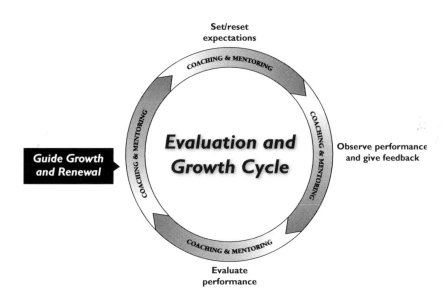

Growth and Renewal vs. Professional Development

Before we discuss of the elements of a growth program, we need to share a word or two about our choice of the term "growth and renewal" instead of the more common "professional development." There is nothing at all wrong with the term "professional development." We find it, though, somewhat narrow compared to our fullest vision of growth and renewal.

In narrow terms, professional development implies adding skills to the professional's toolbox, as it were. This is important and meaningful. Our vision, though, goes beyond this to include deeper growth of the person—to speak to the professional and personal passions that fuel his/her spirit as an individual who impacts the lives of children and communities. Passion must be engaged, lest the development become relegated simply to added techniques.

Moreover, the second part of the term—"renewal"—is equally vital. Teaching is a *giving* profession (as are many service-oriented occupations). Every day, teachers are asked to give their time, talent, and energy to students, fellow teachers, parents, and to the school community as a whole. If not replenished, these energies can become quickly depleted, sometimes to the point where a teacher has nothing left to give.

Thus, renewal is absolutely required—and often on a regular and ongoing basis. It is vital for teachers and administrators not to lose sight of the renewal aspect of their growth programs. Without it, any development program is likely to be reduced over time to a perfunctory exercise rather than one that truly impacts the lives of teachers and students alike.

What a Broad-Based Growth and Renewal Program Looks Like

Inevitably, when we ask teachers and administrators what comes to their minds when they think of professional development, the immediate answer is "workshops"— followed quickly by "in-service days," "graduate courses," and "sabbaticals." While valuable, these items cannot compare to a professional development program that is much more broadly, imaginatively, and robustly conceived.

ISM's research and experience leads us to conclude that an ideal faculty professional growth and renewal program is largely:

- *focused on higher-order behaviors* that expand the teacher's understanding of the teaching profession and spur his/her quest for professional knowledge, skill, and discovery;
- *site-based,* i.e., fundamentally focused on learning in one's own school and from one's own peers and mentors;
- *continual,* i.e., a regular and ongoing part of daily and weekly routines;
- *annually renewed but career-long in nature,* i.e., taking both a short-term view ("how can I teach better now") and a long-term view (as part of the teacher's life-long learning and development efforts);
- *teacher-directed with administrator support,* i.e., propelled by the teacher, but with the administrator ready, willing, and able to provide support and counsel, to help the teacher attain his/her goals;

– *socialized,* when knowledge and insight is gained by a teacher, it is shared freely and actively with colleagues; and

– *focused on skills, perspectives, and behaviors designed to be difference-makers* in the lives of the students in the classroom and outside—i.e., not solely knowledge for knowledge's sake, but knowledge that can be put to use for the best interests of current and future students.

Examples of Professional Growth and Renewal Activities

In line with the above, the following represent examples of growth and renewal activities that speak to higher-order faculty growth (several of which speak to collective faculty growth as well as individual teacher growth, thus enhancing the overall faculty culture):

– *observation of colleagues' classes* within-school or at neighboring schools, as other faculty members work on new and innovative concepts;

– *faculty-led seminars* using regular faculty meetings as setting in which an in-house panel of teachers makes presentations and leads discussion on recent studies, reading, or research they have engaged in;

– *teaching experiments diary,* an informal log of each new thing attempted, including the preparation involved, the outcomes, and ideas for enhancement;

– *journal-coverage responsibility,* reviewing professional journals and discussing them with a designated colleague to draw out ideas and tools that might be useful in their classrooms;

– *brown-bag or after-school snack sessions* in which an individual offers a short presentation and leads a discussion on a special topic that he/she has studied, or observed at another school or in another classroom;

– *professional membership,* energetically participating in professional education organizations, including attending meetings, leading workshop sessions, reading the organization's professional journal, and engaging like-minded members in a variety of settings;

– *faculty summer reading programs,* with faculty members reporting on books that have impacted their teaching practices; and

– *action research,* teachers examining their own practices in the classroom (see details later in this section).

Caveat: It's About the Conversations, Not the Forms

In recommending this growth program, we need to offer one caveat. That is, one can implement a program that is well-structured and efficient, but that is also lacking in heart and passion. Conversely, one can have a program almost wholly lacking in structure, but in which resides deep passion, commitment, and energy. While we suggest and encourage the school to establish a program that combines the best of each (which we believe the following process in fact does), if we had to choose between two extremes, we would always choose passion over structure.

Said differently, "it's not about the program—it's about the *conversation*" that the program engenders. Thus, implementing an efficient process with which teachers and administrators *comply*, but do so reluctantly, adds little to the life of the school (in fact, it detracts from it), and doesn't help students in any way. Instead, the goal is a program that generates, supports, and enhances myriad ongoing, robust conversations among teachers as to teaching techniques, experiments, and all manner of growth regarding the vocation of teaching.

Developing Your Professional Growth and Renewal Program

With the purposes and caveats outlined above firmly in mind, we offer the following recommendations regarding implementation of a highly engaging Professional Growth and Renewal program at your school.

1. ***Prerequisite—Characteristics of Professional Excellence:*** To engage in the growth and renewal program we suggest, the school first needs a well-defined set of Characteristics of Professional Excellence (CPEs). The process for establishing a set of characteristics appropriate to your mission, culture, and values is described in detail in Chapter 3.

2. ***Forming a Professional Growth and Renewal Design Team:*** In much the same way that a team is needed to develop a school-customized evaluation template, the Head will wish to appoint a team of exemplary teachers and academic administrators to translate the school's characteristics into a school-customized professional growth and renewal program. The Head may appoint some, all, or none of the teachers who served on the Characteristics Design Team and Evaluation Design Teams to the Professional Growth and Renewal Design Team.

3. ***The Charge:*** The Head's charge to the team is, using the Teacher's Growth and Renewal Plan Template shown later in this chapter as a model, to customize a process and template for your school.

4. ***The Team's Work:*** Just as described for the team that forms the school's Characteristics of Professional Excellence (CPEs), the Professional Growth and Renewal Design Team may take a few weeks or longer to complete their work. The end product—not the time taken—is the primary focus of the team. During the course of their work, they will want to seek out input and feedback from their colleagues.

5. ***Approving the Growth Plan Template:*** When the team's proposed template is fully formed, it must be reviewed and approved by your Head and the Management Team.

6. *Administrative Training:* Before this program can be implemented, the school's academic administrators will need to be trained on not only the growth and renewal process itself, but also on coaching and mentoring skills. They will then be well-equipped to carry out their roles as managers and mentors. (See the "Coaching and Mentoring" section at the end of this chapter for further details and guidance.)

7. *Introducing the Template to the Faculty:* With the template fully formed and the Management Team trained, the template and overall growth program are ready to be introduced to the faculty. In an all-faculty meeting, the topic should be introduced by your Head and presented by the Professional Growth and Renewal Design Team.

8. *Putting the Plan Into Effect, Teacher-By-Teacher:* Once the program has been introduced to the faculty at large, it should be put into effect in individual coaching meetings between administrators and teachers. The timing of this will depend on when the program is approved and introduced.

9. *Launching the Individual Growth Plan:* At the appropriate time, the teacher and administrator collaborate to develop the teacher's initial growth plan. Once approved, the teacher goes forth and launches the plan—which may begin during the summer break, or early in the fall semester, as appropriate based on the goals involved.

10. *Ongoing Support, Guidance, and Feedback:* Throughout the year, the administrator supports each of the teachers he/she is responsible for, providing resources, learning opportunities, and feedback. The administrator becomes an agent of each of his/her teacher's success—conveying to the teacher his/her desire for the teacher to be successful and communicating that the teacher's success will be felt as a success by the administrator as well.

11. *Concluding One Plan and Launching Another:* As the first year of the Professional Growth and Renewal Program comes to a close, teachers and administrators meet to review the results of the current year's plan. This may happen at the formal evaluation session or shortly thereafter. In concert with reflecting on the teacher's performance and growth needs stemming from that year's performance evaluation, the teacher and administrator collaborate on drafting a growth plan for the coming academic year—and the cycle begins anew.

The Question of Timing (Calendar)

The Professional Growth and Renewal Program may be initiated toward the end of a school year, e.g., May, for purposes of mirroring the annual academic calendar (i.e., planning in May for the new academic year to begin in August/September). However, as the need for growth and renewal is constant and ongoing, its use can begin at any time that makes sense practically and administratively for your school. Some schools, in fact, choose to operate the program on a January–December basis, because that works best for them in terms of providing time, attention, and resources. Timing is an important consideration that the design team will need to grapple with.

The Question of (Administrator) Time

In terms of allotting administrative time to guide and mentor teachers during the process, time spent will vary (sometimes considerably), based on the type of goals selected and the experience levels, styles, communication preferences, and needs of the teacher and administrator involved. It is difficult to estimate exactly how much of an administrator's time the growth program will take up, because a good portion of the administrator and teacher's coaching sessions might involve items and aspects of the teacher's growth program.

Due to the intertwining of coaching and growth and renewal, schools are cautioned against spending too much time trying to distinguish between the two. In the end, the distinction is unimportant and possibly harmful. That is because the value of both coaching and growth is not in the program per se, but in the behaviors and perspectives that they spur, which ultimately translate into the performance, satisfaction, and enthusiasm of your students. It is unimportant whether a teacher-administrator meeting is a coaching session or a growth and renewal session. Both are important; the distinction is not.

Going back to where we began this book, we believe strongly that the primary responsibility of academic administrators is building the capacity of faculty to deliver the mission with excellence. Coaching, mentoring, and growth and renewal conversations are a primary means by which this happens, and thus is time well- and importantly spent (up to 25%–50% of the administrator's time).

That being said, we understand and sympathize with the need for schools to anticipate time burdens on their administrators. For planning purposes, the following broad example might be helpful.

- **Situation:** An academic administrator is responsible for coaching, mentoring, and evaluating 10 faculty members.

- *Coaching:* The administrator visits each teacher once per month. The classroom visit is 10 minutes, followed by a 10-minute coaching conversation. Connected to these conversations, they spend 10 minutes each time discussing the progress the teacher is making in his/her growth plan. Thus, 30 minutes are spent with each teacher each month.

- *Evaluating:* To incorporate all aspects of the Evaluation and Growth Cycle, we will consider that the administrator spends two hours writing the teacher's evaluation and one hour discussing the evaluation with him/her.

- *Calculation:* If the administrator spends 30 minutes per month coaching the teacher and discussing his/her growth plan, that is 30 minutes x 8 months = 240 minutes = 4 hours.

  Adding to the three hours that the administrator spends writing and discussing the teacher's evaluation, we see that actively coaching, mentoring, and evaluating each teacher and helping guide his/her growth can be anticipated to consume seven hours per teacher per academic year.

Teacher's Professional Growth and Renewal Plan Template

Our sample Professional Growth and Renewal template is shown below. As with the evaluation template, ISM's Professional Growth and Renewal Plan template needs to be reviewed and customized to align with and support your school's unique mission, culture, and values.

As a brief overview, key elements of the template include:

- *Introduction:* Overview and Instructions
- *Step 1:* Reflecting on Mission
- *Step 2:* Reflecting on Your School's Characteristics of Professional Excellence
- *Step 3:* Establishing Two Goals
- *Step 4:* Setting a Path for Success
- *Step 5:* Determining the Support and Resources Needed
- *Step 6:* Establishing Milestones and Measurements for Success
- *Step 7:* Anticipating Student Outcomes
- *Step 8:* Joint Accountability: Gaining Commitment
- *Step 9:* Reflections (The Ongoing Conversation)

Introduction: Overview and Instructions

Whether communicated in the form of a separate cover letter from the Head or as the first few paragraphs of the template itself, it is helpful to provide the template's users (i.e., the teacher and administrator) with an overview of the professional growth and renewal program's purpose and meaning within the life of the school. An example is shown below.

Aegis Academy

Faculty Growth and Renewal Program

Overview: Greetings! For both new and returning faculty, I offer you my warmest welcome as we, together, embark on another challenging and exciting year of offering the best college preparatory education for students from nursery through grade twelve.

One of the hallmarks of Aegis Academy has always been the extraordinary energy, creativity, dedication, and passion of our faculty, which the administration strives to support in all ways possible. We understand the commitment you have to our students and the personal and professional sacrifices you make in meeting their needs. We also understand that teachers need to regularly renew and refresh themselves to keep doing what they do with vigor and excitement. To this end, we are proud to introduce our new Professional Growth and Renewal Program.

This program is intended to provide a framework and support for professional development efforts—helping you explore new ideas and gain new insights into teaching and your subject area, and doing so in a way that is meaningful, exciting, and energizing. I ask that you work through each section of this document in drafting a plan to propel your growth and renewal over the course of this academic year—with an eye toward this being one step on your journey as a lifelong learner and communicator.

Directions for drafting your plan are provided on the following page. Please complete your draft and schedule an initial meeting with your Department Chair, who will guide you throughout the year. This meeting should occur no later than September 30th.

Thank you for your commitment to our students, to Aegis Academy, and to private-school education. I offer my fullest support and encouragement as you go forward with a spirit of service and excellence.

Andrew Jones
School Head

Instructions

It will be helpful to provide concise directions to the teacher and administrator regarding how to draft an individual growth plan.

Progressing Through Aegis' Professional Growth and Renewal Program

1. Reflect on Aegis Academy's mission, culture, and values; our Characteristics of Professional Excellence (shown below); and your personal/professional mission and interests.

2. Select two personally and professionally meaningful "stretch" goals/projects to pursue during this school year. (Note: Multiyear projects may be proposed, as appropriate.)

3. Complete the indicated sections of this template, defining your goals, steps to achieve the goals, the resources required, milestones and measures of success, and anticipated student outcomes.

4. Meet with your Department Chair or Grade Coordinator to review your proposed plan and gain agreement/approval for your goals and the resources needed.

5. Begin pursuing your goals, checking in with your supervisor for feedback and guidance on a regular basis (e.g., at least once per month).

6. Upon completion of the goals, meet with your supervisor to wrap up this year's program, summarizing key achievements in the "Final Reflections" section.

▲▲

Step 1: Reflecting on Mission

NOTE: In this step, we offer two options—an active and a reflective approach. In customizing the template, the design team will take into consideration which approach (or modified version thereof) will be most helpful to your faculty.

Active Option: The school invites teachers to actively record both your school's mission statement and their own personal mission statement. The exercise of actively writing down their personal mission and restating the school's mission is designed to help the teachers clarify why they are teaching in your particular school at this particular time in their professional career. Understanding this may help them determine anew what resonates most strongly with them and what they want to achieve professionally now—guiding them toward the type of growth they need and desire at this time, and that aligns with the school's mission.

An example of this active approach is shown in the template below.

Mission Statements

Write our mission statement below—either our formal statement or in your own words. Circle or highlight the words or phrases that resonate most strongly with you. You may find that you wish to focus on these items in this year's individual growth plan.

Aegis Academy Mission Statement

_____

_____

_____

Personal/Professional Mission Statement

Compose your own personal mission statement. This may express why you believe you exist, your core purposes in life, the roles you play, etc.—your reason for being. A well-crafted personal/professional mission statement might identify points at which your personal and professional missions intersect.

Example:

As a son, friend, musician, and teacher, I exist to engage with people in ways that build them up ethically, emotionally, and intellectually; as a teacher, I exist to create relationships with my students that inspire them to deep, lifelong learning.

_____

_____

_____

_____

▲▲

Reflective Option: As an alternative, the design team may choose to ask teachers to reflect deeply on the school's mission, culture, and values—as expressed in the school's mission statement, values statement, or any other related statements which the school may have developed—but not require them to share those reflections in writing in their growth plan. This is a thought exercise only.

An example is shown below.

Points of Reflection

As an aid in developing your growth goals for the year, you are asked to reflect on Aegis Academy's mission, culture, and values, as exemplified in the following statement.

Aegis Academy Mission

As a coeducational college preparatory school, Aegis Academy strives to educate students toward leading a life of character, integrity, global citizenship, and deep commitment to the pursuit of knowledge, intellectual rigor, and constant curiosity.

Personal Mission

We each have our own personal and professional missions—what we intend to pursue and achieve with our time, treasure, and talents. Each faculty member is asked to reflect on his/her personal mission, particularly with regard to the intersection points between his/her personal/professional mission and the school's mission. Consider what opportunities, endeavors, and purposes are suggested as you plan your proposed goals for this year's Professional Growth and Renewal Program.

▲▲

Step 2: Reflecting on Your School's Characteristics of Professional Excellence

Teachers next are encouraged to reflect on the school's defined Characteristics of Professional Excellence (CPEs), described in detail in Chapter 3. Teachers may wish to focus on one or two of the characteristics that strike them most deeply—or, they may wish to reflect on the set of characteristics as a whole, considering the impact that the entire statement may have in shaping the direction of their growth efforts this year. (See next page.)

Step 3: Establishing One or Two Goals

This is where the rubber meets the road. In this step, the teacher translates his/her work to this point—reflecting on the school mission, his/her personal/professional mission, and the characteristics of excellence—into one or two rigorous professional growth and renewal objectives for the next school year.

It is strongly recommended that the number of goals be strictly limited to two. This is so that they can receive sustained attention from the teacher (and support from the administrator) throughout the year. To undertake more than two goals risks the whole plan collapsing onto itself, with even the most determined of teachers quickly being overwhelmed by the size, scope, and volume of tasks and projects before him/her (in addition to carrying out his/her "day job" as a teacher, of course). For this reason, many schools—especially those implementing this program for the first time—ask teachers to select only one goal, so that goal can receive the teacher's maximum effort and attention.

The sample below illustrates what goals proposed by a faculty member might look like.

My Professional Growth and Renewal Goals

Briefly describe your proposed goals for this year in the lines below. You must limit your objectives to two. Please recall that these objectives are designed to be higher-order behaviors that will make a difference to your students and promote your own long-term professional growth and renewal.

Goal No. 1:

Research and implement best practices in incorporating social media into instruction.

Goal No. 2:

Improve my ability to assess individual student progress by learning and implementing two new tools or techniques.

NOTE: For purposes of focus and clarity, we will use Goal No. 1 as our example for the remainder of this section.

Aegis Academy

Characteristics of Professional Excellence

*The faculty of Aegis Academy commit to these characteristics as the foundation
of our efforts to serve the needs of our students, colleagues, and school.*

- *Professional Growth:* I dedicate myself to daily and lifelong professional development, continually seeking opportunities to improve my teaching in service to my students and colleagues.

- *Setting and Maintaining Standards:* I set and support clear and appropriately challenging standards for both student academic performance and student behavior. My students know what they're accountable for and are confident that they will be held to these standards.

- *Real-Life Applications:* I strive to relate all of my lessons to real-life conditions and events, to help students make the connection between the subjects we are studying and the world they observe and experience outside the classroom.

- *Enthusiasm:* I bring my "A" game every day, passionately and energetically demonstrating my enthusiasm for teaching and learning, and striving to engender similar enthusiasm in all my students, so that they may become lifelong learners, seekers, doers, and innovators.

- *Commitment to Mission:* I strive to live the mission in word and deed, working every day to help make our mission come to fruition in the lives of our students, families, and graduates.

- *On Their Side:* In all of our interactions inside and outside the classroom, I find ways to make it obvious to all students that I am eager to teach them, I believe in their abilities, and I work for their success every day.

- *Engaging and Supporting the Whole Person:* I strive to have meaningful and healthy emotional engagement with my students and colleagues regarding their out-of-school lives, without crossing privacy barriers—so that we can support each other in the most vibrant, professionally appropriate ways possible.

- *Healthy Learning Community:* I work hard every day to contribute to a healthy learning, growing, and mutually supportive environment for and with my colleagues—sharing knowledge, resources, insight, and aid freely, openly, and energetically.

Required Goals: Linking the Written Evaluation to the Growth and Renewal Plan

When the teacher is performing at a high level and there are no obvious gaps or areas of needed improvement, he/she is free to select two goals that inspire and drive her. In many cases, though, the teacher-administrator coaching conversations that occur during the year will suggest areas for skill or technique improvement that the teacher will wish to focus on.

For teachers experiencing notable performance difficulties, the "suggested" goals would become *required*—i.e., the teacher wouldn't be free to select his/her own goals; areas of improvement would be mandated by the administrator. In the most serious cases, the teacher wouldn't complete an individual growth plan at all; rather, he/she would be placed on corrective action (described in detail in Chapter 8). In these cases, the teacher's employment is at risk, and he/she wouldn't be free to pursue individualized growth goals until after the performance matter is resolved and he/she comes off of corrective action.

An illustration of a suggested goal is shown below. Let's say that the annual written evaluation for our sample teacher, Annette, included the following comments.

> *Consistency and Reliability:*
>
> Annette demonstrates consistent and reliable behavior in all areas of her work in the classroom. As we have discussed at several times during the year, however, these otherwise good and desired characteristics can become a negative if they are taken to the extreme—i.e., if consistency becomes "rigidity" or "inflexibility" in ways that don't help support students. I know from our conversations that Annette understands and agrees with this concept but still has struggled applying this in the classroom at times.
>
> As one example, when working with a student with ADHD issues, Annette struggled with adapting her teaching style to engage this student as fully as possible. Providing flexibility in how he participated in discussions and presented papers and other assignments may have permitted the student to perform at a higher level in the subject matter. I am asking Annette to focus on differentiated learning and teaching styles as one of her professional growth and renewal goals in the coming year.

After reflecting on this assessment by the administrator, Annette proposed the following as the second goal for her professional growth plan.

Goal No. 2:

> Engage in intensive study of differentiated instruction, to enhance my ability to assess individual student progress, and then to modify my instructional approaches accordingly.

This demonstrates an excellent coordination between the written evaluation (as informed by a year's worth of coaching and mentoring conversations) and the teacher's professional growth plan.

Step 4: Setting a Path to Success

The next task for the teacher is to develop a basic outline of the steps she plans to take for each goal. At this stage, it will be impossible to describe the steps and actions that need to be taken with great precision in most cases. Rather, the intent is to develop a best-guess outline for the project—subject to developments, new information, course corrections, etc., which will inevitably come to light as the project proceeds. The effort at this time is simply to chart a thoughtful course that provides direction without being unduly restrictive or too narrowly construed so as to preclude serendipitous moments and graces that come the teacher's way in due course.

One important element of the teacher charting his/her preliminary course in this way is that it enables both the teacher and administrator to consider both resource and time line issues. Thus, if the steps to be taken will require significantly more resources than are available (described in the following step), then this may suggest that a course correction is necessary before setting sail on the project.

Steps to Achieve My Goals

Please indicate the main steps you need to take to achieve your professional goals.

Goal No. 1:

- Attend "Social Media in Teaching" webinar

- Participate in online discussions on this topic on at least a weekly basis

- Conduct research into the variety of ways that social media is currently used in instruction

- Make arrangements to visit at least two schools using social media in their upper school classrooms

- Prepare to report my findings at an in-service meeting

Special Issue: Socializing Knowledge

One of the primary intents of robust professional growth programs is the socialization of the knowledge gained—i.e., where faculty share with their colleagues the new knowledge they have gained. Sharing can take on many forms, including:

- publishing an article;
- giving a presentation at the monthly faculty meeting;
- sharing findings with department colleagues over a brown-bag lunch;
- designing and displaying a poster board at the annual Faculty Research Exhibition; or
- a blog with write-ups, pictures, and video snippets describing faculty research.

What's important is that the teacher's newly gained knowledge gets out for others to use, to comment on, to add to, to be challenged, to affect teacher behavior, and ultimately to impact classroom practice and student achievement. Accordingly, administrators may wish to ensure that all growth plans include an aspect of socializing knowledge in the project plan.

Step 5: Determining the Support and Resources Needed

The teacher is then asked to list the type of support and resources that he/she will need to carry out the projects. This should flow from the list of steps to be taken and may include access to colleagues, journals, networks, associations, and other sources—some of which involve time, money, or both.

An example (*flowing from the Sample Goal No. 1 shown above*) might look like this.

Resources/Support Needed to Achieve My Goal

Please indicate the key resources you will need to achieve your professional goals.

Goal No. 1:

> Approval and reimbursement for webinar registration

> Reimbursement for appropriate textbook (to be determined)

> Time off (up to 2 days) to visit schools selected to observe their use of social media in the classroom

> Weekly planning period to consult with the school's IT Director and social media experts in the Marketing/Communications department

NOTE: Demonstrating support by providing necessary resources is a critical issue. Particularly in the first years of the program, teachers will be looking for signs that the school is serious about this endeavor. They will silently assess if you are willing to commit resources to the effort—and thus, if you are worthy of their trust and commitment—or, if this is simply the "flavor of the month" and will soon be forgotten. You are making commitments around dollars, time, relationships, etc. that the faculty member will be looking to you to fulfill. Once you have agreed to this support structure, you must deliver on it. If not, the credibility of the entire program will be severely diminished, perhaps beyond repair.

Step 6: Establishing Milestones and Measurements for Success

Now that the teacher has described her two goals and resources have been determined, it is important to consider how you (the teacher and the administrator) will know if she has successfully attained her goals. Accordingly, the teacher is asked to forecast what success looks like with respect to the goals selected—and what milestones will help you both know that she is progressing along the right path.

Milestones and Measures of Success

Please indicate the key milestones for keeping on track for attaining your professional goals, as well as the measures that will indicate successful completion of the goal.

Goal No. 1:

> Dec. 15—Identify two schools using social media in the classroom and arrange to conduct visits prior to holiday break

> Feb. 15—Present research and observation findings to the in-service meeting in February

> March 15—Implement at least one social media element in my classroom

> May 15—Assess student outcomes relating to the new social media element

Depending on the nature of the goals involved, identifying milestones—i.e., dates by which interim steps should be begun or completed—may be critical for giving the project forward momentum and structure.

Measures of success may take a wide variety of forms, including:
- a product (e.g., a log, a diary, a portfolio, a video, a report);
- objective accomplishment of a particular skill (e.g., a new instructional technique, mastery of a new piece of software or computer technology, a new approach to grouping students for particular activities, a new class-control approach, a revised parent education plan);
- an assessment point (e.g., a Division Head's assessment of the product and/or result); and/or
- an assessment process (e.g., a parent survey or a standardized testing event).

Failure Is an Option: Measures need not be strictly quantitative or tangible. Rather, the only requirement is that the teacher and the administrator agree on what success might look like within the context of professional growth. This leads to the question of whether or not "success" is even required at all.

As one school administrator said to us, "***Failure*** is an option. ***Not growing*** is not." This is to say that achieving a particular forecasted outcome may or may not indicate whether the teacher accomplished the goal. It may be the case that the goal was, on one level, completely unsuccessful. For example, it could turn out that the teacher wasn't able to identify any effective uses of social media in the classroom.

From a superficial level, the teacher failed to achieve the goal. At the same time, however, if we consider the goal more broadly, he/she may have succeeded fabulously well. That is to say, if the overarching goal was really the teacher's professional growth through rigorous inquiry of new topics, he/she may have achieved this in spades—e.g., in the course of the research, the teacher may have learned two new nonsocial media techniques that are used in the classroom to great effect; or he/she may have developed a working partnership with the IT department that will enhance and inform his/her future teaching efforts in innumerable ways. Therefore, the frame of reference used to define success should be carefully considered.

Technique: Conducting Action Research: One way in which the teacher may assess success by engaging in action research. One form of action research is for the teacher to introduce a new technique to the classroom and then assess the impact of the technique on student learning—such as, for example, the impact of the new social media technique described in our "Goal No. 1" example. Conducting action research may be a goal itself (i.e., learning a new research technique to add to the teacher's toolbox of resources), or it may be a data point when measuring the success of a particular goal (such as the use of the new social media teaching technique, for example). By assessing the impact of a new technique through action research, the teacher is fulfilling the highest aspirations of the professional growth program—to enhance his/her abilities in ways that impact student performance, satisfaction, and enthusiasm.

Step 7: Anticipating Student Outcomes

The final piece of the goal proposal process involves anticipating student outcomes. Here, we return to Covey's maxim about "beginning with the end in mind." If the end goal of teacher professional growth is impacting student learning, then it is important for the teacher and administrator to try to forecast what some of the outcomes might be with regard to students.

Some outcomes might be straightforward (e.g., "being able to use a new technique to spur student learning"), while others might be more subtle (e.g., "renewing my enthusiasm for my subject area, so that I can communicate new passion for the topic to my students"). In either case, trying to put the potential outcomes on paper early in the program will help both teacher and administrator keep the true purpose of pursuing the goal in sight throughout the project.

Consider the following example.

Anticipated Student Outcomes

Please try to forecast what you believe might be the impact of these goals on your teaching and on your students.

Goal No. 1:

Learning this new technique will provide me with another instructional method to serve the needs of my students. It will also enable me to stay true to Aegis's core principle of applying real-world lessons to classroom topics, by bringing the real-world into the classroom in the form of social media that the students use in all aspects of their lives outside of school.

Step 8: Gaining Commitment

While a signature may seem a perfunctory part of the process, in the case of a teacher's Professional Growth and Renewal Plan, the implications of this page are profound. The administrator and teacher should be encouraged to reflect on what they are truly signing off on. We say this not from a legalistic perspective, but from the perspective of engendering deep commitment and accountability on the part of both teacher and administrator.

- The teacher is committing to a significant professional growth and renewal effort—embarking on a year-long (or a career-long) conversation with his/her administrator about increasing his/her skills in ways that impact student performance, enthusiasm, and satisfaction.

- The administrator is committing to being an active success agent, cheerleader, coach, guide, and mentor; to providing needed resources; and to engaging in a professionally intimate conversation with the teacher that will form the basis of their collaborative relationship.

Commitment and Joint Accountability

A teacher's commitment to professional growth and renewal is critical to our students' performance, enthusiasm, and satisfaction, and ultimately to the success of our school and its mission.

An administrator's commitment to the teacher's growth and renewal is central to his/her role as leader, coach, and mentor. By signing below, both parties formally accept the teacher's growth plan for this school year and agree to pursue it with the greatest professional vigor, dedication, and enthusiasm possible.

With this understanding, we wish to jointly commit to and be held accountable for this plan.

TEACHER'S SIGNATURE: _____ DATE: _____

ADMINISTRATOR'S SIGNATURE: _____ DATE: _____

Step 9: Reflections (The Ongoing Conversation)

We believe strongly in the power of self-reflection to help us learn and grow from our own experiences. Accordingly, the final step in the professional growth and renewal process is designed to help teachers discern lessons learned from pursuing their professional growth goals. Journal space is provided to encourage teachers to reflect on the projects they undertake both while they are ongoing and afterward.

See the following example.

Year-End Summary and Reflections

Teachers are asked to reflect their thoughts throughout the course of their projects (either below or in a separate document, as appropriate).

Entries may be in the form of status updates, musings, or any comments that reflect their feelings, perceptions, learning, questions, and concerns throughout this process. Questions that you may wish to reflect on include:

- In what ways have my classes improved due to what I've learned from this project?

- In what specific ways have I been renewed? (Or, have I been renewed?)

- What new characteristics do I see my students developing (e.g., sense of hope, confidence, and belief in their efforts) that I can tie back to my efforts on this project?

- What surprises, obstacles, and frustrations did I encounter during this journey?

- What insights, ideas, or perspectives did I gain by pursuing these goals?

TEACHER'S SIGNATURE: DATE:

Considerations in Guiding Professional Growth and Renewal Plans

Issues to consider when guiding teachers in developing the growth plans include:

- *Flexibility:* While planning is needed to provide the growth plan with appropriate structure and direction, no plan should be considered as set in stone—all plans should be viewed as open to change as conditions and needs change. To adhere too rigidly to the original plan when circumstances may have changed is to fall victim to carrying out the plan for the plan's sake, rather than carrying forth with the spirit and purpose of growth that is at the plan's true core.

- *Guiding the Conversation:* During their meetings to form the year's professional growth plan, the administrator's role is to listen, to clarify, and to be as supportive and encouraging of the teacher as possible—as, in its most ideal form, the growth plan should be driven by the teacher and reflect his/her professional goals, interests, and passions.

  In good-case scenarios, i.e., when a mission-appropriate teacher presents a well-conceived initial plan, it is often the case that the plan can be accepted and put into action with little reworking or fine-tuning.

  In less ideal scenarios, such as a teacher who submits a poorly conceived or unambitious initial plan, the teacher and administrator may need to collaborate on several rewrites before a satisfactory plan is developed.

  In worst-case scenarios, where the administrator is requiring the teacher to pursue one or two specific goals due to poor performance, the resulting document is really a corrective-action warning or performance improvement plan, rather than a true growth and renewal plan. These circumstances are described in more detail in Chapter 8.

- *Check-In Meetings:* Subsequent meetings between the teacher and his/her supervisor should occur at intervals that are determined by the nature of the goals. Some goals may require only occasional meetings; others may require several clusters of meetings to help the teacher move forward. The administrator's availability and eagerness to give feedback, serve as sounding board, or just provide a sympathetic ear is vital to maintaining trust in the teacher-administrator relationship.

- *Time Frame for Completing Goals:* We made brief reference earlier to the notion that goals aren't necessarily confined to one-year time periods. The nature of the teacher's goals might be that they require an 18-month or two-year period to complete. As long as the teacher keeps the administrator apprised of his/her progress and he/she seems to be accomplishing the milestones set out in the plan, the length of the plan itself shouldn't be of concern—it is the continual learning and growth that is occurring that is the true purpose of the growth program in the first place.

Required: Full Support of the School Head

The visible and vocal support of the Head is critical to the success of teacher evaluation and growth and renewal programs. As in many other areas of school leadership, mixed messages or signs of weak executive support will undermine these programs—communicating that these programs are the current flavor of the month—which, if teachers are patient, can be safely ignored as the school moves on to other topics of interest.

Since many schools do not currently engage in robust evaluation and growth processes of the type recommended here, implementation of this program represents a significant organizational change effort. As such, the dynamics of implementation will vary considerably based on the history, culture, and faculty-administration relationship present at the school. In general, we suggest the Head must clearly communicate to faculty and administrators that:

- all teachers will be evaluated annually, assessing their overall performance inside and outside the classroom;
- all teachers will develop and carry out robust professional growth and renewal plans, guided by their supervisor as coach and mentor;
- the primary responsibility of academic administrators is to develop and enhance the capacity of faculty to deliver the mission with excellence; and
- appropriate resources will be provided to support growth and renewal efforts (especially in the form of time for administrators to coach and mentor faculty, time for teachers to pursue their plans, and adequate funding to support their approved growth plans).

By repeating these messages consistently in word and deed, the Head will be doing a great deal to ensure the success of these programs—i.e., ensuring the ability of the faculty to impact student performance, satisfaction, and enthusiasm in meaningful and vibrant ways.

VIGNETTE: Establishing Growth and Renewal Goals

In the prior vignette regarding an evaluation discussion, we encountered a teacher who was initially resistant to and suspicious of the school's aims in implementing a new evaluation system. In this vignette, we consider a different and opposite circumstance—a teacher who embraces growth and renewal too vigorously. Their enthusiasm is so intense and their initial growth plan proposal is so ambitious that she is likely to fail and overshadow her responsibilities to current students.

The following dialogue imagines how an understanding, perceptive, and firm coach and mentor might help the teacher focus her efforts and energies more effectively—creating a growth and renewal plan that will help her grow without the negative side effects of overextension or burn out.

SET-UP: Aegis Academy, a K–12 coed day school, has had a vigorous professional development program in place for several years now. Today, Roger, the Middle School Principal, is meeting with Vanessa, a Science teacher in her second year of teaching, to discuss her growth plan for next year.

NOTE: You may wish to read the "dialogue" column in full, and then loop back to the "commentary" column for notes and perspectives on the dialogue.

It is important for the coach to be engaged and supportive, even when being directive.

In these type of circumstances, it is often important for the coach to reiterate—and to model—ideas about work/life balance, gently guiding the teacher toward greater balance.

Dialogue

Roger: Vanessa, I really appreciate the great deal of thought and effort that you put into your development goals for next year. Very impressive!

Vanessa: Thanks, Roger. You know I get very wrapped up in things … it's just so exciting to be here, doing this. I've had *such* a great experience with the students this year, I just want to keep *going and going*!

Roger: [chuckling to himself] I understand. We all need a break to rest and renew, though.

Vanessa: Oh, I know. Believe me. I'm a little exhausted right now, I have to admit. I am looking forward to a little time off with my family once the semester ends. I really need it.

Roger: I'm glad to hear you say that. Sometimes new faculty work so hard for so long that they burn out prematurely, and that's not good for anyone.

Vanessa: I hear you—my parents and my fiancé remind me of that all the time. I'm not always great at taking a break, but I do understand. I'm trying!

Roger: That's great. Well, in that regard, I wanted to talk with you a little bit about your proposed goals for next year.

Vanessa: Yes—what did you think? Were they "stretchy" enough? I know that Ellen really stressed that part in the in-service meeting a few weeks ago.

> *Vanessa clearly got the "stretchy goals" message. The coach's role here is to "reel her back in" and help her avoid overextending herself (which would benefit no one).*

Roger: They are definitely "stretchy" enough. Actually, I think we have the *opposite* problem. They're *too* ambitious.

Vanessa: Really?

Roger: Absolutely. To begin with, you wrote *four* goals. We really only like to see teachers working on two goals each year … or, if it is a really challenging or demanding goal, sometimes only one.

> *In coaching faculty, the administrator strives to strike the proper balance between encouraging the teacher and being directive enough.*

Vanessa: But I have lots of energy. I want to learn. I want to serve my students better. I know it's a cliché, but I really consider it my personal mission. Why shouldn't I try to do as much as I can?

Roger: That is admirable, of course. I'm just not sure it's effective. You're already stretched since you teach the whole middle school science curriculum. If a teacher sets too many goals, it is usually the students who suffer, ironically enough, because the teacher is pulled in too many directions that don't have to do with the students in her class *today.*

Vanessa: But there are so many things I want to learn and try!

Roger: I appreciate that. I really do. But trust me on this. You will get a lot more out of it if you limit your focus than if you try to cover too much ground.

Vanessa: OK … I guess. I still want to take it all on, but I defer to your judgment.

Roger: Great. OK, then. Which goals do you want to keep and which do you want to defer to the future?

> *Guiding the teacher toward making her own selection decisions is a wise approach for the coach to take, as the teacher's goals should always feel self-selected rather than imposed.*

Often, a simple reading out loud of proposed goals will help make it apparent when overreaching occurs. To even the casual observer, Vanessa's proposed goals would clearly be too many to adequately attend to in any one school year.

Calm consistency and resiliency are important characteristics for administrators to display during coaching interactions.

It is often the job of the coach to help teachers group or summarize their ideas in ways that make them more useful or in ways that make the answer more readily apparent. Here, Roger's grouping of three of the goals as like items helps Vanessa see the prudence in picking one of the three similar goals.

The coach appropriately segues to his role as supporter and resource-provider, which is a key element of supporting professional growth.

Vanessa: I think I'm the wrong person to ask about that. I mean, I want to do them *all,* remember?

Roger: Right. Well, here's what you came up with originally: "1: Research the latest developments in nanotechnology as they relate to chemistry. 2: Get up-to-date on NASA's chemical research with respect to the Mars program. 3: Speak with a scientist from a major pharmaceutical company about the role of chemistry in their research and development projects. 4: Enhance my teaching skills with regard to engaging students in labs, experiments, and other experiential learning."

Vanessa: You're *really* going to make me narrow it down, aren't you?

Roger: Yes, I really am.

Vanessa: Hmmm …

Roger: Let me suggest an approach, if I might. The first three that you listed all have to do with "scientific" knowledge itself. What if you picked *one* of those? Then, the last one talks about engaging students in lab activities. That has to do with teaching technique. If you went with one of the science goals and the one teaching goal, you would have a nice balance.

Vanessa: Hmmm … I see what you're saying. That makes sense.

Roger: Great. Think about that a little more, then let's meet again next week to finalize the goals and start looking at the resources and support that you'll need.

Vanessa: Sounds good, Roger—will do! Thanks so much!

Roger: My pleasure.

Vanessa: Whewww, I feel a whole lot better. Thanks for helping me focus. Now, I just have to pick one of the three—but which one? Maybe I'll talk to a few other teachers in the middle school. They might have some suggestions on which way to go.

Common Element: Coaching and Mentoring

Before we close this chapter on the Evaluation and Growth cycle, we need to discuss in more detail the element that connects all steps and stages of the cycle—the coaching and mentoring of the teacher by the administrator.

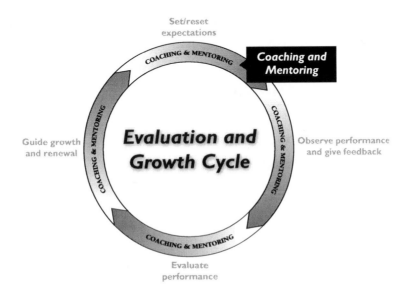

This responsibility, which is at the center of the administrator's role in expanding the capacity of faculty, runs throughout each step of the cycle—from setting expectations, to observing performance and providing feedback, to evaluating performance, to guiding growth and renewal. It is vital that administrators be trained and become skilled at the coach/mentor role, and it is equally vital that the School Head and the Management Team organize the school's processes, schedules, and resources to enable this coaching/mentoring relationship to occur.

Coaching and Mentoring Defined

The dictionary provides us with definitions of coaching and mentoring as both nouns and verbs.

Coach: (n.) a person who trains an athlete or a team; (v.) to give instruction or advice

Mentor: (n.) a wise and trusted counselor; (v.) to influence, sponsor, and support

NOTE: For our purposes in this book, we are not attempting to distinguish between the terms coaching and mentoring, but are rather using them as a combined idea (i.e., coaching and mentoring)

All of the definitions above come into play in our concept of coaching and mentoring. We see the coach/mentor as someone who:

– trains the teacher (particularly in the case of those new to the profession);
– gives advice or direction;
– helps teachers see "the big picture" and understand where they fit into it;
– is trusted (credible) and wise (takes a long view of events);
– encourages (influences) the teacher and builds his/her confidence (supports); and
– functions as a success agent (sponsor) for the teacher, helping provide resources, people, materials, and information that aid the teacher's growth and development.

In practical terms, this can be reduced to two key aspects. That is, the administrator as coach/mentor:

– communicates expectations; and
– provides guidance, support, encouragement, and resources necessary to attain expectations.

If the administrator is executing his/her role with excellence, then it is highly likely that mission-appropriate, competent teachers will respond positively to the coaching and mentoring and will grow and thrive.

The Question of Subject-Specific Coaching

Teachers and administrators alike may question the ability of someone to train teachers outside of his/her discipline or specialty (e.g., an administrator who was a history teacher training a new chemistry teacher). In such cases, two considerations come into play.

1. A skilled administrator's focus will be on coaching and mentoring the new chemistry teacher on techniques and approaches to teaching that transcend any particular discipline (i.e., such as by helping him/her reinforce the principles of predictability and supportiveness in his/her teaching).

2. The success agent part of the administrator's role will come to the fore here, as well. It is not necessary for the administrator to be the individual training the teacher directly. Rather, he/she may broker the teacher's training by arranging for discipline-appropriate guidance to occur (such as arranging for a veteran science teacher to mentor the new chemistry teacher on science-specific teaching techniques, approaches, etc.).

Managing Through Coaching and Mentoring

One of the foundational principles of the Comprehensive Faculty Development (CFD) Model is "managers must manage"—that is, academic administrators must actively, purposefully, and systematically manage their interactions with faculty in a way most likely to support faculty in delivering the school's mission with excellence. As noted previously, managing is not meant to conjure up images of micromanagement or control. Rather, our recommended approach focuses on managing by providing faculty with an environment based on predictability and support—in essence, *managing through coaching and mentoring*.

Our research and long experience indicate that teachers perform best in environments that are:

- *Predictable*—i.e., where faculty know and understand what is expected of them; and
- *Supportive*—i.e., where faculty feel that their academic leaders are working hard to help them and provide them with the tools, resources, and encouragement to succeed.

In such environments, coaching and mentoring occurs naturally throughout all stages of the Evaluation and Growth Cycle. In these schools, coaching and mentoring is simply the order of the day—i.e., the way in which faculty and administrators interact as a regular course of business.

The Question of Administrators' Time and Focus

Concern may be raised that, by recommending this approach to faculty development, we are suggesting *another* time-consuming task for administrators to fit into already overburdened schedules. With specific regard to evaluating faculty, it is true that preparing for, writing, and delivering annual evaluations will represent some measure of *additional* time and tasks for administrators, if evaluations are not currently taking place regularly (or at all) in your school. However, the central question is whether the evaluation of faculty—and more broadly, the overall coaching and mentoring of faculty—is central to the administrator's job, or not.

Like evaluating, coaching and mentoring faculty is a crucial element of enhancing faculty capacity, it is integral to the administrator's role and thus exactly the place in which considerable time, effort, and focus is worthwhile and required (thus, pushing less essential tasks to the margins). For many schools, this will require rethinking the academic administrator's job description—with the attendant practical and financial implications, as noted below.

Administrative Span of Control—and the Resulting Financial Implications

In a sense, the success of this approach to faculty development lies in the numbers— as coaching and mentoring requires realistic ratios of supervision. Any one administrator—no matter how talented, hard-working, or insightful—can only effectively coach and mentor so many teachers. We recommend that administrators evaluate no more than 12–15 teachers. When the number of teachers exceeds these limits, the teacher-administrator relationships inevitably become less effective, as there is simply not enough time to engage deeply with so many teachers.

When an academic administrator's span of control (i.e., the number of teachers he/she supervises) exceeds the recommended ratio, adjustments need to be made. This has several practical implications regarding time, money, and other resources. Remedies may include:

— ***empowering Department Chairs*** (or, in the middle school or lower school, team leaders or grade level coordinators) so that their roles become much more actively managerial than ceremonial in nature;

— ***reducing Department Chairs' teaching schedules,*** to free them up for more active engagement with faculty, including evaluation, coaching, and mentoring;

— ***reducing Division Head tasks that are not related to faculty*** (such as administrative and clerical duties that can be handled by others) to focus their efforts on coaching and mentoring faculty; and

— ***adding administrative positions or reconfiguring reporting relationships*** to achieve a more manageable supervisory ratio for administrators.

Schools that wish to implement this process will need to do so with careful planning and forethought, of course. Typically, if additional resources are required, these need to be factored into the school's upcoming budgets and/or strategic financial plan. Given the powerful effects of robust evaluation and growth programs on faculty culture and school sustainability, the benefits should clearly outweigh the costs— but patience and resilience is needed. It may take one to three years to put all of the necessary resources in place. Management Teams need to be steadfast in seeing this process through, or else the program will wither from lack of attention and resources.

NOTE: A full consideration of the nuances, dynamics, and considerations involved in effective strategic financial planning is beyond the scope of this book. Readers are directed to ISM's Web site *(www.isminc.com)* for The Strategic Board Series and other publications and articles offering guidance on strategic financial planning and the related topics of scheduling and Management Team design.

Administrator as Coach and Evaluator

It is critical that all involved understand fully the dual, parallel roles of the academic administrator as evaluator (i.e., performance assessor) *and* coach and mentor (i.e., supporter and guide). Since this is exactly the kind of dual role that all teachers are called upon to play with students, it is a role that one might imagine most academic administrators (as former teachers) slipping into comfortably. However, we repeatedly hear administrators voice their concerns with the duality of the role—convinced that if they truly engage in critical evaluation, the teacher will never accept them as coach.

To this dilemma, we suggest that administrators imagine their role as similar to that of the most student-supportive teachers in the school. These are teachers who confidently go about assessing the quality of student work, insisting upon high standards, but always clearly "on the students' side." Similarly, the evaluator role calls for an administrator to examine the quality of his/her teacher's contributions to the life of the school, while acting as a coach and mentor supporting the teacher and his/her work—all with the institutional mission and its implications as the overriding standard against which all faculty results must be measured.

We encourage School Heads to have candid conversations about the evaluator/coach dichotomy with any potential administrators before hiring them for the role. For those who are already in place and are struggling to reconcile the duality of the role, they may simply need to seek a different position from which to contribute their talents. Serving as coach and evaluator is central to the duties of an academic administrator—and these need to be duties that the administrator takes on with relish to be successful within the Comprehensive Faculty Development approach to managing the school.

Reporting Relationships

Reporting structures can get complicated. Some schools, for example, have Deans of Faculty or Curriculum Coordinators, positions which technically are not supervisory positions (i.e., faculty members do not report directly to them), but which are certainly regarded as academic administrator posts in a general sense. Regardless of how such positions are placed in the hierarchy, they can almost always serve as a supplementary coach and mentor. Clarity around the nature of the relationship is the key to success in these cases.

When nonsupervisory academic administrators interact with teachers, a clear reporting structure is particularly critical. All parties must be aware to whom the teacher reports—e.g., is it to the Dean of Faculty, or is it to the Division Director? A teacher's direct supervisor must have authority over the teachers he/she leads—authority in this case to formally evaluate the teacher, guide his/her professional growth, and recommend nonrenewal of a teacher's contract. Absent this authority, the supervisor will be ineffective. Teachers will not be bound to accept the guidance, knowing that the immediate supervisor has no real power to hold him/her accountable for his/her performance.

Nonsupervisory administrators (such as Deans of Faculty) can play a vital role in teacher development without ever having teachers report to them. They should be integrated into the professional growth and renewal process in ways that allow them to support both teachers and administrators in appropriate ways. For example, the Dean of Faculty may be the logical person to help provide resources that support the teacher's growth—i.e., offering a wide variety of contacts, networks, associations, and other sources from which teachers and administrators can benefit. Operating in this way, Deans of Faculty and other similar positions can support teachers as well as administrators tasked with guiding their growth.

Peer Coaching

As noted, there is no need for the academic administrator to be the sole mentor of the teachers under his/her charge. Rather, it is often the case that individual teachers may benefit from some feedback from one or more of his/her colleagues or other individuals outside of the formal chain of command. In our experience, peer coaching works well when:

— the peer mentors take up the task eagerly, with a sense of excitement (and even honor to be asked), rather than with a sense of dread or obligation;

— the mentoring happens as part of a mutual exchange (i.e., pairs of teachers observe each other several times per year, providing mutual coaching suggestions in brief follow-up sessions after each set of observations); and

— mentoring choices aren't limited to individuals teaching at the same grade level and/or within the same subject area. Often, helpful coaching tips come when observers cannot attend to "scope and sequence" of material (because they are not familiar with or expert in the details of either the content or the curriculum). Sample pairings might include a second-grade teacher with a fourth-grade teacher, or an upper-school history teacher with a middle-school science teacher.

Such peer coaching arrangements can arise in a multitude of ways. One teacher, experienced in a teaching practice or subject, may be asked by another teacher to mentor her around a specific goal that is part of her growth plan. Or, the teacher will ask her Department Chair or Division Head for a mentor, and the administrator will recommend an appropriate individual. Or, an experienced teacher will see a colleague struggling with a teaching practice and volunteer to mentor the teacher. This is the ideal arrangement—as teachers see a colleague in need and initiate action, and the teacher accepts his/her colleague's assistance.

Teachers who are asked (or who volunteer) to mentor a peer may need to be coached on offering feedback in a way that will make the peer receptive. If the mentor (however well-intentioned) comes across in a way that is off-putting, the good purposes of the mentoring arrangement might be inadvertently sabotaged. Thus, eagerness—though primary—is not the only attribute that a good mentor requires. Tact and sensitivity in offering constructive feedback are a necessary skills of all good mentors. In this way, administrators should take care when assigning mentors, so that the relationship is likely to be successful once initiated.

The Role of Classroom Observations in Coaching and Mentoring Faculty

As noted before, while we don't believe that a single-class observation can serve as a valid evaluation of a teacher's full-year performance and overall contribution to the life of his/her students, we do believe that frequent classroom observations play a vital role in coaching and mentoring faculty. They serve as a primary means through which an academic administrator gets to know—and builds trust and credibility with—the teachers under his/her charge. Ways to get the most from these interactions include the following.

Length: Classroom observations can range from the brief and informal (five to10 minutes) to extensive (a whole period). The length should vary, dictated by the circumstances. The short ones will be a "check in" to watch the teacher, get to know him/her and his/her teaching practices better, and to "catch the teacher doing good work." The longer ones will more likely be for a particular purpose—to watch a lesson or activity that may be a formal part of the teacher's goals or because the teacher is proud of the quality of that lesson and wants to share it directly with his/her coach/ mentor/supervisor.

Frequency: As a general rule, informal observations by the administrator should be frequent (e.g. once or twice per month, at minimum). Brief, informal visits help the administrator gather impressions and information about the teacher, which can be turned into immediate (and in most cases, positive) feedback. Frequency of interaction helps develop and maintain the teacher-administrator relationship, begetting comfort, which begets openness to feedback, which begets innovation and breakthroughs.

Context: Another benefit of frequent observations is that, over the course of time, they help develop and maintain a "culture of observation." That is, teachers get used to having administrators in their classrooms—even to the point of seeking out observation eagerly. When this occurs, the school is proceeding down the path of truly becoming a learning organization, where constructive feedback (and the resulting growth) is central to how they operate every day.

Revisiting the Characteristics of Professional Excellence

In our experience, it is helpful if, several times a year, administrators discuss as a group the individual Characteristics of Professional Excellence (CPEs) to ensure broad understanding of what they mean in the context of the school's mission, goals, and values. If a Characteristics Design Team has helped form the characteristics, this committee could certainly be included at appropriate points in these discussions. By renewing their focus on the characteristics, the academic administrators are reminding themselves "what to look for" in their coaching and mentoring sessions—that is, if the characteristics are truly vital to the life of the school, then they should be coaching teachers on the strong (or weak) presence of the characteristics in their teaching. In this way, the characteristics will become more deeply embedded as central operating principles of the school and become ever more useful as points of evaluation, growth, and development for teachers and administrators alike.

Coaching and Mentoring the Coaches and Mentors

School Heads have a unique role in the Comprehensive Faculty Development Model, in that they are called upon to coach the coaches (i.e., the Division Heads, Department Chairs, grade coordinators, etc.). Just as a primary role of the academic administrator is to expand the capacity of faculty, a primary role of the School Head is to expand the capacity of his/her administrators to coach faculty. As this is a subject fit for an entire book unto itself, we will offer just a few brief thoughts on the subject here— recommending that School Heads seek out any number of books and resources around the subjects of coaching, mentoring, leadership, and development.

'Do as I Say, Not as I Do' Doesn't Work: All too often, we see administrators struggling to coach and evaluate teachers who are not coached and evaluated by their own supervisor (often the School Head). At the least, this sends a decidedly mixed message to administrators (i.e., "if coaching and evaluation is so important, why doesn't the Head coach and mentor me?"). In addition, it represents a huge missed opportunity to impact the life of the school by increasing the skills and confidence of the academic administrators.

To get administrators and faculty members to truly buy into the value of coaching and evaluation, the School Head needs to be the first to "walk the talk"—and to do so diligently. You need to set up your schedule to permit adequate time each week to interact with and coach your administrators—which comes in the form of being available to them as a set of sympathetic and perceptive ears, as well as actively seeking them out, observing them as they go about their daily duties. In addition to building their skills and reinforcing the value of coaching and mentoring, engaging with administrators in this way builds your relationship and professional comfort level with them, something that will benefit all of the individuals involved and the team as a whole in many ways.

To be clear: Coaching and evaluating administrators includes the idea that School Heads evaluate their administrators in writing annually. The excuse, "I don't need to evaluate them. We're in close contact every day—they know how I value their work," isn't any more valid for the Head than it is if an academic administrator were to use it with regard to a teacher with whom they've worked closely. If the School Head believes in the principles outlined in this book, he/she will take the time to evaluate academic administrators in writing. Period.

NOTE: As the job of the academic administrator is quite different from that of the teacher, we *don't recommend* that School Heads use the same form or template for evaluating administrators that we suggest for evaluating teachers.

Help Them Practice: All administrators want to be as good at their jobs as possible. In the same way that athletes require practice and repetition to achieve skill proficiency and excellence, so do administrators. One way that a School Head can coach administrators is by helping them practice their own coaching and mentoring.

The Head may hold practice or role play sessions with administrators before they hold their first coaching and mentoring sessions or professional growth plan development meetings with their faculty members. Guidance can be given on feedback, listening, and observing techniques. For example, when guiding the teacher in the development of his/her professional growth plan, the administrator needs to anticipate questions that may occur. As demonstrated in the prior vignette, teachers may struggle with deciding on goals, or may not see clearly patterns in their interests that suggest particular goal paths to follow. By playing out different scenarios, the Head can help administrators fine-tune their listening skills and suggest techniques for guiding teachers toward goals that match both their personal interests and the mission of the school.

Again, the above thoughts provide just snippets of information and techniques that Heads can use in coaching and evaluating faculty. What is most critical is that Heads endeavor to enhance their own coaching and mentoring skills, so that they might enhance those of their administrators—forming a virtuous cycle of professional growth and renewal that models those attributes that the school is seeking in its faculty, as well.

Coda: Encouragement

Our notes above represent just a drop in the bucket of potential approaches to coaching and mentoring. Many books are written each year, expressing new ideas, tools, and techniques for effectively coaching and mentoring employees (in general) and teachers (in particular). Just as the healthiest faculty cultures are composed of individuals who vigorously pursue continual professional development, so too are the healthiest administrative cultures. We encourage all school administrators to engage in ongoing study of ways in which they can best guide their faculty. We're sure that you will make wonderful discoveries along the way, heightening your impact on the teachers you guide, and the students whom they guide, as well.

COMPREHENSIVE FACULTY DEVELOPMENT MODEL

HIRING
&
INDUCTION

CORRECTIVE
ACTION
& SELECTIVE
RETENTION

Characteristics
of Professional
Excellence

EVALUATION
& GROWTH

Reward
&
Recognition

Reward and Recognition

Now that we have reviewed methods for hiring and inducting teachers, evaluating their performance, and helping them grow professionally, the next issue for us to grapple with is how to reward (i.e., compensate) faculty. We will briefly touch on traditional (nonperformance-based) methods of compensation, quickly moving on to the central focus of this chapter: the question of providing pay in a way that recognizes and rewards excellence, aligns with the school's mission, and supports a healthy faculty culture.

Traditional Compensation Structures in Schools

For decades, private-independent schools have used one of two primary methods for compensating faculty:

- salary grids: where teacher pay is based on years of experience and educational degrees
- individually negotiated contracts: where the teacher's pay is based on direct negotiation between the teacher and the School Head.

Both of these methods have their positive and negative points, as discussed below.

Salary Grids

Also known as the ladder system, this structure is based on the approach used by most public schools. Under this system, a teacher's starting salary is determined by years of credited teaching experience, as well as the highest degree earned. A sample is shown below.

YEARS OF EXPERIENCE	DEGREE		
	Bachelor's	Master's	Doctoral
0	$28,000	$29,500	$31,000
1	$29,500	$32,000	$33,500
2	$31,000	$35,000	$37,000
14	$48,000		
15	$50,000		

NOTE: The above chart is presented for illustration purposes only. The figures shown should not be considered benchmarks or recommendations in any regard.

The benefits of this system are that:

- salary growth is completely predictable for both the school and the teacher;
- the system is transparent (everyone understands the basis for his/her salary); and
- the grid supports the collegial nature of healthy faculty cultures, where many teachers prefer that everyone be treated equally (i.e., based on years of experience and degree).

The downside of this system is that:

- it implicitly assumes (inaccurately, in ISM's view) that there is a direct relationship between years of experience, degrees, and teacher performance (i.e., "we should pay teachers with more experience and advanced degrees more than less-experienced/lesser-degreed teachers because they perform better and have a greater impact on students"). We know of no research that suggests such a correlation between experience and performance; and

- there are no pay-related consequences for mediocre or poor performance (since pay is solely based on experience and degree). This can lead to the unfortunate situation in which salary raises for high-performing faculty are restrained due to the need to pay long-serving but mediocre-performing faculty ever-increasing salaries as time goes on.

The Individual Negotiation Model

This model, which is popular with a fair number of private schools, leaves salary offers (as well as annual raises) at the full discretion of the School Head. Under this system, when a new teacher is hired, the starting salary offered is determined not by a fixed grid (as above), but is rather determined by what the individual can negotiate.

The benefits of the individual negotiation model are that it:

- responds to the labor market. If competitive conditions make it necessary to make higher salary offers to secure desirable candidates, the Head is not restrained from doing so by a fixed grid specifying what her offer must be. For example, if the school is hiring a Chemistry or Physics teacher, and labor market conditions and competition dictate that starting salaries for such positions are x-percent higher than for World Language or English teachers, then the Head is able to craft a market-competitive offer for the candidate; and

- enables the Head to recognize and reward excellent performers with higher-than-usual year-to-year increases. For example, when determining next year's salary offer, the Head can take into account an individual's performance along with competitive pressures such as whether the school is at risk of losing this person to a competitor.

The downside to this approach is that it:

- is completely nontransparent. Teachers do not know the basis on which their peers are paid, which can damage the collegial nature of faculty cultures (i.e., it diminishes the faculty's sense that they are all being treated equally);

- is not predictable for either the school or the teacher. That is, for the school, it cannot determine in advance what its salary budget will be, because it does not know how dramatically (or not) market pressures may force larger-than-usual starting salary offers or salary increases for incumbent faculty. For the teacher, he/she cannot predict what his/her salary will be from year to year, as it depends

> both on economic/labor market conditions as well as the teacher's ability to be an effective negotiator; and

– is open to claims of favoritism and discrimination, because there is no fixed basis on which salaries are set. In the example above, the Head made a higher-than-usual starting salary offer to an incoming Science teacher due to market and competitive pressures. Taken at face value, such an offer is completely legal and reasonable. However, if we add in the fact that the new Science teacher is a friend of the Head's family, is the only male on the Science faculty, and happens to be making more than the long-time Science Department Chair (who is female), etc., we see that a claim of favoritism and discrimination can easily be raised. While the claim may or may not succeed in court, the school leaves itself open to costly litigation or settlement talks, to say nothing of the attendant negative publicity.

As a pertinent aside, recent ISM research has revealed a consistent gap between the salaries of male and female teachers in private-independent schools—with males consistently being paid 5%–15% more than females across virtually every slice of data. If such a situation is present in a school with individually negotiated contracts, the school has little with which it might protect itself if sued by female teachers claiming gender discrimination. (See the Lilly Ledbetter Fair Pay Act referenced in Chapter 2 for further details.)

Merit-Pay Structures

Having examined the main elements of traditional pay structures, we will now focus our attention in the remainder of this chapter on merit-pay approaches that are steadily gaining adherents in private schools.

Factors Impacting the Rise of the Merit-Pay Model

The risks and downsides noted for salary grid as well as individual negotiation models, combined with burgeoning societal changes, have served to elevate merit pay as a third pay model being used in private-independent schools. While the concept of merit pay (also known as "pay for performance") previously has been anathema for most private schools, conditions in the past 15–20 years or so have prompted school leaders to consider the topic anew. These conditions and pressures include:

– Board members increasingly calling for pay-for-performance models similar to those they are familiar with from their "day jobs" in for-profit organizations;

– 21st century competitive pressures forcing schools to focus intently on ensuring high performance from all faculty members, in addition to the extended recession making schools less financially able to "carry" mediocre or poorly performing faculty until they choose to retire of their own accord; and

– changes in the perspectives, attitudes, and expectations of newer faculty regarding their ability (and need) to influence their compensation, particularly their ability to grow salary in ways that aren't dependent on "putting in their time and paying their dues" over a number of years.

The Needs and Expectations of Gen-X and Gen-Y Teachers

Examining the last factor in more detail, our experience is that it is largely (but not exclusively) the younger and less-experienced teachers who are most concerned with increasing their pay aggressively. From a generational perspective, these teachers reflect different motivations than their predecessors. As we enter the second decade of the 21st century, school leaders continually report that Gen-X and Gen-Y (aka "Millenial") faculty:

– want a defined way to grow their salaries,
– want to be recognized for the value they add to the school,
– are willing and able to negotiate their salaries, and
– will leave a school when their salaries fail to correspond to their perceived personal and professional investments (of time, energy, commitment, etc.).

The View Ahead

Taking all of the above into account, it is our view that the traditional compensation systems (i.e., the salary grid and individual negotiation models) used by schools are quickly reaching the end of their usefulness for many schools. The salary grid does not adequately compensate faculty for their level of skill or contribution to the school (compensating, as it does, experience rather than impact). And while individually negotiated contracts provide schools with significantly greater flexibility than the salary grid, the fact that these negotiations are not explicitly tied to objective measures (i.e., performance evaluations) leaves schools open to significant risks and vulnerabilities. Therefore, we believe the time has come for all schools to carefully consider (and for many to implement) some form of merit-based pay.

Preparing Your Faculty for Merit Pay

Schools wishing to start down the path of pay-for-performance will need to address the following items before they are fully prepared to implement a merit-pay system.

- **Evaluation Systems:** For merit-based pay to succeed, the system must be perceived to be fair and reasonable. In our estimation, the evaluation system must have been in place and operating smoothly for at minimum one year (but better two or more) before it can be universally regarded as fair and reasonable. Only after this is achieved can merit-pay increases be effectively implemented in any form.

Schools that are overeager to institute merit pay and which thus implement merit increases at the same time that they establish a new evaluation system risk gravely damaging the credibility of both the evaluation system and the merit-pay program. Patient, sequential implementation (i.e., first evaluation, then merit pay) allows the faculty to acclimate to the new evaluation system and criteria before having to adjust to the even more dramatic and direct impact the new system may have upon their pay. Building credibility by implementing evaluation and then merit pay is critical to the success of the entire endeavor.

- *Communication:* When a well-regarded evaluation system has been in place for at least one to two academic years, the school may then be ready to move toward merit pay. Early in the new academic year, the Head will wish to communicate to faculty that the following year's contract renewal and salary offer will be based on the results of the teacher's annual evaluation (assuming that the evaluation system is, by that time, well-understood by faculty and fully credible in their eyes). In simple form, this means that, rather than across-the-board salary increases, the next increases faculty will experience will reflect their evaluated performance (i.e., not everyone will receive the same rate of increase).

A well-founded concern may be raised that springing merit pay on faculty in this way, even a full academic year in advance, may feel like a "bait and switch" tactic to faculty (i.e., "You told us two years ago when you implemented the new evaluation system that it was to help us grow. Now, we see that your ulterior motive all along was to force a new pay system on us"—with the underlying implication being that merit pay will be used as a way to limit rather than to grow salaries). To avoid the significant skepticism and negativity that would accompany an announcement regarding merit pay handled in this manner, the Head is encouraged to communicate the school's intention to move toward merit pay when the new evaluation system is announced. This way, the merit-pay announcement noted above is a reminder to faculty of something they were informed of years prior, rather than a "bolt out of the blue" that sends them into a tailspin of suspicion and concern.

This approach will give faculty at least two years to acclimate to the idea of merit pay. While there will always be ripples of discontent when any change of this magnitude occurs, fully revealing the school's long-term intent when the initial evaluation announcement is made will go a long way toward avoiding misgivings arising about the school's motives.

- *Addressing Concerns about Competing for Salary Increases:* Concern may arise from faculty and administrators alike that merit-based increases will damage the faculty culture by placing faculty in competition with one another. Any concerns about damage to the faculty culture should, of course, be reviewed and considered carefully by the administration before implementation. In this case, though, such concerns, while understandable, should not come to pass.

This is because the school's evaluation system is based on its defined Characteristics of Professional Excellence (CPEs). As long as the school's list includes or emphasizes some form of collegiality, collaboration, and support for colleagues, these characteristics will also naturally be part of its evaluation process. This should resolve the issue, as faculty will see that they are rewarded for collaborating with and supporting one another rather than for competing with one another.

That is to say, if collaboration and support for colleagues is a criterion of the evaluation, faculty should be highly motivated to help colleagues (in addition to their own personal, intrinsic motivation to help colleagues, of course). In this way, what had the potential to be a vice (i.e., promoting damaging competition among faculty) is actually turned into a virtue (i.e., helping colleagues not only supports and enhances the faculty culture, it also helps an individual receive a stronger evaluation—and conceivably, a larger salary increase), thus becoming a virtuous cycle of support and reward begetting more support and reward, etc.

Types of Merit-Pay Systems

With the prerequisites taken care of, the school is now prepared to assess what type of merit-pay system it is interested in implementing. We suggest two potential forms of merit pay for your consideration:

- *Simple Merit Pay*—a basic framework that provides the school with salary increase ranges based on the past year's performance; and
- *Broadbanding*—a more complex structure that incorporates evaluation-based merit decisions along with considerations of related, sophisticated measures of teacher contribution and impact.

We will now describe and analyze both pay-for-performance frameworks in detail.

The Simple Merit Framework

This framework sets up a simple rubric that guides the Head and Management Team in making decisions about annual salary increases for faculty based on individual performance. An example is shown below.

PERFORMANCE LEVEL	INCREASE
At-Risk *Very weak evaluation; placed on corrective action; at risk for nonrenewal next year*	0%
Below Expectations *Less than satisfactory performance; fell short on one or more expectations or characteristics; will watch closely and increase coaching efforts over the next year*	0%–2%
Strong Performance *Solid evaluation; performing well in all areas.*	2%–4%
Exemplary Performance *Outstanding contributions in all areas of the teaching role inside and outside the classroom; a role model and mentor for other teachers*	6%–8%

The process for using this framework is quite straightforward, comprising four main steps:

1. Business Manager (in concert with the Head and the Board of Trustees) determines the pay increase budget for the coming year (e.g., 4%).

2. The Business Manager and Head collaborate on a rubric (such as that shown above) that sets out categories of performance and the corresponding potential range of increase.

3. The academic administrators evaluate faculty (see Step 3 of Chapter 6 for details).

4. The academic administrators and the Head collaborate to determine salary increases for each of the teachers under their charge, within the guidelines of the agreed-upon rubric.

The final decision the school needs to make is how and when to communicate the salary increases. Some schools may choose to have administrators communicate the teacher's raise during the annual evaluation meeting, whereas others may choose to schedule separate meetings after the evaluation meetings are concluded, so as to avoid having the compensation portion of the discussion overshadow the performance portion of the discussion. Both approaches have their pluses and minuses; the school should choose the approach that best fits its culture and the message it intends to send regarding the links between salary and performance.

Comparing Simple Merit Pay With Salary Grids

To help us illustrate some key points of the simple merit-pay approach, let's consider the following example.

- **Situation:** After working through its annual budgeting process, in accord with its overall strategic financial plan, the school determines that its salary increase budget for the coming school year will be 4%.

- **Grid System:** Under the grid system, the school would make sure each grid was 4% higher than the prior grid (e.g., a 4% increase for moving from seven years of experience with a master's degree to eight years of experience with a master's degree). In effect, all teachers would receive an across-the-board 4% increase.

- **Simple Merit:** Under the simple merit-pay approach, the same 4% budget would be in place. However, now, an individual teacher might receive anywhere from a 0%–8% increase, based on his/her performance evaluation. This is where the philosophy of "managers must manage" comes back into play. In this case, managing means making judgments about performance that lead to judgments about pay.

- **The Question of Trust:** It is important to reiterate that judgments about performance (particularly those that link to pay) must be seen by faculty to be credible—i.e., if faculty perceive that so-called performance judgments are really poorly disguised personal opinions of the administrators (playing favorites, as it were), the whole system will come crashing down in a heap of distrust. Rather, the judgments must be seen to be (and must be in actuality) derived directly from an objective, "predictable" evaluation of their performance (i.e., the evaluation system described in the previous chapter).

Under a simple merit-pay system, the Head's salary increase decisions might look something like the following example.

TEACHER	INCREASE	REASONING
Angela Jones	0%	*Very weak evaluation; placed on corrective action; at risk for nonrenewal next year*
Danielle Smith	8%	*Outstanding evaluation; exemplary assessment on all Characteristics of Professional Excellence*
Cherise Robertson	4%	*Solid evaluation; shows high potential; seems poised for substantial performance growth in the coming year.*
Bob Markham	6%	*Strong evaluation; consistent high-performer; an established leader among his peers*
Kris Andrews	2%	*Somewhat disappointing evaluation; fell short on a key characteristic; will watch closely and increase coaching/mentoring efforts over the coming year*

- ***End Result:*** For budgetary purposes, the school is in close to the same financial position as it would have been by providing across-the-board 4% increases to all faculty under the grid system. In terms of its focus on high performance and attention to its defined Characteristics of Professional Excellence, the school emerges in a significantly stronger position. It has rewarded high performers for their excellence, thus aligning its salary increase budget with its mission-focused evaluation.

NOTE: This example is admittedly simplistic, as it is designed to illustrate the difference between merit-pay increases and salary grid increases. For the math to work out as cleanly as it does above, the example assumes that all faculty are currently paid equally, which is rarely the case. Where faculty are currently paid different salaries, the impact of a 4% merit-pay budget on the overall salary line will vary somewhat, depending on the particular increases granted to particular faculty. For example, a 6% increase for a faculty member earning $50,000 per year costs more than a 6% increase granted to a teacher earning $40,000, of course. All in all, though, the end result should be a total increase figure close to budgeted amount.

Starting Salaries in the Simple Merit-Pay Approach

The one gap that the Simple Merit-Pay structure doesn't explicitly address is the question of how you set the starting salary for a teacher new to the school. Since Simple Merit Pay is based on the last year's performance—and you have no way of accurately assessing last year's performance for a new teacher—the school must find another way of establishing starting pay. In this case, the school can either use a "starting salary grid" or an individually negotiated approach. This plays out as follows.

- *Salary Grid:* The school would establish either a fixed starting salary for new teachers (e.g., $35,000) or a simple grid based on years of experience and education (e.g., starting salary for a teacher with a master's and five years' experience is $42,000). The difference between this and the traditional salary grid noted above is that this grid would only be used for teachers entering the school for the first time. From that point forward, their salary increases would be determined based on performance, according to the Simple Merit-Pay rubric.

- *Individual Negotiation:* Under this approach, the Head would set the individual's starting salary at whatever he/she felt was appropriate and necessary based on the competitive environment (and what the new teacher agreed to accept). The Head would then explain that, from that point forward, all increases would be based on performance (again, according to the rubric put into place each year, as illustrated above).

Benefits and Downsides of Simple Merit Pay

Just as with the traditional pay plans noted earlier—as well as with all conceivable pay plans—the Simple Merit-Pay approach has both benefits and downsides. These include the following.

- *Benefits:* Under this system, the school is explicitly connecting pay with performance. This is an active way of recognizing and rewarding excellent performance while holding poor performance accountable by financial means. This system responds to Gen-Y and Millenials' need to impact their pay faster and more directly than the traditional grid system would allow. It also permits Business Managers to plan for the next year's salary increases in a way that is relatively stable and predictable.

- *Downside:* Critics of merit pay argue that any form of competition for salary increases has the potential for damaging the collegial nature of faculty cultures.

Ultimately, of course, the School Head needs to determine if merit pay is right for the school—and if so, which form it should take. To further this discussion, we will now examine another merit-pay approach known as broadbanding.

Broadbanding

After the school has used a simple merit-based approach (as above) for a number of years, it may wish to move to a more complex and sophisticated version of merit pay known as broadbanding. Alternatively, if the Head determines that conditions are in place for introduction of broadbanding without first taking the interim step of using a simple merit increase process, the school may move from a salary grid or individual negotiation model directly to a broadbanding model. In either case, it is important to keep in mind that the same prerequisites apply as were outlined above (i.e., successful use and acceptance of a well-conceived evaluation program for at least one to two academic years, etc.).

In its essence, broadbanding is a strategy that outlines a salary *path* without guaranteeing a predetermined salary. Rather than seeing annual increases as discreet events based solely on that year's performance evaluation, consideration is given to multiple years of performance—in the form of accomplishments that take several years or more to achieve. In a nutshell, bands of qualifications are set up to help faculty and administrators identify increasingly impactful levels of contribution to the life of the school. Faculty must meet specific criteria to advance their salaries (i.e., to earn annual increases and to move upward from band to band) and remain employed by the school.

Goals of Broadbanding

The broadband structure is designed to achieve several objectives.

- It gives the school maximum flexibility to recruit and retain high-performing faculty by allowing the Head to reward outstanding performance with differentiated starting salaries and pay raises.

- It enables the teacher to have maximum influence over his/her salary growth, by allowing for annual increases based on that year's performance while also providing the opportunity for additional leaps in salary when moving to a higher band/performance level.

- It communicates both predictability (e.g., "here are the high levels of performance that we are expecting of you—and here is what your salary will be like when you achieve those levels of performance") and supportiveness (e.g., "we fully expect that you will achieve these levels of performance and we are dedicated to helping you do so").

- It aids the Business Office in planning the salary line of the operating budget by providing a reasonably predictable (though more expensive) structure and framework around salary increases.

Factors Influencing Your School's Move to Broadbanding

Similar to our comments regarding merit pay in general that opened this chapter, we see the move to broadbanding structures in private-independent schools as being driven by several market realities, including:

- – increasing competition for the best teachers (in every discipline);
- – competition with the corporate sector for teachers with particular kinds of training (such as in technology, science, and math);
- – need to provide differentiated compensation to attract the above categories;
- – desire to compensate exemplary faculty so that they aren't compelled to go into administration simply to improve their financial position; and
- – desire to enable faculty to make lifestyle choices (impacting compensation choices) as they move from one life stage to another (such as potentially choosing to downshift from the rigorous expectations of a higher band to the slightly less taxing requirements of a lower one, to spend more time with their family).

Establishing a Design Team

The first decision a School Head must make when embarking on a broadbanding implementation is whether or not he/she and the Management Team will design the band criteria, or whether they will appoint a committee to drive this effort. At several points in this book, we have recommended appointing teams of faculty members to create necessary structures (e.g., a Characteristics Design Team to develop the school's Characteristics of Professional Excellence, an Evaluation Design Team to customize the evaluation template, and a Professional Growth and Renewal Design Team to customize the school's professional growth and renewal program).

- ■ The Head may choose to appoint a similar committee to develop the banding criteria. If so, the committee's recommended appointment of mission-appropriate, exemplary members follows the same suggestions as for the other noted teams/committees.

- ■ Alternatively, depending on the dynamics of the situation (i.e., whether exemplary faculty are available for the committee assignment, whether there is a broad relationship of trust between faculty and administration, etc.), the Head may instead choose to task the Management Team with development of the bands and criteria.

This is a matter of judgment on the Head's part. Our only caution is that if the bands are developed by the administration rather than a faculty committee, the Head and the deputies will have to work harder to communicate the purposes of the system and gain buy-in from faculty when the bands are introduced. If the bands are developed, however, by a faculty committee, there will ordinarily be more up-front buy-in from faculty, given the credibility of the team members as well-known, exemplary faculty members.

Regardless of its membership, the Broadbanding Design Team's charge would be to establish bands (or levels) that describe groupings of teacher skill and impact as teachers progress through their careers. While this will ultimately translate to money, money is not the team's concern or purview—dollars will be attached to the bands later by the Business Officer and School Head. Rather, the team's focus is solely on developing the bands and the associated criteria for moving up from one band to another.

Establishing Band Criteria

The design team's primary tasks are developing broadbands or levels of faculty performance and achievement, as well as defining the criteria for band membership. As with prior design teams that we have recommended, the team may take six to eight weeks (or longer) to complete its work. Just as with the design of the school's characteristics, evaluation template, and growth program, it is the quality of the work that counts, not its brevity. Accordingly, the Head will wish to check in with the committee on a regular basis to offer encouragement and support, and to provide any resources or guidance that might be necessary. The final result of the team's work might look something like the following example from our fictional Aegis Academy.

Criteria for Moving From Band to Band

In reviewing the Aegis Academy sample broadband (facing page), it is important to note that the goals in Band A are relatively easy to obtain, emphasizing professional development and participation in school activities. This helps teachers early in their careers to focus upon classroom basics while placing increasing responsibility upon veterans. A teacher should clearly understand what is expected of him/her at Band A, as well as what he/she must do to progress to Band B, and beyond that to Band C and possibly Band D.

Bear in mind the following elements when developing band movement criteria.

- Except for the entry-level band (i.e., Band A), faculty ordinarily should be required to remain at a given band a minimum of three or more years. This is to ensure that skills and experiences gained at each level are truly embedded in the teacher's makeup, rather than demonstrated on a short-term basis solely for purposes of progressing up the band structure.

- As one moves up the bands, professional quality and excellence should increase.

- ISM does not recommend that graduate degrees be required to move to higher bands, as we do not believe advanced degrees necessarily correlate with teaching excellence. However, we understand that many schools have traditionally encouraged or required teachers to gain advanced degrees as a means of career progression.

Broadband Faculty Compensation Structure

A dedicated team of faculty members and administrators has collaborated on the following structure that represents performance levels sought and expected by the school of its faculty, and through which faculty are recognized and rewarded.

Band A

Teachers with 0–5 years of total teaching experience (e.g., a novice educator entering the field and the Aegis Academy culture) are placed in this band. To progress to Band B, the teacher must:

- successfully complete two annual professional growth and renewal plans in Band A
- complete at least four of the following:

  - work with the Department Chair to arrange a class observation and follow-up debriefing meeting at least once per quarter,

  - participate in a professional education association/group,

  - develop a lesson study and debrief with a mentor,

  - attend a beginning teacher institute,

  - shadow a teaching mentor for one day, and/or

  - maintain a reflective journal of professional readings and/or experiences.

Decision point: *Following three years at Aegis Academy, a teacher must qualify as either a Band B or Band C teacher with the endorsement of his/her Division Head, or they will be released from employment.*

Band B

Teachers with 4+ years of total teaching experience. A committed educator. The goal at this level is to provide professional growth experiences that promote a teacher's further commitment to the school and to optimize his/her potential to positively impact the lives of the students. To progress to Band C, the teacher must:

- successfully complete four professional growth and renewal plans in Band B; and
- complete at least four of the following:

  - join and participate in a group that provides professional collaboration (e.g., Critical Friends),

  - receive training and demonstrate competence in differentiated learning principles,

•••▶

- participate in a national or regional educational conference,
- attend a conference or seminar addressing technology in the classroom,
- maintain a reflective journal of professional readings and/or experiences,
- serve actively on a faculty committee addressing a student-related issue,
- develop a lesson study and debrief with a mentor, and/or
- conduct an action research study and report the results to an in-service faculty session.

Decision point: *When the teacher believes that he/she is ready to progress to Band C based on the above criteria, he/she must submit a self-evaluation and band progression report to the Division Director.*

Band C

An educational leader interested in professional growth and career, committed to a continuing relationship with Aegis Academy and the larger profession. A person who has demonstrated commitment to students and who is open to learning from a broadening circle of professional relationships inside and outside of Aegis in a particular discipline area or in curriculum and teaching. To progress to Band D, the teacher must:

- successfully complete four professional growth and renewal plans in Band C; and
- complete at least four of the following:

  - present an advanced or experimental lesson to colleagues each year,
  - demonstrate through classroom practice outstanding use of differentiated learning principles,
  - lead a group that provides professional collaboration (e.g., Critical Friends),
  - present a session at a national or regional educational conference,
  - lead a faculty committee,
  - develop and deliver a curriculum or program that serves to enhance the lives of Aegis Academy students and community members,
  - acquire professional certification in an area related to the teacher's discipline, and/or
  - serve on an association visiting/accreditation team.

Decision point: *When the teacher believes that he/she is ready to progress to Band D based on the above criteria, he/she must submit a self-evaluation and band progression report to the Division Director.*

Band D

An expert well-versed in the research and best practice methods of his/her discipline. A "Pied Piper" who draws students and other educators to him/her; highly respected by students and faculty alike; a teacher of teachers. A model of excellence and curiosity. A passionate keeper of the school vision, a paragon of the core values of Aegis Academy, a champion of the strategic plan, and a well-rounded, well-respected member of the community. This professional's presence is felt throughout all areas of the school, both formally and informally. To retain membership in Band D, the educator is expected to:

- complete a robust professional growth and renewal plan each year and assist the Department Chair in guiding the growth of junior faculty members; and

- participate in several of the following each year:

  • teach a "master's course" lesson on an advanced or experimental educational topic to peers,

  • present at a national or regional conference on a topic related to his/her discipline,

  • publish an article or research study in a journal related to his/her discipline,

  • achieve advanced certification in a field related to his/her discipline,

  • develop and deliver a curriculum or program that serves to enhance the lives of Aegis Academy students and community members, and/or

  • serve on or lead an association visiting/accreditation team.

▲▲

- Choice can be built into the bands (e.g., a faculty member must meet at least four of five or six requirements to move to the next band). This helps faculty buy into the program by enabling them to act on their passions and interests rather than being overly restricted by criteria that may not be meaningful to them.

- Faculty should be required to "apply" to move to a higher band and present a professional growth portfolio demonstrating forward progression. Requiring "work" to progress from band to band will help teachers recognize the serious purpose (performance improvement) that is behind the band structure, rather than seeing the structure as a set of easily attained criteria that every teacher passes through without particular effort or commitment.

The Question of Naming Bands

ISM suggests careful consideration be given when deciding to name the bands (such as "Novice," "Experienced," etc.). There are two schools of thought on this matter.

- Some schools prefer to use general labels such as "Band A" or "Range A" (as in our example, above), so that no faculty assigned to any particular band feel dispirited or demotivated by their assignment (i.e., "How can I still be considered an 'Apprentice' after all of these years?").

- Conversely, other schools may find that the bands' criteria serve as a guide and motivator to the faculty as they gain in skill level, impact, and contribution to the life of the school and of their students and colleagues—causing the school to decide to name the bands.

The Head must determine which approach fits the school's culture and values best.

For schools that decide to name the bands, one of the strongest examples we have seen is as follows:

- *Band I (Learn)*
- *Band II (Commit)*
- *Band III (Lead)*
- *Band IV (Give Back)*

In this example, the names of the bands clearly communicate the focus, purpose, and expectations of those in each band.

Assigning Faculty to Bands

Once the bands and criteria are established, the School Head and the academic administrators must assign each teacher to a band. This may be accomplished by reviewing each teacher's current performance evaluation and history with the school against the criteria of the bands. Many of the assignments will be straightforward (such as assigning the first-year teacher straight out of graduate school to Band A and the eight-year veteran who is a steady performer to Band C). Other assignments may require more reflection (such as the 15-year veteran who might have been considered a shoo-in for Band C based on past performance, but whose contribution has declined considerably in recent years and is now perhaps more accurately slotted into Band B). Assignments should be solely on the basis of performance/contribution factors, with salaries playing no role in band assignments.

Attaching Dollars to Each Band

After the design team completes its work establishing the bands and criteria to the Head's satisfaction, the project is then turned over to the Business Officer so that dollars (representing annual salaries) can be assigned to each band. This may occur at the same time that the academic administrators are assigning individual faculty to bands.

Continuing our Aegis Academy example, the financial component of the broadband structure might look like this chart.

NOTE: As with previous charts shown in this book, the salary figures shown at the right are provided for illustration purposes only. Schools should not consider these figures benchmarks or targets in any way, nor do they represent recommendations for the band structure of any particular actual school.

AEGIS ACADEMY BROADBAND SCALE	
Band A	$32,000–$38,000
Band B	$36,000–$49,000
Band C	$46,000–$58,000
Band D	$52,000–$69,000

When attaching dollars to the band levels, the minimum and maximum salaries at the extreme ends of the structure will generally conform to the current salaries present in the school. It is recommended that the salary ranges overlap between bands, giving the administrator flexibility when placing each teacher in a band. In this way, teachers have the opportunity for salary growth within their current band, as well as when moving from band to band.

Using the Bands: Movement From Band to Band

From an administrative perspective, when teachers are ready to progress to a new band, the Head has complete discretion regarding where a teacher is placed in his/her new band. Consider the following example.

- A teacher earning $57,000 in Band C is approved to move to Band D.

- Her salary already exceeds the low end of Band D, so no particular salary increase is necessary to get her into the band.

- Therefore, the administrator is free to determine the appropriate salary, beginning with the current salary up to the band maximum of $69,000.

- In this case, the administrator might choose to set the teacher's new salary at $60,000 in the year she moves from Band C to Band D.

- Two things of significance have happened, then: (1) the teacher's performance contribution is being recognized as being at a Band D level; and (2) the teacher, who was previously at the upper end of Band C with limited salary growth potential within the band, now has significant growth potential within the band (i.e., she has $9,000 of upward potential until she hits the current maximum of the band, with the maximum likely to progress upward itself over the course of years).

Using the Bands: Red-Circling

A key benefit of the band structure is to that it gives the Head guidance (in the form of parameters and boundaries) with regard to salary movement, without being overly rigid. Altering the above example slightly, let's say that the teacher's current salary is $59,000 instead of $57,000, and that she is clearly a Band C—and not a Band D-level performer—and, in fact, her performance appears to be on a slightly downward path over recent years. In this case, her $59,000 salary exceeds the maximum of Band C (which is $58,000).

Situations such as this are likely to happen during your first few years of using the band system (and even afterward, if teachers choose to ratchet-down their performance level due to lifestyle commitments). In this case, the school would likely "red circle" the teacher and discontinue salary increases, until:

- the teacher's performance rebounds and warrants moving her up to Band D (where she would be well within the bounds of the salary range for the band and would not need to be red-circled or limited in salary growth for quite some time), or

- the dollar ranges associated with each band are increased and the teacher again falls within the range of Band C (and once again has room for salary growth while remaining in Band C).

By establishing criteria under which a faculty member can enter and move within the bands, the school places appropriate constraints on the administrator's discretion and provides balance between holding to a rigid system and using unfettered discretion.

Annual Salary Decisions Within a Broadbanding System

Once the broadband system is in place, the Head (and the academic and financial leadership team members, as may be appropriate in your school structure) have a few decisions that they need to make annually with regard to each faculty member.

- For those faculty members staying within their current band this year, what is an appropriate merit increase?

- For those faculty members who have applied and been approved to move up in band this year, what is an appropriate promotional as well as merit increase? (The term "promotion" admittedly has a corporate tinge. In simple terms, though, movement from band to band may be considered a promotion in a manner of speaking, with the attendant rise in salary, as shown in the above example).

Depending on the level of analysis the school chooses to engage in, the answers to both of these questions are influenced by several factors, including where the teacher's salary stands relative to:

- the band in which he/she resides,
- the salaries of others in the same band, and
- relative performance/impact compared to the performance/impact of others in the band.

Comparing Salaries Within the Band

The first two factors noted above (i.e., assessing where the teacher's salary stands relative to the band's boundaries and relative to the salaries of others in the band) are easily assessed by creating a simple chart, listing all faculty members in order of salary. The following example includes Aegis Academy faculty assigned to Band C.

NOTE: Band C extends from $46,000 to $58,000

FACULTY MEMBER	SALARY	COMMENTS
Nelson	$74,500	Because both Nelson and Martinez are well over the top of Band C's $58,000 maximum, they will likely be red-circled until such time as either the band maximum increases above their salary or they progress to Band D based on performance and achievement.
Martinez	$66,200	
Wisinski	$57,400	Because Wisinski, and D'Angelo are relatively close to the top of the band, their annual increase will likely be modest until they are ready to progress to Band D.
D'Angelo	$56,100	
Christiansen	$54,800	Since Christiansen, Anderson, Hale, and Sandstrom are in the middle of the band, the school is able to provide normal salary increases based on performance. For example, if they demonstrate particularly strong performance, they might receive an increase of 6% this year, to reflect and reward their strong performance—or, relatively weak performance might generate only a 2% increase. This assumes that the school's salary budget allows for an average of 4% in salary increases. As they approach the top of the band in future years, though, they can expect their salary growth to slow (even with strong performance), until they are ready to move up to Band D.
Anderson	$54,500	
Hale	$54,100	
Sandstrom	$52,900	
LaBelle	$47,800	Being at the low end of the band, even more salary growth potential exists for LaBelle than it does for her four colleagues immediately above.
Gilbert	$45,800	Since Gilbert and Esposito are both below the minimum of the band, they can expect fairly aggressive increases this year that bring them at least to the band minimum.
Esposito	$42,100	

The Question of Performance/Impact: Advanced Analysis

The salary analysis above is both easily conducted and easily explained to each teacher (discussing only his/her particular salary, of course—"You are being offered x% salary increase this year because of your performance as well as your relative position in the broadband"). Ordinarily, this will more than serve the purposes of schools just starting out with merit-pay structures. Schools that are more experienced in robust performance evaluation of the type suggested in this book (as well as those more experienced in managing a broadbanding structure) may wish to engage in advanced analysis when assessing faculty pay.

For these schools, we recommend engaging in impact analysis. In brief, impact analysis takes the basic salary comparisons suggested above and layers them with consideration of the teacher's performance contribution and impact on the life of the school.

Quantifying Performance: To accomplish this analysis, we need to quantify each teacher's performance. As you will recall from the evaluation section of Chapter 6, we specifically recommended *against* assigning ratings or labels to the performance evaluation elements—focusing instead on writing substantive comments that provide examples of the teacher's performance vis-à-vis. the defined Characteristics of Professional Excellence. However, for purposes of comparing performance to salary (i.e., assessing the teacher's impact relative to the financial resources— salary—spent for their services), working with strictly qualitative measures such as comments is too cumbersome. Therefore, we will need to assign numerical ratings to each performance characteristic for ***purposes of this exercise only.***

The simplest way to accomplish this is to assess each teacher on a 1–5 scale with respect to each of the school's defined Characteristics of Professional Excellence (which make up the core content of the annual performance evaluations previously described). With regard to the same Aegis Academy teachers shown in the example above, a numerical analysis of performance might look something like this.

NOTE: This example assumes that the school has established a quite lengthy list of 12 Characteristics of Professional Excellence. The numbers in the sample calculation would shift, depending on exactly how many characteristics your school designates.

FACULTY MEMBER	AEGIS ACADEMY CHARACTERISTICS OF PROFESSIONAL EXCELLENCE *(rated on a 1–5 scale: 1–characteristic never demonstrated; 5–characteristic consistently demonstrated in exemplary fashion)*					TOTAL POINTS *12 characteristics x 5 points = 60 points maximum*
	Professional Growth	*Personal Renewal*	*Supportive Demeanor*	*Consistency/ Reliability*	*Socializing Knowledge*	
Nelson	3	3	5	4	3	36
Martinez	4	4	2	3	4	40
Wisinski	5	3	4	4	2	44
D'Angelo	3	3	3	4	3	39
Christiansen	4	4	5	4	4	50
Anderson	2	3	4	3	2	33
Hale	3	3	5	4	3	39
Sandstrom	4	4	4	4	3	46
LaBelle	3	3	2	3	2	32
Gilbert	4	2	4	3	4	37
Esposito	3	3	5	4	4	42

The teachers' performance/impact scores (above) can then be compared to their current salaries.

Comprehensive Faculty Development

FACULTY MEMBER	SALARY	PERFORMANCE/ IMPACT SCORE
Nelson	$74,500	36
Martinez	$66,200	40
Wisinski	$57,400	44
D'Angelo	$56,100	39
Christiansen	$54,800	50
Anderson	$54,500	33
Hale	$54,100	39
Sandstrom	$52,900	46
LaBelle	$47,800	32
Gilbert	$45,800	37
Esposito	$42,100	42

A side-by-side comparison of salaries versus scores enables the Head to quickly see outliers in both directions—that is, teachers whose salaries appear to be quite high or low as compared to their performance/impact.

- Nelson's score of 36 (which might be termed a fairly mediocre score against the 60 maximum points) stands in sharp contrast to her relatively high salary of $74,500 (which, again, well exceeds the Band C maximum of $58,000).

- Conversely, the scores of Christiansen, Sandstrom, and Esposito are much more positively aligned with their salaries ($54,800 vs. 50 points for Christiansen; $52,900 vs. 46 points for Sandstrom; and $42,100 vs. 42 points for Esposito).

- Teacher-to-teacher comparisons can be even more eye-opening. As one example, the school is paying Nelson $32,400 more than Esposito (almost 75% more) and getting weaker performance.

Scattergraph Analysis

It is often helpful to review this type of comparative data in visual form, so that outliers are even more readily identified. The prior chart is shown below plotted graphically.

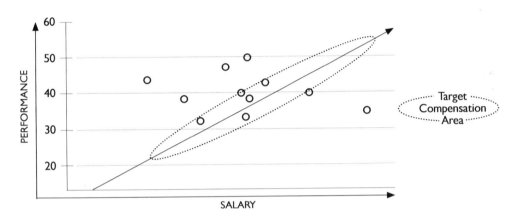

Salary

Graphing the salary vs. performance data in this way tells us several things.

- Ideally, we would like to see performance/impact increasing as salaries increase, which is the ultimate goal of a merit-pay system.

- Whether this is happening can be assessed by how well salaries correspond to the upward trend line (in the graph, the arrow running from lower left to upper right). Ideally, most salaries will fall relatively close to this line (i.e., performance and salary trending upward at relatively similar trajectories).

- It is impossible for any faculty's salary/performance comparison to hew perfectly to the trend line (nor is it necessary to achieve such precision). For this reason, it is helpful to draw a general range around the trend line (represented by the elliptical, shaded figure on the graph), which can be considered the *"Target Compensation Area."*

- Data points that fall within the Target Compensation Area can be considered to reasonably correspond with the salary-to-performance ratio that merit-pay structures seek.

- Data points that veer considerably away from the trend line and are also outside the bounds of the target compensation area are outliers—which can either be positive or negative.

- *Positive outliers* such as the four data points that are above and to the left of the trend line and outside of the target compensation area—represent faculty members whose performance exceeds that which would be expected for their compensation level. For these faculty members, the school would ordinarily wish to increase their salaries more aggressively (i.e., provide above-average annual merit increases) until their salaries move closer to the target area.

- *Negative outliers* such as the data point that is below and to the right of the trend line and outside of the target compensation area—represents a faculty member whose performance is below that which would be expected for their compensation level. For faculty members such as these, the school would ordinarily wish to limit or suspend (i.e., red circle) their salary growth, until such time as their performance places them within the target compensation area.

Implications of the Graph: General Salary Action Recommendations

Generalizing from the example above, schools will ordinarily wish to take the following actions with teacher salaries based on their position within the Target Compensation Area (TCA):

- increase the compensation of those above the TCA as a factor in ensuring they stay with the school as teachers;
- restrict the compensation of those below the TCA (or provide minimal cost-of-living increases), with a plan to improve their impact or counsel them out; and
- provide "normal" (for your school) compensation increases for those within the TCA to keep them within that band.

The principle behind these recommendations is that equity (fairness) in teacher salaries is achieved when compensation and impact are in sync.

Before Taking the Plunge: Reassessing Your School's Readiness for Merit Pay

As the foregoing examples demonstrate, pay-for-performance structures—particularly those of the broadbanding variety—require considerably more planning and preparation than other compensation approaches. Putting a merit-pay structure in place is a significant undertaking for any school, given the potential impact upon the school's culture, finances, and way of operating. We urge schools to carefully assess their readiness before beginning this journey.

In our experience, four factors are critical indicators of a school's readiness to implement any form of merit pay (whether Simple Merit Pay, Broadbanding, or another pay-for-performance approach). We believe that these factors are necessary prerequisites for successful implementation of merit pay.

1. *The faculty evaluation system must be regarded as fair and accurate.* Faculty must understand what is expected and evaluated—and must regard the process for arriving at these determinations as fair and accurate. Without this, any connection of pay to performance is likely to have a disastrous impact on the faculty culture.

2. *The faculty culture must have a professional-growth ethos.* Teachers must be positively engaged in professional growth before implementing merit pay. If the school's faculty culture is one of entitlement rather than one that is committed to continual growth, faculty will not eagerly embrace a system that helps them progress to higher levels of performance, because performance is not necessarily their focus. The culture must be changed before any merit-pay efforts can be successful.

3. *The school's Board must operate strategically.* That is, Trustees must understand and plan for the impact that merit pay (particularly broadbanding) can have on tuition—and they must be willing to adjust tuition to provide funds for improving salaries. In addition, the Board must be committed to establishing adequate funding for a proper management structure.

4. *A well-defined Management Team must be in place for faculty to be adequately evaluated and supported.* In most schools, the Head must be supported in the evaluation, coaching, and mentoring of faculty by Division Heads, Department Chairs, or the like. (See Chapter 6 for further discussion of this point.) This links back to point No. 1—that is, if adequate management staff isn't in place to coach, mentor, and evaluate faculty, there is little chance that evaluation can be carried out properly—and thus, little chance that the evaluation system will be credible in the eyes of faculty.

Broadbanding can be an effective strategy to address competitive faculty salaries, reward professional growth, and build institutional effectiveness. However, not every school should implement this strategy—and even fewer should attempt to do so without a number of years of preparation time. Evaluating and understanding your school's current culture, management systems, and readiness is essential before attempting to implement a broadbanding system. Heads are encouraged to ensure the above predictors for success are in place first and only then implement broadbanding.

COMPREHENSIVE FACULTY DEVELOPMENT MODEL

Characteristics of Professional Excellence

HIRING & INDUCTION

EVALUATION & GROWTH

REWARD & RECOGNITION

Corrective Action & Selective Retention

Corrective Action and Selective Retention

We have come to the final process in the Comprehensive Faculty Development Model: Corrective Action and Selective Retention. While this process is connected with the other three processes in the model through the common thread of the Characteristics of Professional Excellence, it is distinct from the other segments in one regard.

- *All* faculty members will go through the hiring and induction, evaluation and growth, and rewards and recognition processes.

- However, *only a small portion* of faculty will be subject to formal corrective action at any point during their careers—and *even fewer* will be asked to leave the school as part of the selective retention process.

That distinction firmly in mind, we'll now explore a recommended approach to both corrective action (i.e., addressing performance issues) and selective retention (i.e., determining when a faculty member can no longer continue employment with the school) that is consistent with keeping the mission, culture, and values at the center of the conversation, as it has been throughout each of the other steps in the model.

Corrective Action: Proceeding Down Dual Tracks

Most academic administrators enter the teaching profession because they are interested in helping others improve their knowledge, skills, and abilities (i.e., improving performance). The good news is that under the corrective-action process that we are recommending, administrators can happily devote 95% of their coaching and mentoring efforts toward helping teachers improve their knowledge, skills, and abilities.

The bad news is that, as noted earlier, because ours has become a litigious society, administrators need to devote some portion of their attention to documenting their actions—to help protect the school when and if a lawsuit or claim should ever arise. The reality is that being mindful of developing proper documentation is an inescapable part of contemporary management duties.

Taken together, then, we see that administrators need to operate on dual tracks— the majority of their energy being focused on enhancing teacher performance, while also being aware of the need to document actions for the protection of all involved. All of the actions that we suggest in our four-step Sample Corrective-Action Policy are designed to honor both of these goals—focusing on performance improvement while documenting for legal protection.

A Brief Word of Definition

It might strike some that the terms "corrective action" and "selective retention" are simply euphemisms for the more straightforward and realistic terms "warnings" and "termination." This is both true and untrue, in different regards.

- It is true that these terms developed in the past as part of an effort to "soften" what seemed to be the overly harsh or punitive nature of words and ideas like "warning" and "termination."

- At the same time, while softer, the labels "corrective action" and "selective retention" actually describe the intent and effect of these actions better than the more limiting terms of "warning" and "termination." As described below, the intent and purpose of corrective action truly is to *correct* poor behavior or performance—not as *punishment*, but rather as *performance improvement*. Similarly, selective retention is just what it claims to be—a process for actively (selectively) deciding whom to retain in the school (i.e., those whom are most able to deliver the mission with excellence).

Euphemisms? Perhaps somewhat. But most important, these terms get at the essence of what is being attempted in each action. Keeping this perspective in mind will help us get the most out of the steps and actions involved, to serve the best interests of all involved.

Elements of Effective Corrective-Action Practices

Broadly stated, mission-appropriate corrective-action practices in private-independent schools should be:

- predictable and supportive,

- performance improvement-focused rather than discipline-focused,

- well communicated,

- well documented, and

- consistently (but not blindly) followed.

We will examine each of these factors in more detail below.

- *Predictable and Supportive:* As noted, our research strongly indicates that schools that provide predictable and supportive learning environments for students enable them to perform at their highest potential (and with the greatest satisfaction and enthusiasm). We believe that the same is true of the school's relationship with its faculty.

  By communicating its expectations clearly and consistently—in the form of its Basic Teacher Expectations and Characteristics of Professional Excellence—the school establishes a *predictable* environment in which employees know what the standards are as well as the consequences of failing to meet the standards. At the same time, by interacting with employees in ways that demonstrate that they wish—and are working to support—the employees' great success, the school establishes a *supportive* environment in which faculty can grow and thrive.

  By creating and sustaining a culture built on predictability and support, schools not only reduce their legal risks (such as from a discrimination claim), but also their social risks (such as the risk that a termination tears at the fabric of the school's culture if teachers feel the termination was random, unfair, or unjustified). The two themes of predictability and support are applied practically through each of the elements of corrective action noted below.

- *Performance Improvement-Focused Rather Than Discipline-Focused:* Consistent with the purpose and spirit of the Comprehensive Faculty Development (CFD) Model, we strongly recommend that corrective-action efforts be oriented toward *improving performance* (i.e., building up employees so they can meet the school's high standards) rather than punishment-oriented (i.e., focusing on catching employees doing things wrong so that they can be disciplined). This is true for several reasons, including:

    - consistency with a growth-focused faculty culture;
    - alignment with the school's mission, culture, and values; and

– fair treatment and acting to support faculty members, which not only sustains healthy employee morale and the overall faculty-administration relationship, but also provides significant legal protection, should the situation devolve into legal claims.

■ **Well-Communicated:** Increasingly, courts are deciding against employers (including schools) whose actions appear to be in any way *unfair*—whether or not the actions are actually *illegal*. Perceptions of unfairness develop when standards are not well communicated to employees. We recommend communicating performance and behavior expectations *early and often*, including from the school's first interactions with the employee (i.e., during the hiring process).

For example, we recommend including several of the school's required characteristics of excellence in the employment advertisement—as well as using the characteristics as the basis for the interview questions. In this way, the school is communicating to employees what is important and expected at the school up front, and in no uncertain terms. (See Chapter 4 for details.) This same communication of characteristics and expectations is carried through each of the other CFD steps (e.g., induction, evaluation and growth, and rewards and recognition—see Chapters 5, 6, and 7 for details).

■ **Well-Documented:** Courts expect termination decisions to be well-documented. To this end, the school's records should contain a clear statement of:

– the standards that were communicated to the teacher;
– the steps taken to help the teacher achieve satisfactory performance;
– the stated consequences for failing to attain required standards; and
– should termination result, the manner in which those standards were applied.

Incomplete, shoddy, or ill-considered documentation will significantly damage a school's ability to defend itself against any claims or suits brought by terminated employees. See recommendations below, which detail proper documentation in full.

■ **Consistently (But Not Blindly) Followed:** When dealing with lawsuits and claims, it greatly aids a school's defense if it can show that similarly situated employees were treated in the same (consistent) way. This is not meant to imply, however, that the school needs to blindly defer to precedent, without room for judgment. In any given situation, the Head needs to do what he/she needs to do in the best interests of the school—even if this differs from what was done in seemingly similar situations in the past.

The School Head in particular (and the Management Team in general) is entrusted to manage the school using sound judgment. Judgment necessarily implies taking into account subtleties and nuances that serve to distinguish situations from one another. While written corrective-action policies are intended to provide predictability (consistency) of actions taken, it is not possible to write policies that address all possible situations that may occur in the future. To this end, the corrective-action policy should avoid "writing itself into a corner."

That is to say, *policies* should serve the *school*, not the other way around. In any written corrective-action policies, it is vital to protect the discretion of the Head to act in the best interests of the school, according to his/her best judgment. We will examine how exactly to protect this discretion.

Model Corrective-Action Process

Corrective-action processes generally have several steps, each one leading to progressively more serious consequences (giving the process its other name, progressive discipline). The goal of the process is to help the teacher return to satisfactory (or better) performance levels. If this does not occur, the situation— and the risk of termination—becomes increasingly more serious.

This plays out in several simple steps:

1. *First Warning*

2. *Second Warning*

3. *Third Warning*

4. *Termination/nonrenewal decision*

We will examine each of these steps in detail below.

1. *First warning:* When poor performance crosses the threshold from a minor (coaching) issue to a significant problem, the teacher's supervisor speaks with him/ her to discuss the issue and lay out a plan for remedial (corrective) action, which is presented in writing. If the teacher does not correct the issue to the level required, the administrator will ordinarily move the process to its second stage.

2. *Second warning:* If the first warning is not effective in changing the behavior or improving performance to satisfactory levels, then a second warning may be issued. This is similar in nature and substance to the first warning, only with the explicit proviso that the situation is now more serious and the teacher is at greater risk of termination if the issue is not corrected.
   NOTE: Recommendations as to what information should be contained in all warnings is detailed below.

3. *Third warning:* If the behavior or performance issue continues after the second warning, the process will then proceed to the third or final warning stage. As with each prior step, a written warning document is prepared and the employee is provided with an appropriate amount of time and support to rectify the performance/ behavior issues involved. In accord with the concept of progressive discipline, the

teacher is advised that the situation is at its most serious—that they are now at the final step before which termination will be considered.

4. *Termination or nonrenewal:* If the first three steps are not successful, then a decision may be made to proceed to termination—which could be immediate (in the case of severe behavior or performance issue) or result in nonrenewal at the end of the term (which is the more usual case). This is the aforementioned selective retention decision. Specific considerations around communicating and carrying out this action are discussed in further detail later in this chapter.

Considerations Surrounding the Corrective-Action Process

In our experience guiding school administrators through the corrective-action process, common questions and concerns arise with regularity. These include the following.

- *Who is the supervisor—and what authority does he/she have?* In some schools, it may sometimes be unclear exactly who the "supervisor" is—and who is invested with the authority to issue a warning and/or make a termination decision? Is it the Department Chair, or is it the Division Head—or only the Head?

  Exact levels of authority will vary from school to school. In the most common case, the Department Chair or Division Head is considered the direct supervisor, with the power to issue warnings and recommend termination—but only the Head is empowered to make the actual termination decision. Regardless of who communicates the warning or termination decision, the teacher must be made aware that the person with the appropriate authority has made the decision and supports and enforces the actions being taken.

- *When does the situation move from 'coaching' to warning?* This is perhaps the most difficult issue for administrators to grapple with. It is largely a matter of experience in knowing when something is serious enough to be deemed a warning rather than a friendly coaching or counseling session. The line will vary based on the circumstances involved. In general, though, we would suggest that this occur when—after repeated coaching sessions—the situation does not seem to be improving and when moving to a more serious level of interaction seems to be the best means for holding the teacher accountable for improving his/her performance.

  In the coaching and mentoring discussion in Chapter 6, we put forth the idea that the School Head needed to serve as the "coach of coaches." This is such an instance. Inexperienced academic administrators will often require considerable coaching around corrective-action matters, so that they can discern when moving to formal corrective action is the necessary and appropriate step for the school to take. School Heads need to be prepared to spend significant time with junior administrators helping guide them through the emotionally and intellectually draining efforts of managing a teacher through a corrective-action process.

- *How much time do I need to give them to improve?* It is important for the time frame to correspond to the nature of the issue. If the issue is *behavioral* in nature (e.g., not turning in grades on time), it is reasonable to expect immediate improvement. For more nuanced performance issues—such as poor classroom management, for example—it is not realistic for skills to improve overnight. In these cases, time frames of a month, or a quarter, or an academic year might be appropriate. In all cases, the appropriate time frame should be clearly stated when providing the warning—to provide appropriate predictability (knowing what is expected).

When the Corrective-Action Process Shouldn't Be Used

Returning to the theme that all processes should work *for* the school and not against its interests—i.e., not restrict it from taking necessary action—the corrective action needs to be understood in context. That is, while one aim of the corrective-action process is to provide a predictable framework of action and response for both administrators and teachers, it is not designed to be used at all times and in all situations—especially those situations involving student, teacher, or community safety.

Egregious, dangerous, harmful, or risky behavior (e.g., theft, violence, inappropriate conduct with students and parents, and the like) may require immediate action—being dealt with promptly and decisively (though still fairly and prudently) outside of this process. Example: If a teacher is shown to have placed a child at grave physical danger due to careless behavior or dereliction of duty, a school should not feel compelled to progress through multiple warning steps before terminating the teacher. Often, after time is taken to investigate the facts, such behavior would often prompt termination—or a final warning—without proceeding through each of the steps of the process.

Judgment must be used to decide when to apply the corrective-action process, and when the situation warrants other, more urgent action outside of the process.

Customizing the Process for Your School

The sample four-step process shown above is a model only—one that needs to be adapted to the particular culture and values of each school. This may result in more steps being added (e.g., a fourth warning)—or some variation thereof (e.g. use of verbal and written warnings). We urge you to reflect on your culture and values and modify the process as needed to make it your own.

For example, if patience and forgiveness are core values at your school, more steps (or chances) might be warranted in the process. Conversely, if your school operates with considerable urgency toward teacher performance generating student results, your process might include only two warnings before termination, rather than three.

One common question that we're asked regarding customizing the process involves when to put the warning in writing. In many schools, the first warning is often positioned as a *verbal* warning—to convey the idea that "the situation is serious, but not yet serious enough for us to put it in writing." This leads to several dilemmas, along the lines of, "Shouldn't a warning be documented in writing—and, if you document it in *writing*, doesn't that make it a *written* warning?"

To avoid confusion, we recommend that all warnings be written warnings and that they be progressively more serious in nature (i.e., each warning moves the teacher closer toward a risk of termination). That being said, a school may determine that a verbal warning is the appropriate first step, flowing from the manner in which it has historically addressed performance issues at the school. Whether the process starts with a verbal or written warning, it is vital for all concerned to understand that they have now entered into a formal process with particular consequences. Clarity is the key here, whether expressed verbally or in writing.

Putting the Process in Writing

Some description of the corrective-action process should be published in the employee handbook—for the purposes of meeting the *predictable* and *well-communicated* goals noted. The school may choose to describe the process in brief, general terms, or in more detail. Sample language for both types of descriptions is shown below.

Aegis Academy Corrective-Action Policy (Brief)

Any employee who violates the school's policies, guidelines, rules, and/or standards of conduct or performance may be subject to corrective action up to and including termination. Depending upon the severity or frequency of the violation, corrective action may involve a short series or warnings becoming increasingly more serious in nature, potentially leading up to and including termination of employment. The school expressly reserves the right to determine the severity of the problem and the preferred method of proceeding in each individual case based on the facts and circumstances involved.

▲▲

A more extensive description of the process is shown in the next sample. Note that both versions of the policy (brief and detailed) expressly state the school's right to alter the process in its sole judgment, based on the facts involved. This is a crucial provision to prevent the school from unduly restricting its ability to act as needed, as discussed earlier.

Aegis Academy

Corrective-Action Policy (Detailed)

Aegis Academy encourages our employees to develop and perform to their fullest potential at all times. When an employee's performance or conduct does not meet established standards, we do not look to punish but rather to quickly, effectively, and eagerly support the employee in correcting the behavior or improving his/her performance. The school has developed the following general procedure for addressing most behavior or performance issues.

Please note: While the school intends to address most common performance issues in the manner described in this policy, employees should be aware that the school maintains all of its rights under the employment relationship (whether those rights are at-will rights or contractual rights, as may apply). The school does not restrict itself from altering its approach to corrective action as circumstances warrant, at the School Head's sole discretion.

Two common exceptions to the corrective-action process of which employees should be aware are:

- *misconduct or other serious behavioral issues,* especially circumstances involving risk to students or other employees, will ordinarily be addressed promptly and firmly outside of the process described in this policy; and

- *with employees who are new to the school,* the school and the employee may quickly determine that there is a misalignment between the employee's skills and interests and the school's needs in the position. In these cases, plans to resolve this misalignment ordinarily may be handled promptly and separately from the process shown in this policy.

•••▶

Step One: First Warning

When a performance or conduct issue arises and informal attempts to resolve the issue or correct the performance are not successful, the employee will be provided with a written warning and a conversation will occur between the supervisor and the employee.

Step Two: Second Warning

If the performance or conduct issue is not rectified in the manner or time period provided in the first warning, the employee may receive a second warning. The supervisor and employee will again meet to review the matter and establish a mandatory action plan to help restore the performance to satisfactory levels. The employee should be aware that ongoing performance issues may place him/her at more serious risk for termination or nonrenewal of contract, as may apply.

Step Three: Final Warning

If the employee's performance does not meet standards within the agreed upon boundaries of the second warning, the supervisor may provide a final written warning to the employee. The employee should be aware that further performance issues place him/her at grave risk of termination or nonrenewal of contract.

Step Four: Termination or Nonrenewal of Contract

If the employee's conduct and/or performance does not improve as required, the school may choose to terminate the individual's employment, or not renew the employee's contract for the following school year.

▲▲

Documenting Poor Performance and/or Conduct

When the corrective-action process needs to be used, the administrator has entered a realm of action in which documentation is crucial for protection of the school. When preparing to carry out corrective action, two key questions arise: (a) *What do I document?* and (b) *How do I document it?* The answer is that essentially the same type of information is documented (i.e., written down) and communicated to the employee, regardless of the step in the process. That is, every conversation (warning meeting) and document in the process should contain the following information.

1. ***Situation or actions observed (what happened).*** The problematic behavior or performance should be articulated as specifically as possible—striving to state the facts and eliminate emotion from the situation.

   For example, you might state: "In the past two months, we have spoken on at least four separate occasions about your communications with parents—including your timeliness when returning e-mails and phone calls and your tone and demeanor when speaking with parents. We've discussed our "24-hour callback" standard—but I continue to observe that you have not met these standards (as you acknowledged in our conversation last week). In addition, on at least three separate occasions during this period, you have responded to parent calls in a way that provoked an angry exchange with the parent, which you also acknowledged during our discussion."

   This explicit, factual description of the situation is different—and much better positioned to protect the school in any ensuing litigation—from an emotional, nonspecific statement such as, "I *always* have to bail you out of conflicts with parents."

2. ***Applicable performance or behavior standards (what should have happened).*** Wherever possible the warning should make reference to established standards. For example, "The school's standards require all teachers to return e-mails/telephone calls to parents within 24 hours, and with the proper tone communicating warmth, professionalism, and caring."

   A statement of *why* this is important (i.e., describing the negative impact of the action) should be added. For example: "Failure to be an effective communicator with parents negatively impacts the school's reputation within the most important constituency and makes retention of students very difficult. It is also mission-inappropriate; our mission clearly states that parents are *partners* in the education of their children and need to be respected and treated as such in all interactions with them."

3. ***Required action and time frame (what needs to happen and when it needs to happen).*** Continuing with our example, the school might indicate that: "Effective immediately, parent communication must correspond with school standards as to tone, demeanor, and responsiveness, and all e-mails and telephone calls must be returned within 24 hours."

4. ***Support available (how the school can help).*** This is where the school will indicate what, if any, assistance is available to the employee. For example: "To assist you, we have hired a communications coach who will meet with you for two hours after school each Tuesday for the next month to work with you on communication skills. We have also provided two stickers with '24 hours!' printed on them for your computer and office phone (these reminders will be made available to all

upper school faculty)." This aspect of the warning communication goes directly to *supportiveness*.

Note that it will not be possible or appropriate for the school to provide help in all situations. In the example above, the school might not have the resources available to provide extensive communications training to the teacher. However, where possible, making school resources available to help the teacher demonstrates a sense of fairness as well as supportiveness on the part of the school—qualities that are consistent with private-school culture and that also help enhance the school's credibility should legal claims ever arise.

5. *Corrective-action step (where we are in the process).* It is important to clarify what step in the process is involved. For example, "This is considered a first warning, which is the first of three potential steps in our corrective-action process prior to termination or nonrenewal decision." A brief summary of the corrective-action process may be provided here, as well as a statement of the steps that have been taken. Even in stating this, however, the school should include the disclaimer statement that it reserves the right to condense or alter the process if circumstances warrant.

6. *Consequences of failure (what might happen next).* Consequences for not meeting the required performance or behavior standards in the specified time frame must be communicated. For example, "Failure to meet the specified performance standards may result in further corrective action, such as issuance of a second warning or further corrective action." Again, this goes directly to the question of clarity (predictability) and reinforces the seriousness of the issue.

Conducting the Corrective-Action Meeting

Corrective-action meetings should be approached as a formal coaching and counseling session. The goal is to engender the employee's recognition of the issue and gain his/her commitment to altering performance or behavior to meet school standards. That said, while it is the time to communicate a serious message from the school, it is also an opportunity for dialogue to explore the employee's ideas for self-correcting the behavior. When used in this way, the meeting has the greatest chance for gaining the teacher's buy-in and commitment to change.

Planning for and conducting the corrective-action meeting should be based on the following principles.

- *Appropriate time and setting:* To communicate the seriousness of the discussion, it should always be held in a private setting without outside distractions. For example, meetings should be held in the supervisor's office or a private room rather than while walking down the hall, sitting in the faculty lounge, or standing on the sidelines watching the school's soccer team play a match. Informal settings dramatically reduce the impact of the meeting as well as the legal protection provided, sending mixed messages about the seriousness and urgency of the issue at hand.

- *Nonemotional discussion of the issue:* While by their nature performance discussions may become personal and emotional, the supervisor must endeavor to stick to the facts. Emotional statements on the part of the supervisor, such as, "You're always so ____" or "You're never____" sound to the teacher's ears like personal attacks rather than substantive, objective judgments. If the administrator communicates the messages in this tone or style, he/she risks having the process perceived as personality-driven rather than job performance-related.

- *Clear communication of the current stage of the process:* For most employees, it is a shocking and deeply personal issue for their performance/behavior to be questioned—even if this occurs in the most respectful, nonemotional way possible. For this reason, it is particularly important to calmly and clearly communicate that you are in a formal corrective action process—and to specify what point in the process you are at, as well.

  As obvious as it may sound, it is nevertheless vital to say the words, "This is a formal warning" in the discussion. Without this being said, it is easy (and understandable) for the employee to perceive that your conversation may be simply a "friendly chat" akin to all of the other coaching discussions with his/her supervisor in the past— which diminishes both the clarity and the impact that a warning is intended to have.

- *Seek their commitment in changing behavior:* The school's goal is to *correct* behavior, not to *punish* it. This is much more likely to occur if the employee understands the seriousness of the situation and commits to righting the ship, as it were. Employee buy-in can be gained by seeking employees' input into the action plan they need to carry out to make the behavior/performance changes a reality.

  Ultimately, the supervisor is always in control—nothing the employee can say will alter the fact that a warning is being issued. However, by opening up the discussion to gain the employee's ideas on how to correct the situation, the supervisor is gaining the employee's engagement—as well as legal protection (i.e., courts ordinarily recognize the fairness and credibility of processes in which the employee was involved in establishing action plans and milestones).

The Question of Witnesses

ISM is often asked if we recommend having a witness present during warning or termination discussions. As a general matter, we **do not recommend** having a third party (such as another administrator) present in the meeting for witness purposes. From a human resources perspective, we do not find that this adds much weight to the school's case (i.e., having *two* people corroborate the school's words and actions rather than *one*), though we fully acknowledge that attorneys often recommend this practice. Instead, we find that the witness' presence immediately sends the employee the message that he/she is not trusted, or that the school feels threatened or otherwise vulnerable (all of which are counterproductive to the aim of correcting the behavior or performance in question).

We do support the inclusion of a third party, though, when that person is brought in to contribute information or ideas pertinent to the problem-solving focus of the discussion (e.g., if the Head is meeting with an employee, he/she may bring in the employee's Department Chair to brainstorm about professional growth opportunities that may aid the employee in resolving the performance issue being discussed). Any third party who is included must, of course, be in a position that is appropriate to being involved in the performance discussion (such as a Department Chair, Division Head, Dean of Faculty, or the like), otherwise his/her presence may seem random, confusing, or unhelpful by the employee.

Coaching the Coaches: Preparing Administrators for Corrective-Action Meetings

The School Head will recognize that often nothing is more daunting to inexperienced administrators than the prospect of conducting a corrective-action meeting. This is particularly true if the administrator in question is considerably younger or less experienced than the teacher involved, or if the teacher is considered to be unusually difficult or aggressive. Regardless of individuals or circumstances involved, it is often productive for the School Head to help junior administrators anticipate and practice responding to issues through role plays and other discussions.

The School Head and academic administrator might sit together (with the Human Resources Director, if one is present in your school) to discuss the written warning document, in preparation for the corrective-action meeting. You might plan the agenda for the meeting, chart out the order in which issues will be discussed, and identify any potential objections to the points being raised. By anticipating objections, the administrator can practice responding in a safe setting—helping him/her respond more clearly and confidently when the actual meeting occurs.

Practicing with junior administrators in this way helps not only build their confidence in dealing with performance issues, it also builds the coaching and mentoring relationship present between the Head and the administrator. Such skill- and confidence-building is sure to pay significant dividends for all involved, including greater legal protection for the school, as well as developing the capacity of administrators to adroitly address thorny performance issues in the future.

VIGNETTE: A 'Drive-By' Warning

It is axiomatic that we can learn from both good and bad practice. In this vignette, generally poor (albeit common) practice is illustrated with regard to providing corrective action to teachers who are not meeting the school's established standards. See how many actions you can identify that violate the principles that we've described in this chapter—and then be sure not to repeat these same errors in your own corrective-action practices.

SET-UP: Sue Williams, Upper Division Head, has been putting off having a verbal warning discussion with Bill Jergensen, American History teacher in the upper school. Sue bumps into Bill as she's leaving her office for a meeting in the lower school building. It is lunchtime and the corridors are crowded and noisy as students bustle past them on their way to the cafeteria.

NOTE: You may wish to read the "dialogue" column in full, then loop back to the "commentary" column for notes and perspectives on the dialogue.

Dialogue

Sue: Oh, Bill. Hi—how's it going?

Bill: Great, Sue. How 'bout you?

Sue: Not bad. Listen, I'm glad I ran into you. Do you have a minute?

Bill: Sure thing.

Sue: Great. There's been something that I've been meaning to talk with you about. But, before I forget, I just wanted to thank you for the fantastic job that you did last week leading your government class on the overnight trip to the state capital. I hear that the kids really got a lot out of it.

Bill: My pleasure. I really enjoyed this year's group. Who knows, we may even have an aspiring politician or two in the class.

Sue: Now that would really be something. Say, I have to run to a meeting in a minute, but there was one other thing.

Bill: Sure. What's up?

> *Corrective-action discussions should always be private, prescheduled meetings, conducted in a manner reflecting the seriousness of the event. They should never be off-the-cuff, spur-of-the-moment conversations—and also never held in public, noisy, and distracting settings.*

> *Warnings should be presented as single-topic meetings. They are different from performance evaluations, which attempt to include both strong and weak performance points from the full academic year. For purposes of clarity, a warning meeting should only be focused on the immediate issue.*

Sue isn't presenting the concern clearly—i.e., is the concern that she's "gotten some calls," or is the concern that Bill's action didn't meet standards? The latter should be clearly stated here.

Sue: I was just wondering, was there a problem getting papers back to students in your classes earlier in the fall? I've gotten some calls and all (voice trails off) ...

Bill: Yeah, I got a little behind at the time. Molly's parents were both ill, so she had to go take care of them while I held down the fort at home with the girls. Plus, my favorite team made it to the World Series this year, as you know— so that distracted me for most of October, I have to admit. Anyway, I just got a little backed up on grading, that's all.

As the bell rings signaling the start of the next class, the conversation continues.

If the behavior/performance is serious enough to warrant a warning, it should never be diminished with phrases like "It's nothing much." That statement presents a mixed message that is in stark contrast with a formal warning.

Sue: Oh, sure. I see. Well, it's just that it seems like I've gotten these calls every once in a while. It's nothing much, I'm sure. You know, it's just that I have to be responsive.

Bill: [defensively] What do you mean, "these calls"?

Sue: [nervously] No big deal, really. You know how parents are these days—all upset if their little darling didn't get their A+ paper back as quickly as expected.

Bill: [offended] You don't think there's a problem, do you? I mean, I've been here eight years, Sue, and I've *never* been questioned before by *anyone*.

Sue: Questioned? No—nothing like that. Just see what you can do, OK?

Bill: [suspiciously] Is there *anything else* that you haven't told me about that I should know?

Again, Sue misses an opportunity to emphasize the importance of standards being met. She diminishes the issue again, and also fails to state the expectation clearly (such as grading papers within "x" days or responding to phone calls within "y" hours, etc.).

Sue: [trying to sound casual] Well, now that you mention it, a few of the parents have complained that you didn't respond to their calls right away, either. It might have all been around that same time, though.

Bill: Sue, you said it yourself. You know how some of these people are. They act like we're the *hired help*, or something—like we have to drop everything to speak with them *immediately*, no matter what else is going on.

Sue: [reassuringly] Listen, I'm sure that it will be fine. Just a little blip on the radar screen. I just had to mention it, that's all. . . . Hey, sorry—I've got to run. Good job again on the trip.

> Sue diminishes the seriousness of the warning with every part of this statement.

As Sue departs down the hall for her meeting, Bill wonders to himself:

Bill: [confused, angry] What was that all about? "All these calls." What did she mean by that? Did I just get reprimanded for something that wasn't my fault? I mean, after eight years, what's with all the questions? Don't they know *how much* I do for this school? Good luck trying to find someone to replace everything *I do*—and at this pay level, too. They don't know how good they have it with me here. I know I don't like it one bit, that's for sure.

... while at the same time Sue is thinking to herself:

Sue: [relieved] Alright, then—check that one off the list. It didn't go too badly, really. What was all of the worrying for? He seemed to take it pretty well. I mean, when you're as established as Bill is, it's got to be pretty shocking to get a *verbal warning*. I didn't want to do it—but I've got to show that I'm on top of things.

> While there are no formal, legal standards for what constitutes a "warning," it would be difficult for a reasonable person to conclude that Sue formally warned Bill. This would certainly be questioned if the situation devolves further and a second warning is necessary—to which Bill would likely respond, "Where was the first warning?"

At least it's done with. I'm sure he got the message. Now, when I get back to my office, I just have to remember to write this down. Our new Business Manager is whispering in the Head's ear and she's making us record everything these days. Great—more paperwork.

When All Is Said and Done: Time to Part Ways

School administrators are generally hopeful individuals by nature, commonly drawn into educational administration by the belief that they can make a difference in the lives of individuals—first students and then adults (faculty and staff). It is this core conviction that makes administrators constantly strive to help poorly performing faculty members fix their performance issues.

Sometimes, though, the situation reaches a point where the school has truly done all that it can do in helping the teacher address performance issues. When this point is reached, the inevitable conclusion is that the school must end the employment relationship with the teacher. Again, this is why we have termed this process "selective retention"—the school is *actively selecting* whom it chooses to *retain* and not retain.

The remainder of this chapter discusses issues related to selective retention (termination), including how to know when it is necessary, how to carry it out, and how to document your actions.

Knowing When Enough Is Enough

We are often asked by School Heads, "How do I know when enough is enough? How do I know when the warning process should end and it is time to terminate the teacher?" In one sense, the answer is "You'll know when you get there … and not a minute before."

While this answer may sound glib and unhelpful, what we mean is that knowing when you're ready is as much an emotional reckoning for the administrator as it is a checklist of items to consult. In our experience, school administrators who sincerely try to give teachers every opportunity to succeed (such as through a credible corrective-action process) have usually done what is necessary to cover the school legally well *before* they come to peace with their decision internally. When both technical and emotional readiness have been achieved, then you are ready to move toward termination.

Administrators can double-check their own emotional readiness and the appropriateness of the decision by consulting the following list of actions and events. Administrators will know it is time to proceed to termination when the following conditions are true.

- The school clearly communicated expectations to the teacher on multiple occasions.

- When the teacher struggled, the school provided resources to support him/her—e.g., coaching, remedial instruction, peer support, and the like.

- When the teacher *continued* to struggle, the school provided additional resources, guidance, or support to assist him/her.

- This continued until the administrator involved:
    - couldn't identify any more resources or support that the school could possibly provide; and/or
    - saw clearly that the teacher was simply not aligned with the school's core purposes, culture, or values and that this was unlikely to change; and/or
    - perceived that students were being poorly served (or were being harmed) by the faculty members' efforts; and/or
    - observed that the individual's poor fit, toxicity, or other behavior was clearly damaging the school's faculty culture.

When this is the case, the school will be ready to either terminate the teacher's employment midyear (for egregious cases) or not renew the teacher's contract for another year.

Types of Terminations

Terminations in private-independent schools are usually one of two varieties:

- *nonrenewal*—in which the contract is not renewed at the end of its term and the faculty member is not invited back for the following school year; or
- *midyear termination*—in which the faculty member's behavior and/or performance is so problematic that he/she must be terminated prior to the end of the contract.

Due to the significant disruption that a midyear faculty termination causes with students (interrupting their learning flow) and faculty (disrupting the faculty culture), midyear terminations are relatively rare. Nonrenewal actions—i.e., deciding not to offer the teacher a contract for the following year—are considerably more common in schools.

Termination Provisions in Contracts

In most contracts—including teacher contracts—the most important provision concerns how the contract is *ended*. Teacher contracts should clearly specify the conditions under which the contract may be terminated by either party. (Reference the "Sample Faculty Contract" in Chapter 4.)

Let us examine two particular issues that arise in contract termination clauses time and again:

- *Permissible reasons for termination*—Many contracts specify that midyear (i.e., midcontract) termination can only occur "for cause." Cause is then spelled out as a short list of particularly egregious behaviors or actions, like being derelict in your duties, placing a student in harm's way, and the like. If the school terminates the employee midcontract for a reason not on the list, the termination would be invalid and place the school in breach of contract.

- *Final pay*—Sometimes contracts will specify a "notice period" (such as 30 days) for which the employee will be paid in the event of a valid termination. In this case, it is clear what the employee is owed. However, what if the contract is silent on the issue of termination payouts? In this case, the court would likely rule that the employee needs to be paid for the rest of the time remaining in the contract, absent any mitigating information to the contrary. This is because a contract is for a set term (e.g., 10 months), and the assumption is that the employee is due pay for the entire contract, as agreed.

Schools should carefully review their contract language with their employment attorney, to ensure that it is clear what is being committed to in the contract, especially regarding reasons for termination and final pay.

Employment At-Will and Employment Contracts

Most U.S. states operate under the doctrine of employment at-will. This means that both the employer and the employee are free to end the employment relationship at any time for any reason, or for no reason at all. However, this doesn't protect most schools because, in schools that use employment contracts with teachers, *employment at-will does not apply*.

By offering the teacher a contract, the school is acknowledging that the *contract* governs the terms and conditions of employment, rather than the employment at-will doctrine governing the employment relationship. Thus, rather than the school being free to end a teacher's employment at any time for any reason, it can only terminate the teacher for reasons and under conditions permitted by the contract that it has entered into voluntarily with the teacher.

Fairness and Nondiscrimination Always Apply

To a large extent, examining the distinction between at-will and contract employment is a matter of concern primarily for the school's attorney—not its academic administrators. What administrators need to keep in mind is that certain principles apply in all terminations, regardless of at-will or contract status. Understanding and acting on these principles will help protect the school in any lawsuits or claims that arise.

- *Fairness:* Courts will be interested in understanding whether the employee had appropriate notice and was given a fair chance to rectify performance issues (such as through the progressive steps of a corrective-action process).

- *Compliance:* Another key issue a court will review is whether the actions taken comply with the relevant policies or legal documents that preside (i.e., the school's policies and procedures or the teacher contract).

- *Nondiscrimination:* Both of the elements above will contribute to the court's judgment about whether discrimination against the employee may have occurred—or whether the school based its actions on job-related skills, experience, and performance demonstrated by the employee (which is nondiscriminatory and thus safe and legal).

Following a well-conceived corrective-action process will go a long way toward helping a court determine that no discriminatory intent was motivating the school's actions and that the steps the school took were solely job-related (i.e., legal).

Conducting the Termination Meeting

Once a termination decision is made, put documentation in order and schedule
a meeting. Key principles involved in conducting the meeting include the following.

- *One-way communication.* A termination meeting is one instance in which dialogue
  is not sought. This meeting is essentially a one-way communication, in which the
  employee is informed of the decision and its reasons, but isn't engaged in discussing
  the decision—as doing so would only serve to heighten emotions and create
  additional risks for the school.

- *Be firm.* The School Head should not schedule the meeting if he/she is at all
  uncertain or wavering in a decision. Regardless of the employee's response to the
  termination news, the School Head needs to be committed to carrying out the
  decision in full. If the faculty member hears or perceives mixed messages—such as,
  "*I* wanted to keep you on, but the *Board* won't agree"—the opportunity for legal
  claims rises substantially. The employee now becomes aware of differences of opinion
  within the Management Team and a divide-and-conquer legal strategy is born. In
  that case, the plaintiff's attorney can claim that the split of opinion reveals that the
  termination wasn't based on objective, irrefutable facts, but rather on the personal
  and perhaps discriminatory animus of one of the parties.

- *Script your remarks.* Ad-libbing the reasons for termination is risky, so you will
  want to carefully prepare the key points to be communicated during the meeting.
  For example, a termination meeting agenda will ordinarily include:

  - the reason for meeting;

  - why this action (termination or nonrenewal) is being taken;

  - what has led up to this (review of previous warnings, dates, and results);

  - what this action means in the short-term—i.e., whether the teacher is being
    asked to finish out the semester, and under what conditions;

  - what documents are being provided—such as termination letter, final paycheck,
    COBRA information, etc. (see below); and

  - how the return of keys, laptops, equipment, etc. will be handled.

- *Prepare documents.* You will need to work closely with your school's employment
  attorney on this point, as requirements may vary by state. Documentation in typical
  terminations includes:

  - termination letter (briefly recounting the process that led up to the termination
    and providing details around final pay, when continuation of benefits (COBRA)
    information will be sent to them, etc.); and

  - final paycheck, if required to be provided immediately in your state or under the
    terms of the contract.

- ***Arrange the logistics.*** For immediate terminations (i.e., when the date of the meeting is the employee's last day with the school), security and IT personnel should be consulted (in confidence and as appropriate) prior to the termination meeting to make necessary arrangements for the protection of the school and its systems (e.g., computer log-ins, keys).

- ***Prepare for your emotions.*** Last, but definitely not least, is the need to prepare yourself (the School Head) for the emotions that inevitably bubble-up during termination meetings. Given the fact that Heads are often faced with terminating a teacher who is a friend, a fellow member of one's church or civic group, a neighbor, a parent, etc., terminations in private-independent schools carry with them more emotion than in many other organizations. Accordingly, even the most experienced Head needs to deal with the considerable emotion inherent in the task. Role-playing "what-if's" and rehearsing your message may be desirable, if an appropriate individual is available to serve as a sounding board and confidante.

See the following role-play for a real-life example of the emotion involved in termination meetings.

VIGNETTE: Managing Through an Emotional Nonrenewal Meeting

Termination discussions are never easy, even for the most skilled and experienced school leaders, due to the emotions and economic and career realities that come to the fore. It is important for Heads to anticipate and practice dealing with their emotions in advance—such as in role-play or other practice discussions with an appropriate sounding board. The vignette below is designed to bring to life some of the emotions and conflicting issues and influences that are often present in termination meetings.

Note: While the Head shown here does a generally good job of handling the discussion, she stumbles at a few points and implements a few solutions that are strongly recommended against, as noted in the commentary column below.

SET-UP: Mary Jane Young, the School Head of a K–8 private-independent school, is meeting with Tom Cunningham, Physical Education instructor.

In his fourth year of employment, Tom is affable and congenial. He participates whole-heartedly in faculty events and activities. He has two children in the school and receives substantial tuition remission, which enables him to afford the excellent education his children are receiving. Many of the students adore Tom and take private tennis and golf lessons from him on breaks and during the summer.

Mary Jane has asked to meet with Tom at 4 p.m. today. It is the Friday before Spring Break.

NOTE: You may wish to read the "dialogue" column in full, then loop back to the "commentary" column for notes and perspectives on the dialogue.

Dialogue

Tom: Hi, Mary Jane. I got a note that you wanted to see me. Is this a good time?

Mary Jane: Yes, Tom. Thanks for coming. Please have a seat. So how are things going today?

Tom: Terrific! Thanks for asking. We started our softball module this week, which is always the kids' favorite. Plus, I'm helping out at the middle school's tennis tournament this weekend. How are things going with you?

Mary Jane: Well, to be candid, it has been a tough week. I've been meeting with the admin team all week looking at our staffing for next year and we've had to make some tough decisions about personnel—which is always the hardest part of my job.

Tom: I can imagine. They say "it's lonely at the top," you know!

Mary Jane: Yes. Well, that is what I wanted to talk to you about, actually.

Tom: [uncertain] OK.

Mary Jane: I need to talk with you about your contract situation.

Tom: Hmmmm.

Mary Jane: Tom, over the past three years, we've spoken on a number of occasions about student behavior in your classes. I've tried to help you—along with Linda, your Division Head—to improve your performance in this area through workshops, observations, and classroom visits. However, we both continue to receive complaints about

> *Mary Jane does a good job of getting to the point in a respectful manner without digressing too far into excessive pleasantries (which would be common, due to nervousness).*

Given the serious impact of a termination as a "professional death," as it were, it is not uncommon for employees to react with emotions akin to dealing with death and dying (e.g., denial, anger, etc.). Heads may wish to consult Elisabeth Kubler-Ross' model of the "The Five Stages of Grieving" described in her book **On Death and Dying** as a reference regarding stages of emotion that might be experienced and communicated by an employee being terminated.

Mary Jane properly communicates the prior steps in the corrective-action process that have led to the termination decision.

Tom begins his emotional appeal here. This is to be expected, especially when the facts of the performance issue are not on the employee's side.

The emotional appeal continues.

this from parents. After serious consideration, Tom, we just don't see the situation improving. Therefore, we've made the decision not to renew your contract for next year.

Tom: Wow. I can't *believe* you're saying this! I just had no idea the situation was this serious. Why didn't you say something to me sooner—or *at all*, for that matter?

Mary Jane: *We did,* Tom. Reviewing my notes, I see that you and Linda had conversations about this on October 20th, November 18th, and January 7th, as well as the warning memo that we gave you in February.

Tom: Sure, we talked a few times—and I admit that Linda has been pushing me to run a tighter ship in class— but I thought that I had time to get things to where they needed to be.

Tom's statement indicates that there may have been poor clarity around the seriousness of the warnings—or, it may be that everything was done and communicated properly, but he was not able to process the impact due to denial issues.

Mary Jane: But Tom, these same conversations have been going on for the past three years—almost as long as you've been with the school.

Tom: Wow, Mary Jane. I'm really seeing a different side of you today. You know how much I care about this school, and how much my girls love it here. How are they going to feel when I take them home today and tell them they can't come to school here anymore because their daddy's been fired?

Mary Jane: I appreciate your commitment to the school, Tom. You've been a role model in many ways. But we have to make decisions based on what is best for our students.

Tom: Can't you give me *just one more chance*, Mary Jane? I don't know what I'll do without this job. I mean—we haven't told anyone yet, but we just found out that my wife, Jeannie, is expecting again. One of the girls is just starting with the orthodontist. We bought a new car recently, because our old one died. I don't know how we're going to make it.

Mary Jane: Tom, I understand that this is startling news. But please know that the school does care about you. That's one of the reasons I felt the decision needed to be made now. The last thing I wanted to do was to string you along for another year believing that everything was OK when it wasn't.

Tom: It just doesn't seem *fair.* I mean, whenever Linda and I talked, it was always pretty informal. I think one of the times you mentioned was a two-minute discussion on the sideline at the soccer game. Nothing that led me to think, "Hey, this is *serious.*"

Mary Jane: I'm sorry if there were any mixed messages, Tom. But I believe that we gave you every opportunity to succeed.

Tom: Isn't there *anyone else* I can talk to about this? What about Jerry Richards, the Board Chair. We really hit it off at last year's golf outing. If I was able to convince him to give me another chance, would that get you off the hook—so you didn't have to do this now?

> *Drawing on the bargaining aspect of the grieving process, it wouldn't be unusual for a teacher to attempt to bargain his/her way out of the termination by calling in the influence of a third party. It is vital that the Head has the implicit and explicit support of the Board in all termination matters, otherwise a breach can be opened that is dangerous to the school on several levels.*

Mary Jane: I'm sorry, Tom, but my decision is *final.* I've discussed each of the staffing moves that we're making with Jerry, and he supports me *fully* on this. Now, I need to explain—

Tom: It's just not fair, Mary Jane. You know, Linda – she's a *piece of work* sometimes. One day she's my friend, and one day—well, she's always had it out for me, ever since I started here. I know that she wanted to hire a female phys ed teacher instead of me. She didn't like me breaking up the all-girl party in the lower school. I bet that's it. I really should probably see my lawyer about that. It all makes sense now. I always knew that there was something I couldn't trust about her. She's so two-faced—gosh, I've always disliked her.

> *Tom's broad claim of potential gender discrimination should be reported to the school's attorney when debriefing on the results of the meeting. However, if the school's facts are in order and if it has considered all pertinent information in the lead-up to the termination decision, new claims ordinarily shouldn't derail the process at this point (i.e., during the termination meeting).*

Mary Jane appropriately redirects the discussion from personality and interpersonal issues back to the facts of the termination decision, properly placing the needs of the students first.

Again, Mary Jane calmly turns away Tom's attempt to divert the discussion and returns to the idea that the conversation must move forward.

Termination discussions are commonly nonlinear due to the teacher's emotions and reactions. Some time and patience should be used to accommodate the inherent emotions, but not to extremes. Ultimately, the conversation needs to go forward in due course—allowing, of course, for appropriate attending to emotions.

Mary Jane: Tom, this isn't about *Linda,* or about anything else other than your *performance* and whether you are a fit with the position. It was a hard decision, but we had to make it, for the good of the students.

Tom: For "the good of the students"? What, do you think my teaching was harming them or something?

Mary Jane: No, Tom—that's not what *I mean* at all. Please listen to me. Our decision is made and we need to put this behind us now and move forward. We've prepared a few documents to provide you with the information that you need. The first one—

Tom: I can't believe it. I got *fired.* I got fired. How am I ever going to explain this to Jeannie and the kids? How am I going to tell them that they have to switch schools and that we may have to move, all because their dad is a loser who couldn't even keep his job? This is a nightmare, just a nightmare.

Mary Jane: Tom, please don't say those things about yourself. They are not true. You're a *very good* person and great with kids—just not in a *classroom,* necessarily. Your true talents may lie elsewhere. Please know that we're going to do everything we can to help you land on your feet. I know that this is an emotional time—I understand that. Maybe you want to take a moment to compose yourself?

Tom: What? I mean, no, thanks, Mary Jane. That won't be necessary. I'll be fine. It's just that it's now hitting me like a ton of bricks—the reality of it, that as of June 15th I'll be unemployed. I know that you've always been good to me, Mary Jane. You've looked out for me. And while it's hard to understand, I believe that you're looking out for me now, even though I don't deserve it. I appreciate it, I really do.

Mary Jane: OK, then, Tom. If we can continue—let me explain the documents that we've prepared for you. Is that OK?

Tom: Yes, of course.

Mary Jane: The first document, for our files, is a letter informing you that we won't be renewing your contract for next year, for the reasons that we've discussed. It also explains that you will be paid through the end of June, and we are asking you to fulfill your job duties for the rest of the term.

The second is a letter of reference. It says that you were "laid off due to budget cuts." We felt that this would help you in finding your next job.

Tom: Am I really being laid off? Is that true? Does that mean I might get rehired—maybe I won't have to leave after all?

Mary Jane: I don't want to give you any false hopes, Tom. It doesn't mean that. Your contract is not being renewed. It isn't a lay-off and you won't be rehired. Do you understand that?

Tom: Oh, OK. (dejected) I understand. But what am I going to tell people, the other teachers? I don't know how I'll be able to face them these next three months.

Mary Jane: What you choose to tell people is up to you, of course. Officially, the school's files will simply indicate that your contract was not renewed—nothing more, nothing less. And the reference letter states that it was due to budget cuts. If anyone asks me about it, I will tell them, as I always do, that we do not comment on personnel issues, as a matter of policy.

Tom: OK, thank you. I appreciate that. I'm going to have to think about what to say. I need to talk with Jeannie.

Mary Jane: Between now and the end of the school year, the Business Office will provide you with—

Tom: I'm sorry, Mary Jane. I'm just thinking now about applying for jobs. Can you help me with that—pass along a good word for me with people you know, other Heads, that is? Can I put you down as a reference on an application?

> *The first document, stating the reasons for the termination, is absolutely appropriate. It is helpful to lay out the pay-related consequences, too, as Mary Jane has done.*

> *The second document is where Mary Jane makes her first significant mistake. Schools should **never** create or distribute documents that misrepresent the facts. The fact is that Tom is not being "laid off due to budget cuts." This greatly blurs the message and creates documents that could potentially put the school at risk of losing a lawsuit in the name of trying to protect Tom's feelings. False documentation is never recommended in any circumstance.*

> *Communicating the reason that a teacher is leaving is always a delicate matter. Mary Jane does a good job of leaving this to Tom's discretion as a personal courtesy— except of course, for the false documentation involved.*

It is not uncommon or necessarily inappropriate for the school to negotiate a letter of reference in cases such as this. However, it is important for the school to scrupulously avoid saying or implying anything in writing about the employee's performance or service that it doesn't believe and can't document (either positive or negative).

We recommend that all discussions of unemployment benefits be deferred, pointing the employee toward the appropriate government agency. To enter into this discussion suggests that the school has control over the matter, which it does not. Mary Jane does a good job of communicating this (except, of course, for the false reason of termination).

Mary Jane: The letter of reference is supposed to serve that purpose, Tom. Officially, it is our policy not to provide verbal references for any employee. However, given the circumstances, I promise you that I will do whatever I can to help.

Tom: Will I be eligible for unemployment? I mean, if I don't end up with a job in another school, it may take me a while to land on my feet. I just need to know if I can plan on getting unemployment—the $350 a week, or whatever it is, will sure make a big difference.

Mary Jane: I can't say for sure, Tom. That is up to the Unemployment Department. All I can tell you is that we'll tell them you were laid off due to budget cuts. They make their determination. The school is not involved at all.

Tom: Right. I understand.

Mary Jane: Now, I realize that this has been difficult news for you to hear, Tom. I know that you will probably have more questions as time goes on. So, once we're back from break, please feel free to make an appointment and we'll discuss any other questions that you have. In the meantime, the Business Office will be in touch with you to talk about benefits, final paychecks, and those sorts of things.

Tom: I know that Jeannie will have lots of questions. Is it OK if I call you at home during the break?

Mary Jane: It would probably be best, Tom, for us to handle things in the office once we're back from break. (Pause) However, if it is an emergency, yes, I'll be home this week and you are welcome to call—if it is urgent.

Tom: Thanks, Mary Jane. I really appreciate that. *I just still can't believe it.*

Special Topic: Separation Agreements and General Releases

From time to time, there may be unique circumstances related to the termination of a faculty member that require special considerations above and beyond the ordinary termination process described above. This may include situations which the school has not managed well (such as a long-time teacher with performance issues that haven't been actively addressed until now) or in which the facts are not fully in its favor (such as the teacher who is clearly not competent but to whom a supervisor has also made inappropriate remarks about gender, ethnicity, etc.).

These cases should not arise often. However, when they do arise, they should be handled with appropriate humility and discretion—acknowledging that, due to a blurring of facts and circumstances, the school has some complicity in the matter and needs to resolve the situation in a way that protects itself. In these cases, the Head may wish to consider use of a Separation Agreement and General Release.

NOTE: Consult with your legal counsel prior to putting such an arrangement into place.

In such an agreement, you are essentially offering the employee an "exchange."

- You are providing the teacher with additional compensation that you don't otherwise owe him/her.

- In exchange, he/she is providing you with a *release from liability*—i.e., agreeing that he/she will not file a lawsuit against you for actions that occurred during his/her employment (such as for discrimination, wrongful termination, etc.).

Two key ideas must be considered when offering a separation agreement.

1. The compensation (called "consideration" in legal terms) must be significant enough for the employee to validly waive his/her right to file a claim (e.g., two or more months of pay is probably the minimum acceptable figure; two weeks pay is generally deemed insufficient).

2. Legal time frames must be observed (most particularly for employees over the age of 40). The employee must be given up to 21 (or more) days to consider the written agreement when it is presented, and then up to seven days to revoke his/her consent once the agreement is signed.

Again, the circumstances that warrant this agreement should be few and far between. However, when it applies, it should be an option that is reviewed by the Head and the school's employment attorney.

Coda: Knowing When You Are Safe

Any school (or other employer) can be sued at any time for any reason. As an administrator, you have long ago come to grips with this reality, otherwise you wouldn't be able to open your doors to teachers and students every morning. That being said, terminating an employee is a particularly risky venture in today's litigious environment. The paradox here is that this *risky* action is also *necessary* for the school's *protection*—i.e., to protect the students, faculty, and culture of the school— when it comes to removing a teacher who is either underperforming, or misaligned with the school's culture and values, or both. Therefore, the action *must* be taken where warranted—but taken in a way that is most likely to protect and support the school in all realms.

How do you know if terminations are being handled in a way that protects the school and its highest purposes? Our best advice is to review school's actions against the following questions.

- Has the school reflected seriously on its mission, culture, and values and identified specific Characteristics of Professional Excellence that describe the core behaviors and attitudes you required in your teachers?

- Have these characteristics been communicated consistently, starting from the school's recruitment advertising and job posting notices?

- Have these characteristics been used as the basis for interviewing qualified candidates?

- Have these characteristics been used as the criteria for selecting candidates for hire?

- Have these characteristics been emphasized and explained during the school's induction process?

- Have these same characteristics and behaviors been established as key criteria in the school's performance evaluation and professional growth and renewal programs?

- Have these characteristics served as the key criteria and standards upon which progressive corrective action was initiated for poor-performing teachers?

Of course, nothing can provide 100% protection to a school, especially when terminations are involved. However, when the school has made the above the foundation of its interactions with faculty, it can feel confident that it has done the best it can do to protect itself and its students and teachers. Job well done!

Assessing the School's Faculty Development Efforts

Now that we have reviewed all of the elements of the Comprehensive Faculty Development (CFD) Model, one task remains. We would like to close this book by offering suggestions on how the school can assess how effectively each process is operating, once implemented, and determine what cumulative effect these processes are having on the school's faculty culture.

We have two purposes in mind here.

- Just as it is important for faculty to continually grow and enhance their skills and performance, it is vital for the school (through its administration) to continually improve its employee programs, processes, and interactions—so that it might continue to attract, develop, retain, and inspire the highest-quality faculty possible to deliver its mission to its students. By assessing each program and process, we can work to continually refine these processes, raising their level of excellence to the highest level attainable.

- All of the school's employee-related interactions serve to shape the school's faculty culture. A healthy faculty culture—one in which faculty are focused on creating predictable and supportive environments for students, as well as one in which faculty perceive the administration as being predictable and supportive towards them—is a primary correlate with student performance, satisfaction, and enthusiasm. Thus, assessing the culture helps the Management Team ensure that the school is heading in the right direction, toward long-term success and sustained viability.

General Approaches to the Assessment and Monitoring of Processes and Culture

Faculty-related processes and the faculty culture may be assessed and monitored in two primary ways:

- *anecdotally*—such as through stories, vignettes, and anecdotes gained through the academic administrators' interactions, observations, collaboration with individual teachers and groups of faculty in all aspects of their jobs inside and outside the classroom; and

- *formally (and statistically)*—through surveys of the faculty as a whole, as well as surveys of individual teachers or groups of teachers impacted by particular programs or processes.

Anecdotal Observations and Impressions

Anecdotal observations of the success or impact of particular processes or programs can be easily gathered by the Head simply asking questions at regular faculty meetings and Management Team meetings. Questions might include the following.

- What does the "temperature" of the faculty seem to be at the moment? (All)

- What common concerns, irritations, high points, or success stories are teachers experiencing and talking about? (All)

- How are we progressing with our hiring process this year —i.e., do our top candidates seem stronger/weaker than in prior years; do we seem more/less at risk for losing top candidates than we were in previous years; how are candidates reacting to our interview questions and processes; etc.? (Administrators only)

- How passionately are you (or your direct reports) engaged in your professional growth projects this year? (All)

- How well prepared do you feel for writing this year's performance evaluations? Have you observed and engaged with your teachers frequently enough to have a storehouse of anecdotes and observations to draw from? (Administrators only)

- How did you (or your direct reports) react to the performance evaluation discussions, merit-pay meetings, professional growth and renewal meetings, etc., this year? (All)

The upside of anecdotal feedback is that it is relatively quick and easy to gain— i.e., just by the Head asking questions like the above, opinions and observations are likely to come gushing out from the teachers and academic administrators. This should be true, assuming that an environment of trust exists between teachers and administrators, where candid opinions and sensitive issues can be shared in confidence.

The downside of such feedback is that, just as its name implies, it is anecdotal— judgment is needed to discern whether it accurately represents faculty opinion as whole, or just the opinions of those who spoke up. As with any other area of management, anecdotes can't be taken as true for all cases and discernment is needed to assess the relative weight and importance of each story with respect to the whole of the faculty environment and culture.

Formal Surveys

Formal surveys might be divided into two categories:

1. *Targeted Surveys:* These are short surveys directed to individuals or groups that are impacted by particular programs or processes (example: newly hired teachers could be surveyed regarding the impact of the induction program).

2. *Whole Faculty Survey:* This faculty-wide survey is intended to capture the collective opinions of all faculty, to help assess the culture and climate of the school.

Formal surveys can be provided in simple paper or electronic (such as e-mail) form— or, if more sophistication and/or anonymity is appropriate or desirable, can be quickly designed using an online service such as SurveyMonkey™ or the like. Similarly, they can be conducted in-house, or third-party survey vendors can be contracted with to help boost the faculty's confidence in the anonymity of the surveys.

Targeted Surveys (Processes and Programs)

We have sketched out a small handful of targeted surveys that the school may wish to use with various segments of the faculty population, to gain feedback on processes contained within the Comprehensive Faculty Development Model. Assessing the survey results will help the school know how predictable and supportive (or not) its programs and processes are, as considered from the faculty members' perspective.

All surveys can, of course, include space for comments and additional explanations, in addition to yes/no and rating or ranking answers.

NOTE: Under each survey, we have provided a mini-action plan, to help spur thinking on the ways in which the particular survey results may be used.

Survey No. 1

New Hire "Nuts and Bolts" Survey

Shortly after a new "class" of teachers comes on board, the school could survey them to make sure that they have the information and tools that they need:

1. *I have received keys/access codes to all rooms or equipment that I need in my role.* (Yes, No)

2. *I have communicated my payroll preferences (e.g., 10-month or 12-month pay cycle, if applicable) to the Business Office.* (Yes, No)

3. *I have provided payroll with my banking information for direct deposit purposes.* (Yes, No)

4. *I have completed my benefits enrollment forms and submitted all forms to the Business Office.* (Yes, No)

5. *I have received a copy of the employee handbook.* (Yes, No)

6. *I have read the employee handbook and understand the policies and procedures that apply to me.* (Yes, No)

- *Action Plan:* Depending on the responses, the Head might confer with the Business Officer, HR Director, or other individuals responsible for processing incoming employees and determine an appropriate plan of action. This plan might include ensuring that all necessary documents, forms, resources, etc., are provided to the new employees promptly, if this is not the case, based on survey results. (See Chapter 4 for details.)

Survey No. 2

Post-Induction Process Survey

This can be sent to new faculty members shortly after they complete the school's induction process.

1. *I participated in the school's new employee induction program.*
   (Yes—I attended all days, Yes—I attended some of the days, No—I missed all of the days)

2. *The induction program helped me understand the school's mission better.*
   (Strongly agree, Somewhat agree, Neutral, Somewhat disagree, Strongly disagree)

3. *The induction program helped me understand my classroom responsibilities better.* (Strongly agree, Somewhat agree, Neutral, Somewhat disagree, Strongly disagree)

4. *The induction program helped me understand my cocurricular (coaching, advising, etc.) responsibilities better.* (Strongly agree, Somewhat agree, Neutral, Somewhat disagree, Strongly disagree)

5. *I am confident that I know where to go or whom to approach when I need an answer about school policies/procedures or my job responsibilities.* (Strongly agree, Somewhat agree, Neutral, Somewhat disagree, Strongly disagree)

6. *I feel that I need more information about the following topics/issues/ procedures in order to do my job better at this time.* (Please describe.)

- *Action Plan:* The Head and administrators responsible for the induction program would meet to determine ways to strengthen the school's program for the following year. This might include establishing an administrator-faculty committee to study and enhance the induction process, and following up with recent hires to proactively answer any questions or concerns that might not have been addressed fully during the induction process. (See Chapter 5 for details.)

Survey No. 3

Pre-Performance Evaluation Survey

This can be sent to all teachers two months prior to their annual performance evaluations.

1. *I am aware of the expectations and criteria on which I will be evaluated.*
   (Strongly agree, Somewhat agree, Neutral, Somewhat disagree, Strongly disagree)

2. *I am aware of who will be conducting my annual performance evaluation.*
   (Yes, No)

3. *I am aware of the approximate date (e.g., month) when my annual performance evaluation will be conducted.*
   (Yes, No)

4. *I am confident that my annual performance review will fairly and objectively take into account all aspects of my job performance at the school.*
   (Strongly agree, Somewhat agree, Neutral, Somewhat disagree, Strongly disagree)

- *Action Plan:* Reviewing the survey answers will assist the Head and academic administrators in preparing for the upcoming performance evaluation cycle. If the faculty members are largely unaware or ill-informed regarding the process, expectations, etc., then considerable communication may be required prior to conducting the evaluations. (See Chapter 6 for details.)

Survey No. 4

Post-Performance Evaluation Survey

This can be sent to all teachers two weeks after the annual performance evaluation cycle is completed.

1. *My supervisor met with me to discuss my annual performance review.*
   (Yes, No)

2. *I was provided with a copy of my annual performance evaluation.*
   (Yes, No)

3. *Circle the word(s) that best describe your reaction to the content of your evaluation:*
   (Pleasantly surprised, Pleased, Happy, Inspired, Reassured, Shocked, Angry, Confused, Demotivated, Depressed)

4. *I feel that my annual performance evaluation fairly and objectively reflected all aspects of my job performance at the school.*
   (Strongly agree, Somewhat agree, Neutral, Somewhat disagree, Strongly disagree)

5. *I had the opportunity to ask questions and voice my opinions during the annual evaluation meeting.*
   (Strongly agree, Somewhat agree, Neutral, Somewhat disagree, Strongly disagree)

- *Action Plan:* This survey can serve as an effective follow-up mechanism for the Management Team. Anything less than 100% "Yes" answers to the first two statements would be cause to follow-up with the direct supervisors to ensure that the evaluation process is carried out appropriately with all faculty members (absent any mitigating circumstances). Any degree of negative response to statements 3 and 4 may warrant retraining for supervisors regarding the evaluation process, and may call for more general communication to faculty about the aims and processes of the evaluation program. (See Chapter 6 for further details.)

Survey No. 5

Professional Growth and Renewal Program Presurvey

This can be sent to all teachers at the beginning of the school year, before most professional growth programs begin in earnest.

1. *I am aware of the professional growth and renewal opportunities available to me at the school.*
   (Strongly agree, Somewhat agree, Neutral, Somewhat disagree, Strongly disagree)

2. *I am aware of my responsibility for pursuing professional growth and renewal this year and throughout my career at the school.*
   (Strongly agree, Somewhat agree, Neutral/Uncertain, Somewhat disagree, Strongly disagree)

3. *My supervisor has met with me (or scheduled an appointment to meet with me) to develop a professional growth and renewal plan for this school year.*
   (Yes, No)

4. *I am excited about pursuing professional growth and renewal opportunities this year.*
   (Yes—I think it will directly benefit my job performance, Yes—it is a matter of serious personal interest, Neutral, No—I'm doing it only because it is required)

- *Action Plan:* This survey may assist the Management Team in understanding how strongly a professional growth ethos has taken hold within the faculty, and/or how well the logistics of the program are being carried out. Negative responses to the first three questions would be cause for follow-up with the direct supervisors. More generally, the results may be cause for the Head and the academic administrators to work to re-energize and re-educate the faculty regarding professional growth and renewal, through one-on-one or group meetings. (See Chapter 6 for details.)

Survey No. 6

Professional Growth and Renewal Program Post-Survey

This can be sent to all teachers at the end of the school year.

1. *I carried out a professional growth and renewal plan as part of the school's program this year.*
   (Yes; No—I didn't engage in any professional development this year;
   No—I engaged in professional development but on my own, not as part
   of the school's program; No—I didn't know that professional development
   opportunities were available to me; No – I wanted to participate but
   couldn't find the time; No—I wanted to participate, but my supervisor
   was never available to get the program started)

2. *My participation in professional growth and renewal directly benefited my students this year.*
   (Strongly agree, Somewhat agree, Neutral, Somewhat disagree, Strongly disagree)

3. *My supervisor or other school leader played an important role in the success of my professional growth program this year.*
   (Strongly agree, Somewhat agree, Neutral, Somewhat disagree, Strongly disagree)

4. *Based on the results of this year's program, I am eager to engage in the school's professional growth and renewal program next year.*
   (Strongly agree, Somewhat agree, Neutral, Somewhat disagree, Strongly disagree)

- *Action Plan:* The results of this survey may suggest tweaks to how the program is administered, as well as potential retraining or enhancing of the Academic Administrative Team's skills regarding coaching and mentoring and guiding and enabling teacher growth. (See Chapter 6 for details.)

Survey No. 7

Compensation Program Survey

This can be sent to all teachers after contracts and merit-pay increases are communicated in the spring (where pay-for-performance is used).

1. *My supervisor communicated my new salary for next year to me.*
   (Yes, No)

2. *My supervisor clearly explained how my new salary was derived.*
   (Strongly agree, Somewhat agree, Neutral, Somewhat disagree, Strongly disagree)

3. *I believe that my salary is appropriate with respect to my contribution to the school.*
   (Strongly agree, Somewhat agree, Neutral, Somewhat disagree, Strongly disagree)

4. *I believe that my salary is comparable to what I would receive for a similar role at a competing private-independent school.*
   (Strongly agree, Somewhat agree, Neutral, Somewhat disagree, Strongly disagree)

5. *I am aware of the opportunities available to me to increase my pay in the future.*
   (Strongly agree, Somewhat agree, Neutral, Somewhat disagree, Strongly disagree)

- *Action Plan:* Responses to statements 1, 2, and 5 will indicate how clearly the school is communicating about its pay-for-performance program. Statements 3 and 4 may provide the Head with an early indication of whether salaries may play a role in teacher retention issues.

Background Regarding the Whole Faculty Survey

Before getting into the details of our recommended faculty culture survey, we would like to offer some background and context. Keeping Covey's "begin with the end in mind" maxim ever present, we will offer a brief reflection on what a healthy faculty culture (the goal that is being sought) looks like in action.

Healthy Faculty Cultures Defined and Explored

ISM's Research for School Management (RSM) and Student Experience Study (SES) research studies (referenced earlier) identified and reaffirmed the strong correlation between student performance, satisfaction, and enthusiasm and a healthy faculty culture. This is defined as a culture in which teachers are individually and collectively:

- focused on continual professional growth and are constantly engaged in discussing the difference-makers in the lives of students,
- striving every day to provide a predictable and supportive environment for students, and
- perceive that the administration actively cares about and supports their needs.

These factors operate on individual as well as collective levels. That is, just as it is vital for each teacher to be pursuing his/her own growth and renewal plan, he/she must be able to trust that each fellow teacher is just as focused and just as dedicated to his/her own professional growth. One happy result is that in such cultures, the weight of the culture shifts strongly to the positive—negative or bitter faculty will be spun out to the margins; left outside of the core, positive culture; and increasingly have less and less impact on the whole.

Over the long term, a teacher can't rise above the culture of the whole; if the majority of teachers aren't actively engaged in professional growth, the ones who are will eventually become pulled down and dispirited by the overall faculty culture, leading to bitterness, learned helplessness, and other damaging factors and effects.

You will recognize the ingredients of a healthy faculty culture when you begin to see broad-based examples of:

- commitment by individuals to their own growth and career,
- whole faculty commitment to common goals and purposes (evidenced by a common understanding and practice of professional excellence), and
- teachers' desire to grow in support of each other (evidenced by collegiality and collaboration).

The instrument described below will help the Management Team better assess the strength and health of its faculty culture through use of a formal survey.

Using ISM's Faculty Culture Profile

As we noted in the "anecdotal survey" section above, an engaged observer doesn't require a formal instrument to gain a general sense of how a faculty culture is progressing—he/she can often gain an accurate feel for the culture just by being around and in it for a short period of time. That being said, most schools find it helpful to assess the culture in a more structured and systematic way, as well—which we fully support. For this purpose, ISM has long published a Faculty Culture Profile for school use. The most recent (2012) iteration of this instrument is shown below.

Note: The Head can choose to use this instrument as is, or, customize it to best reflect and assess the school's unique mission, culture, and values. The fixed template version is shown below, followed by notes and suggestions as to how it can be customized for your purposes. Considerations regarding the frequency and timing of the survey are noted below, as well.

The ISM Faculty Culture Profile II

All faculty are asked to answer the following, circling only one number for each question.

1. *I and my colleagues find ways to make it obvious to all students that we wish them success every day, both in school and outside of school.*

   | 1 | 2 | 3 | 4 | 5 | 6 | 7 | 8 | 9 |

   Not true of us at all   Exactly true of us

2. *I and my colleagues find ways to make it obvious to all students that we want them to become better, more virtuous people (in ways consistent with our school's stated purposes and projected outcomes for our graduates).*

   | 1 | 2 | 3 | 4 | 5 | 6 | 7 | 8 | 9 |

   Not true of us at all   Exactly true of us

3. *I and my colleagues set clearly articulated standards for student academic performance.*

   | 1 | 2 | 3 | 4 | 5 | 6 | 7 | 8 | 9 |

   Not true of us at all   Exactly true of us

4. *I and my colleagues set reasonable, defensible standards for student behavior.*

| 1 | 2 | 3 | 4 | 5 | 6 | 7 | 8 | 9 |

Not true of us at all   *Exactly true of us*

5. *I and my colleagues are continually alert to the threat of bullying between and among our students.*

| 1 | 2 | 3 | 4 | 5 | 6 | 7 | 8 | 9 |

Not true of us at all   *Exactly true of us*

6. *In confrontations with students, I and my colleagues conduct ourselves in ways that leave students' dignity intact regardless of the nature of the issue or infraction.*

| 1 | 2 | 3 | 4 | 5 | 6 | 7 | 8 | 9 |

Not true of us at all   *Exactly true of us*

7. *I and my colleagues individually and collectively demonstrate believably high levels of enthusiasm for teaching/learning and for the content of our studies.*

| 1 | 2 | 3 | 4 | 5 | 6 | 7 | 8 | 9 |

Not true of us at all   *Exactly true of us*

8. *I and my colleagues demonstrate through words and actions a genuine, believable commitment to the school, its purposes, its leadership, and each other.*

| 1 | 2 | 3 | 4 | 5 | 6 | 7 | 8 | 9 |

Not true of us at all   *Exactly true of us*

9. *I and my colleagues are glad to arrive at school and to see our students each day.*

| 1 | 2 | 3 | 4 | 5 | 6 | 7 | 8 | 9 |

Not true of us at all   *Exactly true of us*

10. *I and my colleagues create predictable tests (not to be confused either with "simple" tests or with "easy" tests); our students can rely on the test preparation we offer them.*

1	2	3	4	5	6	7	8	9

Not true of us at all · · · · · · · · · · · · · · · · · · Exactly true of us

11. *I and my colleagues provide fair, reliable, understandable grade/reward structures for our students; our students are led to understand why they receive the grades they receive—good or bad—and thereby to see how improvement, if they will seek it, might be possible.*

1	2	3	4	5	6	7	8	9

Not true of us at all · · · · · · · · · · · · · · · · · · Exactly true of us

12. *I and my colleagues enforce our rules, including the dress code, justly, fairly, consistently.*

1	2	3	4	5	6	7	8	9

Not true of us at all · · · · · · · · · · · · · · · · · · Exactly true of us

13. *I and my colleagues are able to present ourselves each day in ways that will be seen by our students as consistent and reliable (i.e., unaffected by outside-of-school problems).*

1	2	3	4	5	6	7	8	9

Not true of us at all · · · · · · · · · · · · · · · · · · Exactly true of us

14. *I and my colleagues individually and collectively pursue career-long professional development as a foremost priority.*

1	2	3	4	5	6	7	8	9

Not true of us at all · · · · · · · · · · · · · · · · · · Exactly true of us

15. *I and my colleagues have mastered at least one pedagogical approach—not necessarily the same one for all of us—that is supported by reliable, contemporary research outcomes.*

1	2	3	4	5	6	7	8	9

Not true of us at all · · · · · · · · · · · · · · · · · · Exactly true of us

16. When I and my colleagues are in casual conversations with each other, those conversations tend to be constructive, upbeat, and professional.

| 1 | 2 | 3 | 4 | 5 | 6 | 7 | 8 | 9 |

Not true of us at all   Exactly true of us

17. I and my colleagues have great respect for our division and/or school administrators.

| 1 | 2 | 3 | 4 | 5 | 6 | 7 | 8 | 9 |

Not true of us at all   Exactly true of us

18. I and my colleagues find that our division and/or school administrators are highly supportive of our division's and/or school's faculty.

| 1 | 2 | 3 | 4 | 5 | 6 | 7 | 8 | 9 |

Not true of us at all   Exactly true of us

19. I and my colleagues find that our division and/or school administrators are highly supportive of our division's and/or school's students.

| 1 | 2 | 3 | 4 | 5 | 6 | 7 | 8 | 9 |

Not true of us at all   Exactly true of us

20. I and my colleagues find that our division and/or school administrators are highly supportive of our division's and/or school's parents.

| 1 | 2 | 3 | 4 | 5 | 6 | 7 | 8 | 9 |

Not true of us at all   Exactly true of us

NOTE: Schools that regularly rate themselves against ISM's Stability Markers™ will observe that the Faculty Culture Profile is used in the scoring of the faculty culture item. To use the above for that purpose, the following instructions are provided. On any item on which 75% of the faculty members score at the top third of the response scale (i.e., 75% of the faculty circling the 7, 8, or 9), award one point. After determining the total (a number between 0 and 20), multiply that number by 0.3, thus converting the outcome to the six-point scale required by that item in the Stability Markers.

Customizing the Faculty Culture Profile (FCP)

You will notice that the first 13 questions of this survey correspond directly to the characteristics derived from ISM's most recent School Experience Study (SES) project—i.e., the 13 research-based Characteristics of Professional Excellence that are included in the Characteristics of Professional Excellence II list that is in the Appendices of this book. We raise this point here, as the school has a choice to make regarding the use of the Faculty Culture Profile survey.

- If the school wishes to base its survey strictly on research-based items, it is encouraged to use the FCPII Survey unaltered, as shown.

- If the school wishes to customize the survey to reflect its customized, unique Characteristics of Professional Excellence (see Chapter 2 for details), it may modify the formal FCPII survey—replacing Questions 1–13 with questions based directly on the school's own characteristics of excellence. For example, if the school ends up with a set of six characteristics of excellence, it would then write one question for each characteristic (i.e., six questions in all), and then pick up the rest of ISM's survey, beginning with Question 14 and continuing through Question 20.

The downside of changing the questions is that the school will not be able to directly compare its results with those of other schools that use the ISM Faculty Culture Profile II over the course of time. However, by customizing the survey based on your school's list of characteristics, you are reaffirming your characteristics to faculty; it is logical and consistent to test how your specific, unique characteristics are being incorporated into faculty attitudes and perspectives (i.e., the faculty culture). The choice is the school's, of course.

Frequency and Timing

Since ISM first developed its Faculty Culture Profile in the 1990s, we have recommended that schools administer the instrument as follows.

- Survey faculty members using the Faculty Culture Profile three times per academic year (approximately November, February, and May).

- The "three-times-per-year" model has been suggested to roughly correspond with what we find to be the emotional cycle in a school year—from its most positive (November), to its low point (midwinter), to its recovery (Spring).

- Following this approach, we suggest distributing the survey at virtually the same times each year (e.g., the first week of November every year, etc.), so that the results can be compared from year to year (i.e., November compared to the previous November, February compared to the previous February).

The three-times-per-year survey method suggested above has been used successfully by a number of schools that follow it scrupulously as part of their faculty-administrator calendar. Other schools, though, may find that three surveys per year generate "survey fatigue" among faculty and administrators, thereby decreasing both enthusiasm for the process and the reliability of its results. For these schools, consideration may be given to pursuing a once-per-year model. If your school chooses this approach, we recommend that you issue the survey at the same time each year (such as the first week of November, for example), so that you can compare results accurately from year to year (owing to the hills and valleys in the school's emotional cycle, noted above).

Administering the Survey: A Consideration

Schools that have used ISM's Faculty Culture Profile in the past have often found it helpful for the survey to be administered by an exemplary group of faculty, such as those appointed for the Characteristics Design Team, or Evaluation or Professional Growth and Renewal Design Teams described earlier. The advantage in doing so is that faculty feel right from the beginning of the process the connection of the survey to the faculty culture, i.e., we are administering it to "ourselves" (the teachers). In addition, under this approach, schools have found it helpful to have the committee available to interpret the results for the administration.

Alternatively, the Head may wish to have his/her office conduct the survey directly, or via an online service, such as SurveyMonkey or the like. Doing so will demonstrate his/her sincere interest in hearing directly the faculty's views. Academic Administrative Teams that are actively engaged and collaborating with faculty (the primary duty of academic administrators, as we have emphasized previously) may not wish to have an intermediary filter and interpret the results—wishing instead to see the unadulterated responses directly. Our only caution here is that in toxic environments where there is little trust between the administration and the faculty, the direct-to-the-Head survey approach may feed suspicions as to the anonymity of the survey, raising questions about the administration's intentions and motives.

In this, as with all other matters involved in running the school, we recommend that the Head assess the conditions at play and uses his/her best judgment.

Final Note: The 'Now What' Issue

As with the targeted program and process surveys suggested earlier in this chapter, the question that all Heads must ask in assessing Faculty Culture Profile results is, "Now what?" That is to say, what can or should the Head do to address the faculty's feelings as reflected in the survey results? A large portion of the answer will, of course, depend on the particular results—and how those results compare to the school's historical results, as well as any new or unusual events that may have influenced the most recent results (example: the midyear termination of a well-known faculty member or similar other disruptive event shortly before conducting the February survey would surely impact the results of the survey).

As with many things on the Head's plate, "what to do now" is a matter of judgment, discernment, and experience. We can, however, offer several general thoughts on the matter:

- If the faculty rate themselves and their colleagues low on the Characteristics of Professional Excellence, it may be that there is insufficient understanding of (or commitment to) these standards. This may suggest that considerably more discussion of the characteristics is needed (in small or large groups, by department, one-on-one, etc.)—any way that will help the characteristics come to life for faculty.

- If an underlying theme to faculty responses is "*I'm* doing these things, but my *colleagues* aren't", this might suggest one of several things. It could suggest that they are right—that other faculty members are mission-inappropriate (which could require improved hiring practices and/or more vigorous corrective action). Or, it could suggest that there are inadequate opportunities for faculty to get to know and work with one another (i.e., rating others low due to lack of exposure to them). This might be addressed by actively seeking and implementing more opportunities for faculty to collaborate (team teaching, knowledge socialization sessions, etc.).

- If faculty grade their colleagues highly but give low marks to the questions centering around *trust of* administrators or *support from* administrators (such as in Questions 17–20), this might suggest that an "us versus them" faculty versus administration divide has opened up in the school. This may come from a lack of interaction, engagement, and collaboration between faculty and administrators (example: administrators having a reputation of never coming out of their offices, or administrators only visiting with faculty when there are problems to discuss).

This may be addressed by proactively engaging faculty in the types of coaching and mentoring relationships noted earlier.

Low trust scores could indicate that Division Heads and/or Department Chairs are trying to coach and mentor but aren't doing it with as much skill as needed. If so, they may require additional training on coaching and mentoring techniques. Low scores could also indicate that the school may have some supervisors who are not well-suited to the demands of leadership of adults (as opposed to the teaching of children). This may suggest a review of the academic leadership team and consideration of whether all of the players are well-positioned to succeed in their current roles, or whether changes are necessary.

There is, of course, an infinite array of possible interpretations of survey results, just as there is an infinite array of potential ways to address issues that are raised. Using the school's mission, culture, and values as the prism through which the results are viewed may assist the Head in determining his/her approach to addressing issues that are identified. The more frequently, passionately, and vibrantly that the school's mission, culture and values are articulated, the more predictable and supportive the environment will become for teachers and students, and therein will lie a key source of the school's ongoing success.

Drawing All the Threads Together

To return one more time to Covey's "begin with the end in mind" maxim that we've referenced throughout this book, the end goal for all private-independent schools is to have a thriving school where students are performing to the best of their ability, are highly engaged and satisfied with the school, and demonstrate great enthusiasm for all things about the school. If this is the end, then the vehicle—or means—to get to the end is an engaged, collaborative faculty that is constantly seeking excellence. And if that is the vehicle, we believe the vehicle is best maintained by a Management Team that acts with great clarity, support, and respect for the vehicle (the faculty). In a nutshell, we have designed the Comprehensive Faculty Development (CFD) Model to help create and sustain this ideal state of affairs.

The CFD Model is founded on the premise that all of the school's interactions with faculty—from hiring and induction, to evaluation and growth, to reward and recognition, to corrective action and selective retention—serve to support this ideal set of circumstances. For this ideal state of affairs to become a reality, we believe that two things must be true.

1. Every academic administrator must be focused on establishing, maintaining, and enhancing a predictable and supportive environment leading to a healthy faculty culture; and

2. The school must provide the administrators and teachers with the structures, tools, processes, and resources that enable the above to come true.

As noted throughout this book, we believe that a well-defined set of Characteristics of Professional Excellence unique to your school can serve as the thread or linchpin connecting all stages of the Comprehensive Faculty Development Model, bringing the model to life.

By working from this framework, a 21st Century School is sending a powerful, supportive, and energizing message to its faculty. That is:

- We've carefully determined the characteristics that are central to delivering our mission with excellence to students, within the context of our unique culture and values.

- We've used these characteristics as the core of our interviewing and hiring processes—aiming to bring in the most qualified, mission-appropriate teachers possible.

- We emphasize these characteristics in our induction program, helping new faculty inculcate these characteristics and values in their professional lives and practices.

- We engage frequently, deeply, and collaboratively with faculty throughout the year, with coaching and mentoring conversations being "the way we do business" here.

- We evaluate faculty members against how they demonstrate these characteristics in all aspects of their work here, taking a comprehensive view of their role in and outside of the classroom.

- We support, encourage, and require all faculty members to continuously improve their skills, knowledge, methods, and approaches through a systematic program of professional growth and renewal.

- We reward and recognize faculty members based on demonstrating these characteristics and impacting the lives of their students in this manner.

- We use the characteristics as a "common language" for discussing performance issues and in trying to help faculty maintain and exceed standards through supportive corrective-action processes.

- Where these efforts are unsuccessful, we agree to respectfully part company in the best interests of the students and community members.

- We monitor the presence and effect of these characteristics in the faculty and we use results to fine-tune and enhance our practices on an ongoing basis.

- If the above reflects your passions, your abilities, and your commitments, please join us for the ride. We're glad to make the journey with you to support and serve our students. Let's begin!

In using this approach as School Head, you are actively supporting your faculty's efforts to deliver the school's mission to students with excellence by supporting your administrators' efforts to coach and mentor faculty—all combining to enhance student performance, satisfaction, and enthusiasm. We encourage you in these efforts and look forward to hearing your results from using this model in your school.

Appendices

Chapter 1

Comprehensive Faculty Development Model

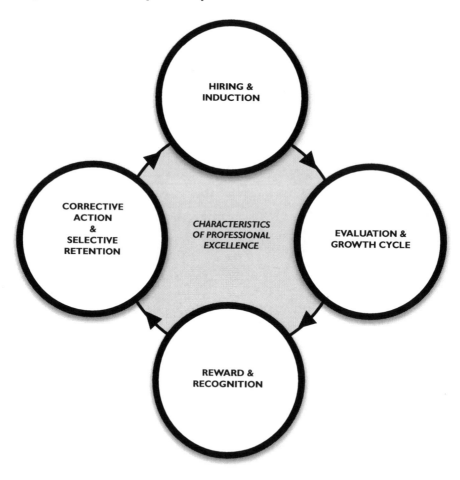

Chapter 2

Equal Opportunity Protected Classes (by State)

Federal regulations—in the form of Title VII of the Civil Rights Act of 1964, the Americans with Disabilities Act, the Age Discrimination in Employment Act, and other related statutes—protect individuals from employment discrimination based on race, color, religion, gender, national origin, age, genetic information, disability, or veteran status.

In addition, states have specified other "protected classes." The following list is accurate as of December, 2011.

NOTE: Cities, counties, and other local governments may enact additional protections not indicated here.

STATE	ADDITIONAL PROTECTED CLASSES (BY STATE)
Alabama	None
Alaska	Physical or mental disability, marital status, changes in marital status, pregnancy, or parenthood when the reasonable demands of the position do not require these distinctions
Arizona	Genetic testing results
Arkansas	Ancestry, the presence of any sensory, mental, or physical disability
California	Ancestry, physical disability, mental disability, medical condition, marital status, sexual orientation, gender identity, gender expression
Colorado	Sexual orientation, ancestry
Connecticut	Marital status, ancestry, present or past history of mental disability, mental retardation, learning disability, physical disability including but not limited to blindness
Delaware	Marital status; sexual orientation
District of Columbia	Sex (including pregnancy, childbirth, related medical conditions, and breastfeeding), marital status, personal appearance, sexual orientation, gender identity or expression, family responsibilities, matriculation, or political affiliation
Florida	Handicap, marital status, sickle cell trait

STATE	ADDITIONAL PROTECTED CLASSES (BY STATE)
Georgia	None
Hawaii	Sex (including pregnancy, childbirth, and related medical conditions), sexual orientation, ancestry, disability ("being regarded as having an impairment" includes an employer's consideration of an individual's genetic information or an individual's refusal to submit to a genetic test as a condition of initial or continued employment), marital status, arrest and court record
Idaho	None
Illinois	Ancestry, marital status, handicap, military status, sexual orientation, unfavorable discharge from military status
Indiana	Ancestry
Iowa	Sexual orientation, gender identity
Kansas	Ancestry
Kentucky	Sex (including pregnancy, childbirth, and related medical conditions), the individual is a smoker or nonsmoker as long as the person complies with any workplace policy concerning smoking
Louisiana	Sickle cell trait
Maine	Sexual orientation, physical or mental disability, ancestry
Maryland	Marital status, sexual orientation, disability unrelated in nature and extent so as to reasonably preclude the performance of the employment, or because of the individual's refusal to submit to a genetic test or make available the results of a genetic test
Massachusetts	Sexual orientation (note, however, that this does not include persons whose sexual orientation involves minor children as the sex object), ancestry, the handicap of a qualified handicapped person
Michigan	Sex (including pregnancy, childbirth, and related medical conditions), height, weight, marital status
Minnesota	Marital status, status with regard to public assistance, membership or activity in a local commission, sexual orientation
Mississippi	None

STATE	ADDITIONAL PROTECTED CLASSES (BY STATE)
Missouri	Ancestry
Montana	Physical or mental disability, marital status, or sex when the reasonable demands of the position do not require an age, physical or mental disability, marital status, or sex distinction
Nebraska	Marital status
Nevada	Sexual orientation
New Hampshire	Marital status, physical or mental disability, sexual orientation
New Jersey	Ancestry, age, marital status, civil union status, domestic partnership status, affectional or sexual orientation, genetic information, gender identity or expression, disability or atypical hereditary cellular or blood trait, liability for service in the U.S. Armed Forces, or because of the refusal to submit to a genetic test or make available results of a genetic test to an employer
New Mexico	Ancestry, physical or mental handicap or serious medical condition, spousal affiliation, sexual orientation, gender identity
New York	Sexual orientation, military status, predisposing genetic characteristics, marital status
North Carolina	None
North Dakota	Sex (including pregnancy, childbirth, and disabilities related to pregnancy or childbirth), physical or mental disability, status with respect to marriage or public assistance.
Ohio	Sex (including pregnancy, childbirth, and related medical conditions), handicap, ancestry
Oklahoma	None
Oregon	Sexual orientation, marital status, or because of race, color, religion, sex, sexual orientation, national origin, marital status, or age of any other person with whom the individual associates, or because of an individual's juvenile record that has been expunged
Pennsylvania	Ancestry, nonjob-related handicap or disability, the use of a guide or support animal because of blindness, deafness, or physical handicap

STATE	ADDITIONAL PROTECTED CLASSES (BY STATE)
Puerto Rico	Social or national origin or social condition, political affiliation, political ideology, for being a victim or perceived as a victim of domestic violence, sexual aggression, or stalking
Rhode Island	Sex (including pregnancy, childbirth, and related medical conditions), sexual orientation, gender identity or expression, country of ancestral origin, arrest record
South Carolina	Sex (including pregnancy, childbirth, and related medical conditions)
South Dakota	Blindness or partial blindness (unless specific vision requirements are necessary)
Tennessee	None
Texas	Genetic information or because of the refusal to submit to a genetic test
Utah	Pregnancy, childbirth, and related medical conditions
Vermont	Ancestry, sexual orientation, gender identity, place of birth, physical or mental condition
Virginia	Pregnancy, childbirth, and related medical conditions, marital status
Washington	Marital status, sexual orientation, the presence of any sensory, mental, or physical disability or the use of a trained guide dog or service animal by a person with a disability, honorably discharged veteran, or military status
West Virginia	Ancestry, blindness, disability
Wisconsin	Marital status, ancestry, arrest record, conviction record, sexual orientation, membership in any military, use or nonuse of lawful products off the employer's premises during nonworking hours
Wyoming	Ancestry, pregnancy, use or nonuse of tobacco products outside the course of the individual's employment

Chapter 3

In Chapter 3, we provided a list of ISM research-based Characteristics of Professional Excellence that was segmented into groupings of characteristics. For those readers interested in more specific details pertaining to this research, the following represents the research-based version of the characteristics listing, as adapted from an article appearing in ISM's *Ideas & Perspectives* management advisory newsletter (Volume 37, Number 9).

The ISM Characteristics of Professional Excellence II

The ISM Characteristics of Professional Excellence II (CPE II) list is divided into two parts: Part A, items derived from the ISM Student Experience Study (these items are identical to those in the Faculty Culture Profile II: Part A except for details of the items' wording); and Part B, items designed for broad administrative use in faculty hiring/dismissal, faculty evaluation, and the development of more general criteria for overall faculty excellence.

Part A

NOTE: These characteristics were derived directly from ISM's Student Experience Study (SES).

1. I find ways to make it obvious to all students that I wish them success every day, both in school and outside of school.

2. I find ways to make it obvious to all students that I want them to become better, more virtuous people (in ways consistent with our school's stated purposes and projected outcomes for our graduates).

3. I set clearly articulated standards for student academic performance.

4. I set reasonable, defensible standards for student behavior.

5. I am continually alert to the threat of bullying between and among my students.

6. In confrontations with students, I conduct myself in ways that leave students' dignity intact, regardless of the nature of the issue or infraction.

7. I demonstrate believably high levels of enthusiasm for teaching/learning and for the content of my studies.

8. I demonstrate through words and actions a genuine, believable commitment to the school, its purposes, its leadership, and my peers.

9. I am glad to arrive at school and to see my students each day.

10. I create predictable tests (not to be confused either with "simple" tests or with "easy" tests); my students can rely on the test preparation that I offer them.

11. I provide fair, reliable, understandable grade/reward structures for my students; my students are led to understand why they receive the grades they receive—good or bad—and thereby to see how improvement, if they will seek it, might be possible.

12. I enforce our rules, including the dress code, justly, fairly, consistently.

13. I am able to present myself each day in ways that will be seen by my students as consistent and reliable (i.e., unaffected by outside-of-school problems).

Part B

The following continuation of CPE II comprises a more comprehensive list of faculty and faculty culture characteristics designed for use in faculty culture enhancement systems, faculty evaluation systems, career-long faculty professional development systems, faculty pay-for-performance systems, and faculty hiring/dismissal procedures.

14. I pursue career-long professional development as a foremost priority.

15. I am knowledgeable of cutting-edge content and developmental theory.

16. I have mastered at least one pedagogical approach that is supported by reliable, contemporary research outcomes.

17. I am practiced in establishing meaningful emotional/psychological engagement with all my students.

18. I am practiced in finding creative and appropriate ways to be involved with my students outside the classroom.

19. I am practiced in displaying an overt, conspicuous interest in students' outside-the-class lives—apart from the previous item—without crossing privacy barriers.

20. I am practiced in applying any subject matter to real-life conditions beyond the classroom, including applications that may be global or universal in their potential.

21. I am practiced in providing private and public positive reinforcement for individual or group (student) successes.

22. I am practiced in giving active support for, and establishing active engagement with, colleagues.

23. I am practiced in making positive contributions to a professional, mission-focused sense of community with all constituent groups.

24. I am practiced in establishing proactive communication with, and service to, each student's parents.

25. I am practiced in making an overt commitment to the personal and professional well-being of colleagues, administrators, and (other) nonteaching staff.

26. I am practiced in giving public support for students, colleagues, and employers (administration and Board).

27. I am practiced in communicating in-class experimentation-and-testing outcomes and findings to colleagues, within and beyond the school.

28. I am practiced in routine (yet enthusiastic) participation in outside-the-school academic organizations whose work is supportive of, and pertinent to, my field(s).

29. I am practiced in making an overt commitment to the life of my own congregation (church, synagogue, etc.) and its core traditions.*

30. I am practiced in serving as a mature role model for a biblically focused lifestyle.*

31. I am skilled in articulating the personal/ethical implications of a lifelong faith commitment.*

32. I am practiced in displaying appropriate levels of public tolerance of, and respect for, other religious points of view.*

33. I am knowledgeable of the developmental history of my school's religious heritage.*

34. I am practiced in participating in (and when appropriate, leading) the explicitly religious components of the school's student and community programs.*

35. I am committed to growing professionally and personally within the framework of my religious traditions.*

*NOTE: Items 29–35 pertain to faith-based schools only.

ISM Articles: Purpose and Outcome Statements

In Chapter 3, we discussed at length our recommendations for defining the school's Characteristics of Professional Excellence. ISM recommends that schools consider the list of characteristics to be one of a trio of documents that we call your Purpose and Outcome Statements—including the school's mission statement and what we term the "Portrait of the Graduate" (explained further below). Taken together, these documents communicate:

- the school's reason for being (mission);
- its end goal (the "portrait" of what students will be like when they graduate); and
- the actions (characteristics) that will make the portrait a reality.

Following are two ISM articles that provide more detailed recommendations for how to form your mission statement as well as your portrait of a graduate.

ISM Article: The Power of the Mission Statement
(Adapted from ISM's former publication, To The Point, Vol. 9, No. 4)

Picture yourself as the new Head at your school, even if you've held the position for several years. Pull out a copy of the mission statement. Is it just a set of words that's dusted off and published in the admission brochure, annual report, and handbooks, then tucked back in a drawer? Or is it a vital part of your school's day-to-day operations, the anchor to windward for all major decisions?

A meaningful mission statement offers more than a concept; it provides focus and clear direction. As a result, mission-driven schools tend to find that they progress more rapidly.

The School's Mission:

- provides the lens through which the school's plan and vision must be viewed, offering guidance in delineating goals, and strategies for achieving them that are consistent with the school's values;
- supports the administration in shaping programs, both curricular and cocurricular;
- defines the qualities of the people the school seeks for its community—families and students, Board, faculty, and staff;
- grounds all fund-raising efforts, defining why the school is worthy of contributions and determining appropriate uses of the proceeds; and
- binds the school community together because the people in it have accepted a set of goals and values they feel is important, want to be part of, and willingly support.

To work well, a mission statement must be practical. How does your school's version stack up in terms of these four characteristics?

- *The mission statement must be short (25 to 30 words).* This concise structure forces you to focus on essential elements and select powerful, descriptive words. The school philosophy can expand on the precepts included in the mission statement and detail the ways they inform pedagogical practices in the classroom, decisions affecting the school's environment, and outside-the-classroom activities.

- *The mission statement must describe your school in ways that distinguish it from other schools.* Focus on your school's competitive advantages—the qualities that set it apart. If your current mission could just as easily be applied to the school up the street or the one across town, it's projecting a blurry image.

- *The mission statement must be compelling.* When it engages the reader concerning the institution, the education it offers, and the benefits it provides, the mission statement encourages support for the school. An excellent mission statement serves as a key marketing tool, both internally and externally.

- *The mission statement must be memorable—and easy to memorize.* For the people in your school to embrace the mission and apply it to their day-to-day decisions and actions, it must be meaningful and easy to remember. This is another reason to keep the statement short and focused.

Creating Your Mission Statement

The more specific your school's reason-for-being, the easier it is to create a distinctive mission statement. Those with religious affiliations may talk about offering an education "within the context of a faith-based community" or be quite specific, e.g., "a Catholic school for students of all faiths."

A Montessori school might focus on student-directed learning. A school for children with learning differences might cite its "structure and support" and "the development of coping skills and accommodations that support students' college success."

Phrases such as "lifelong learning," "challenging curriculum," "academic excellence," and "supportive community" have become commonplace. To generate creative alternatives to these basics of a private school education, examine your program and its outcomes for your students. Your students might "expand their views of the world and put their values into action" or "develop moral and social responsibility" or "pursue truth and justice, and recognize the challenges of tolerance and diversity." Your school might be a place where "the joy of discovery inspires serious study, social responsibility, and strong faith."

Your mission statement must not overreach, however. Do not describe your curriculum as "innovative" or your school community as "diverse" unless you're describing a truly distinctive and broad-based component.

The 30-word limit, a challenging requirement, becomes much more attainable when you:

- eliminate information that is not mission-focused,
- avoid information that may become outdated,
- delete unnecessary words, and
- concentrate on the essential elements.

For a look at how Aegis Academy, our fictional, coed, PK–12 day school, evaluated and rewrote its mission statement, see "What does a strong mission statement look like?" below.

The Aegis Academy Mission Statement (original version)

Founded in 1980, The Aegis Academy offers an education for students in grades 1–12 that ensures they will be able to make learning a lifelong pursuit, achieve successful college careers, and face the challenges of the future. The school offers a strong curriculum in academics, athletics, and the arts with small classes and caring teachers. The school is situated on a beautiful four-acre campus with modern facilities.

The Aegis Academy Mission Statement (2013 version)

We encourage cross-curricular learning, leadership development, active minds and bodies, and moral and social responsibility, as we, students and adults, pursue our potential in and out of the classroom.

Keep the Mission Visible and Vital

A school's mission statement needs to be seen as a living document and a part of the community's day-to-day life. To continually reinforce the mission's centrality in your school's life, use these strategies.

- Post the mission statement in all classrooms and offices.

- Publish it in the front of all handbooks and the Board policy manual.

- Give it a prominent spot in all recruitment and fund-raising materials.

- Make it part of all planning documents.

- Review it annually at faculty-staff orientation, orientation for new Board members, the Board retreat, and back-to-school night, discussing how the mission shapes decision-making.

- In the school newsletter and magazine, letters to parents, and presentations to groups, cite examples of how curricular and cocurricular programs fulfill the mission, and how students benefit from the mission's influence on those programs.

- To validate how the mission is carried out on a daily basis, make this the topic for a half-day faculty retreat. Ask the teachers to describe the ways they see the mission being fulfilled, both in the classroom and throughout the school.

Your school's mission statement must be more than mere words. Drafting a concise, meaningful statement, keeping it vibrant and visible, and anchoring major decisions in the spirit of that mission grounds your school community. It provides a consistent guide to planning and decision-making.

ISM Article: Purpose and Outcome Statements: Portrait of the Graduate

(Adapted from ISM's former publication, To The Point, Vol. 9, No. 4)

The Portrait of the Graduate is a list of five or fewer items comprising short descriptors of your "product"—the student you expect to have developed over the years that she/he has spent under your faculty's tutelage. Examples of such descriptors may include:

- ready to perform with distinction at the next academic level;
- committed to lifelong learning, both inside and outside educational (institutional) contexts;
- conversant with the ethical implications of the school mission statement;
- competent in the use of technological research channels;
- committed to advancing the fine arts;
- eager to engage diverse communities;
- committed to community service principles; and
- able to articulate the major ingredients in a lifelong wellness lifestyle.

Schools with explicitly religious missions will include explicitly religious descriptors in their portraits, such as:

- committed to a biblically focused lifestyle;
- able to articulate fully the personal/ethical implications of a lifelong faith commitment; and
- tolerant of, and conversant with, other religious
- viewpoints.

Keep your Portrait of the Graduate concise. The impact of your portrait on readers diminishes as the list grows.

Developing Your Portrait of the Graduate

The School Head initiates the development of your Portrait of the Graduate. While determination of the exact steps and selection of individuals to participate in the process will be the Head's choice, fitting the particular context, there is an expected series of steps that can be viewed as normative. Form a team, certainly to include faculty members, to spearhead the process. (There may be a pre-existing group to which you prefer to assign the task, e.g., a "design team" of teachers who routinely provide advice and counsel to you; a mixed group with teachers, administrators, and others who regularly take on projects of this sort; or a standing administrative committee to which you could add appropriate faculty representation.)

Having created or designated a group of your choosing, consider the following sequence.

1. Meet with the group members and ask them to select a "convener" (if a Chair does not already exist, as with a pre-existing committee). Provide the members with a written charge: *Produce a short list (containing no more than five items) delineating the expected outcomes of the student experience at your school, a list that denotes in concise language the specific qualities of your graduates.*

2. Resist the temptation to elaborate on the charge, other than to explain the overall purpose of the assignment and to note the subsequent steps. Honor the quality of those selected by allowing the team to work unconstrained.

3. Provide time constraints; six to eight weeks is suggested.

4. When the team has readied a draft, schedule one or more faculty meetings where the team members will make a presentation to their colleagues. In the faculty meetings, provide the introduction yourself (see Nos. 1 and 2).

5. With your second-level academic administrators, listen to the discussion of the proposed portrait; do not preside or speak unless asked.

6. Let the team itself determine the next steps; it may decide that the work is finished, or it may request time to continue its work.

7. Accept the finished product with appropriate expressions of private and public gratitude.

8. Make every effort to accept the finished portrait exactly as produced by your team. If you cannot live with some word or phrase, do what you must, but know that, if the Portrait of the Graduate is grounded in the school's institutional culture—as it must be—it needs to be acceptable to your faculty and leadership in a profound sense.

Future Use of Your Portrait of the Graduate

Once your Portrait of the Graduate is in place, revisit it in conjunction with your quadrennial strategic planning events. Your portrait can be "tweaked" routinely without the kinds of ripple effects (through your community, your alumni, your accreditation agency, et. al.) that ensue inevitably with alterations to your mission statement. Use the portrait to emphasize your school's uniqueness and continue to differentiate yourself within your competitive marketplace.

Chapter 4

In Chapter 4, we completed two forms—the *Faculty Hiring Specifications Form*, and the *Interview Planning and Evaluation Form*—in the course of explaining elements of our recommended hiring process.

Download these form at:
Faculty Hiring Specifications: **www.isminc.com/cfd-hiring**
Interview Planning & Evaluation: **www.isminc.com/cfd-interview**

Legal and Illegal Interview Questions

In Chapter 2, we reviewed the primary employment laws and discrimination issues that present risks for the school. Nowhere in the school's interactions with employees is there more risk than in the interviewing and hiring process (described in detail in Chapter 4). The information below is intended to help guide schools on appropriate and inappropriate interview questions, from the perspective of legal compliance.

General Perspective

When conducting interviews with prospective employees, questions should focus solely on the individual's qualifications for the job. The following recommendations were adapted from the Fair Inquiry Guidelines, established by the Equal Employment Opportunity Commission (EEOC), a federal agency, to provide specific protection from discrimination. Those who conduct interviews should review this list regularly and consult with your school's employment attorney regarding any additional protected characteristics in your state.

Relatives/Marital Status

Unlawful Inquiries:
Whether the applicant is married, divorced, separated, engaged, widowed, etc.

Lawful Inquiries:
NONE, except this specific question: "What are the names of any relatives already employed by our school?"

Residence

Unlawful Inquiries:
Names or relationships of persons with whom the applicant resides, and whether the applicant owns or rents a home.

Lawful Inquiries:
Inquiries about address to the extent needed to facilitate contacting the applicant. (A post office box is a valid address.)

Pregnancy

Unlawful Inquiries:
All questions relating to pregnancy and medical history concerning pregnancy. For example: "Do you plan on having more children?"

Lawful Inquiries:

Inquiries regarding duration of stay on a job or anticipated absences (both to males and females): "Do you foresee any long-term absences in the future?"

Physical Health

Unlawful Inquiries:

Overly general questions ("Do you have any handicaps?"), which would tend to divulge handicaps or health conditions that do not relate reasonably to the applicant's fitness to perform the job. Questions such as, "What caused your handicap?" "What is the prognosis of your handicap?" "Have you ever had any serious illness?" or "Do you have any physical disabilities?" should be avoided.

Lawful Inquiries:

Questions that relate specifically to the job: "Can you lift 40 pounds?" "Do you need any special accommodations to perform the job you've been hired for?"

Family

Unlawful Inquiries:

Questions concerning spouse or spouse's employment, salary, child care arrangements, or dependents: "How will your husband feel about the amount of weekend time you will be working if you get this job?" "What kind of child care arrangements have you made?"

Lawful Inquiries:

Whether the applicant can meet specified work schedules. "Can you work overtime?" "Is there any reason why you can't be at the job at 7:30 a.m.?"

Name

Unlawful Inquiries:

Any inquiries about a name that would divulge marital status, lineage, ancestry, national origin, or descent. For example: "If your name has been legally changed, what was your former name?"

Lawful Inquiries:

Whether an applicant has worked for a prior employer under any other name and if so, what name. Name under which applicant is known to references if different from present name. For example: "By what name do the references you provide know you?"

Sex

Unlawful Inquiries:
Any inquiry. Examples: "Do you wish to be addressed as Mr., Mrs., Miss, or Ms.?" Or Any inquiry as to sex, such as "What are your plans to have children?"

Lawful Inquiries:
None

Age

Unlawful Inquiries:
Any questions that tend to identify applicants age 40 or older, such as "When did you graduate from high school?"

Lawful Inquiries:
"Are you 18 years of age or older?"

Education

Unlawful Inquiries:
Any questions asking specifically the nationality, racial, or religious affiliation of a school. (Faith-based schools may ask candidates religion-related questions if religion is a bona fide qualification for the position.)

Lawful Inquiries:
All questions related to academic, vocational, or professional education of an applicant, including the names of the schools attended, degrees/diplomas received, dates of graduation, and courses of study.

Citizenship

Unlawful Inquiries:
Whether an applicant is a U.S. citizen; requiring a birth certificate, naturalization, or baptismal certificate (again, except if baptism is required by a faith-based school). Any inquiry into citizenship that would tend to divulge the applicant's lineage, descent, etc: "Are you a citizen of the U.S?" "Are your parents or spouse citizens of the U.S.? "On what dates did you, your parents, or your spouse acquire U.S. citizenship?" "Are you, your parents, or your spouse naturalized or native-born U.S. citizens?"

Lawful Inquiries:
Whether the applicant can provide proof of eligibility to work in the U.S. after hiring: "If you are not a U.S. citizen, do you have the legal right to remain permanently in the U.S.?" "What is your visa status?"

National Origin/Ancestry

Unlawful Inquiries:

Everything. "What is your nationality?" "How did you acquire the ability to speak, read, or write a foreign language?" "How did you acquire familiarity with a foreign country?" "What language is spoken in your home?" "What is your mother tongue?"

Lawful Inquiries:

"What languages do you speak, read, or write fluently?" This is only legal when the inquiry is based on a job requirement.

Race/Color

Unlawful Inquiries:
Any questions that directly or indirectly relates to a race or color.

Lawful Inquiries:
None

Religion

Unlawful Inquiries:
Any question that directly or indirectly relates to religion. "What religious holidays do you observe?" "What is your religious affiliation?"

Lawful Inquiries:
None except "Can you work on any day of the week?" and only if relevant to the job.

Note: Faith-based schools may ask candidates religious questions if religion is a bona fide qualification for the position.

Organizations

Unlawful Inquiries:
"To what organizations, clubs, societies, and lodges do you belong?"

Lawful Inquiries:
"To what professional organizations do you belong?" Exclude inquiries regarding organizations whose names or character indicate the race, religious creed, color, national origin, or ancestry of its members.

Military

Unlawful Inquiries:
Type or condition of military discharge. Request for discharge papers.

Lawful Inquiries:
Inquiries concerning education, training, or work experience in the armed forces of the United States.

Height/Weight

Unlawful Inquiries:
Any inquiries not based on actual job requirements

Lawful Inquiries:
Inquiries about the ability to perform a certain job.

Note: Being of a certain weight or height cannot be considered a job requirement unless the employer can show that no employee with the ineligible height and weight could do the work.

Arrests/Convictions

Unlawful Inquiries:
All inquiries related to arrests. "Have you ever been arrested?"

Lawful Inquiries:
None relating to arrests. Legal inquiries about convictions are: "Have you ever been convicted of a crime? If so, when, where, and disposition of case?" "Have you been convicted under criminal law within the past five years (excluding minor traffic violations)?" It is permissible to inquire about convictions for acts of dishonesty or breach of trust. These relate to fitness to perform the particular job being applied for.

NOTE: As we go to press, several states and localities are considering "ban the box" legislation that outlaws questions regarding convictions in many instances. Consult with your employment attorney for regulations in your jurisdiction.

Chapter 6

In Chapter 6, we reviewed our recommended Faculty Evaluation Template and Faculty Growth & Renewal Program. These same templates are provided online in clean form (i.e., blank and without examples).

 Download these forms at:
Faculty Evaluation Template: **www.isminc.com/cfd-evaluation**
Sample Faculty Growth & Renewal Program: **www.isminc.com/cfd-growth**

Chapter 8

Model Separation Agreement and General Release

In Chapter 8, we referenced the option of using a separation agreement when particularly sensitive terminations occur. Below is a sample agreement, for your reference.

NOTE: Schools should not use separation agreements without consulting directly with their employment attorney, who will draft an agreement that is appropriate to their needs and conforms with all federal requirements and the requirements of their particular state. ISM is not a law firm and this document is not intended as legal advice.

PERSONAL AND CONFIDENTIAL

NAME

ADDRESS

CITY/STATE/ZIP

Re: Separation Agreement & Release

Dear _____:

Our conversations to date will confirm that, for the reasons we discussed, your employment as **POSITION TITLE** with *Aegis Academy* ("the school") will terminate effective **DATE**. In accordance with the School's policies, you will receive on that date your final paycheck, which will include salary through **DATE**, as well as all accrued but unused vacation time.

The terms of this separation package are:

1. Your termination from the Aegis Academy will be effective DATE. (Alternative: You will be relieved of your duties and responsibilities on DATE, but your compensation and benefits will continue through DATE.)

2. *Aegis Academy* will pay you severance pay in the lump sum amount of **$DOLLARS**, less legally required withholdings and deductions.

3. Provided you are eligible for and elect continuation of your group health insurance coverage under the Consolidated Omnibus Budget Reconciliation Act of 1985 (COBRA), you are solely responsible for such premium payments pursuant to COBRA.

4. Except for the severance pay and benefits described in this letter, no additional pay or benefits shall accrue or be provided after **DATE.** In addition, the severance pay is personal to you, and *Aegis Academy* has no obligation to continue such severance pay to your heirs, estates, beneficiaries or assigns.

5. You agree to assist *Aegis Academy* in effectuating a smooth transition of your responsibilities.

6. You agree that you have or will return immediately all property, credit cards, keys, records, documents, or other information and materials owned by or pertaining to *Aegis Academy*. You agree that you will not at any time after your employment use, disclose, or disseminate any confidential information or any other information of a secret, proprietary, confidential, or generally undisclosed nature relating to *Aegis Academy* or its operations, methods, or procedures. This includes information of a financial nature and marketing and sales policies and practices. In addition, you agree that you will not solicit any of *Aegis Academy*'s current employees to cease employment and work for any other employer.

7. You fully release and forever discharge *Aegis Academy* and its officers, directors, executives, assigns, agents, independent contractors, shareholders, attorneys, and representatives, jointly and individually, from any manner of suits, actions, or causes of action, including any claim for attorneys fees or costs, whether known or unknown, under any possible legal, equitable, contract, tort, or statutory theory, including but not limited to any claims under Title VII of the Civil Rights Act of 1964, as amended, the Americans with Disabilities Act, the Age Discrimination in Employment Act, the Family Medical Leave Act, the Fair Labor Standards Act, *[State Wage and Hour Laws, if applicable]*, and any other federal, state, or local statutes, ordinances, executive orders, and regulations relating to employment, and any other federal, state, or local law claims of any kind whatsoever arising out of or in any way related to your employment by, and separation from, *Aegis Academy*.

   As part of the waiver set forth above, you voluntarily and knowingly waive rights or claims under the Age Discrimination in Employment Act of 1967 (ADEA), as amended, that may have existed prior to the date you execute this agreement. You recognize that you do not waive any claim or right under ADEA that may arise after the execution of the agreement.

8. You also agree not to make any disparaging comments about *Aegis Academy*, its policies, practices, and procedures, to any persons inside or outside *Aegis Academy*, including but not limited to current and former employees. Please take note that this provision is a material provision which the school deems important to this separation package, and any breach by you of these provisions shall completely relieve the school of any further obligations to continue providing any payments or benefits under this letter.

9. This letter contains the entire agreement between you and *Aegis Academy* regarding these issues, and no modification to this letter shall be valid unless set forth in writing and signed by both you and me. This letter shall be governed by the laws of *[State]* and any dispute regarding the terms of this letter shall be settled by final and binding arbitration in accordance with the National Rules for the Resolution of Employment Disputes of the American Arbitration Association.

10. Your signature below indicates that you are signing this letter voluntarily for the purpose of receiving additional pay and benefits beyond that provided by normal *Aegis Academy* policy. You are receiving consideration in addition to that which you are entitled by law or school policy.

11. Nothing contained in this letter or the fact that either you or the School has signed this letter shall be considered an admission of any liability whatsoever. In addition, this letter and all of its terms shall be maintained in strict confidence by you, except that you may disclose the terms of this letter to your accountant, attorney, immediate family members, or as required by law. Should any portion of this letter be declared void or unenforceable, such portion shall be considered severable from the remainder, the validity of which shall remain unaffected.

12. So that you can review this Agreement as you deem appropriate, the School also advises you as follows:

    - (i) this Agreement does not waive rights or claims that may arise after it is executed by you;

    - (ii) you have twenty-one (21) days from the date you receive a copy of this Agreement to consider this Agreement and whether you will enter into it ("Consideration Period");

    - (iii) you have been advised to review this Agreement with an attorney during the Consideration Period and prior to signing this Agreement; and

    - (iv) at any time within seven (7) days after executing this Agreement, you may revoke this Agreement ("Revocation Period").

Thus, if you accept the separation package, we will mail you the separation payment described above seven (7) days after the Revocation Period ends.

NAME, if the terms of the special separation package as set forth above are acceptable to you, please date and sign this letter below. In addition, if you have any questions regarding the separation package, or any aspect of your employment, please contact me. Finally, if you do not wish to sign this letter and accept the separation package, simply let me know. Regardless, you may, of course, keep your last pay and benefits (including accrued vacation) through DATE.

Whatever your decision, I sincerely wish you well in your future endeavors.

Sincerely,

NAME
Head, Aegis Academy

ACCEPTANCE OF TERMS OF SEPARATION AGREEMENT & GENERAL RELEASE

I have been advised to review this document in detail with my legal counsel. I have read and understand this letter and voluntarily accept and agree to its terms.

_____

NAME   **DATE**